AF478633

International Development Co-operation

Professor Sir Hans Singer: pioneering development economist

International Development Co-operation

Selected Essays by H. W. Singer on Aid and the United Nations System

Edited, with contributions, by

D. John Shaw

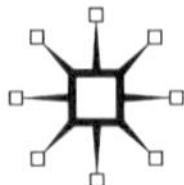

First published 2001 by
PALGRAVE
Houndmills, Basingstoke, Hampshire RG21 6XS and
175 Fifth Avenue, New York, N. Y. 10010
Companies and representatives throughout the world

PALGRAVE is the new global academic imprint of
St. Martin's Press LLC Scholarly and Reference Division and
Palgrave Publishers Ltd (formerly Macmillan Press Ltd).

ISBN 0–333–71129–7

This book is printed on paper suitable for recycling and
made from fully managed and sustained forest sources.

A catalogue record for this book is available
from the British Library.

Library of Congress Cataloging-in-Publication Data
Singer, Hans Wolfgang, 1910–
    International development co-operation : selected essays /
    by H. W. Singer on aid and the United Nations system ; edited,
    with contribution, by D. John Shaw.
        p. cm.
    Includes bibliographical references and index.
    ISBN 0–333–71129–7
     1. Economic assistance—Developing countries. 2. Food relief–
    –Developing countries. 3. Structural adjustment (Economic
    policy)—Developing countries. 4. United Nations—Developing
    countries. 5. International economic relations. I. Shaw, D. John.
    II. Title.

    HC59.7 .S46693 2001
    337—dc21
                                                    2001021743

10   9   8   7   6   5   4   3   2   1
10   09 08 07 06 05 04 03 02 01

Printed in Great Britain by Antony Rowe Ltd, Chippenham, Wiltshire

Contents

Dedication and Acknowledgements

This collection of essays is dedicated to the Fellowship of the IDS, The Institute of Development Studies at the University of Sussex, United Kingdom, and to friends and colleagues in the United Nations system with whom I worked over many years. Regarding the former, I would particularly like to mention Richard Jolly, Dudley Seers, John Shaw, Paul Streeten and John Toye among the early pioneers who created this fellowship. Concerning the latter, I remember with deep affection Paul Hoffman and Sir David Owen.

My chief debt is to John Shaw. This collection of essays is entirely due to his initiative and to Tim Farmiloe, formerly by publishing editor at Macmillan (now Palgrave), who fathered this enterprise. Invaluable assistance was given by my former secretaries, Caroline Pybus and Judy Barrow.

I would also like to acknowledge the permission received from co-authors and publishers of the papers included, in slightly modified form, in this collection of essays.

H. W. SINGER

Preface

The common link between these essays is expressed in the subtitle of this book. Several concentrate on those parts of international co-operation which centre on aid, and especially on multilateral aid through the United Nations system. Today, both aid and multilateral organizations suffer under a cloud of 'fatigue'. Yet, economic inter-dependence between countries, and between North and South, has never been stronger. New technology and expanding trade are creating a global world market and global financial markets. There is a growing recognition that the counterpart of globilization is the establishment of impartial monitoring and safety-nets for those not able to benefit from global markets. The former assigns a new importance to truly multilateral organizations; the latter to continued and improved forms of aid. As has been well said: 'The more you deregulate the greater the need for regulation'. There remains also the need to bring Africa into the mainstream of economic development. Marginalization of so many African (and some other) countries can be dangerous and costly for the rest of the world. Here again, aid co-ordination by multilateral organizations will have to play an essential role.

In all these new tasks, we must learn from history and experience. Hence, it is hoped that these essays, essentially written before the globalization era, will provide some clues to that experience, which should help us in dealing with our current and future development. 'Sustainable development' includes more than the environment and inter-generational equity. It also includes universal participation and inter-country (as well as intra-country) equity. That is the common theme of this collection of essays.

H. W. SINGER

List of Abbreviations

ADB	African Development Bank
CAP	Common Agricultural Policy (of the European Union)
CCFF	Compensatory and Contingency Financing Facility (IMF)
CFF	Compensatory Financing Facility (IMF)
DAC	Development Assistance Committee (of OECD)
ECOSOC	Economic and Social Council (United Nations)
EPTA	Expanded Programme of Technical Assistance (United Nations)
FAO	Food and Agriculture Organization of the United Nations
G7	Group of seven leading industrial countries (Canada, France, Germany, Italy, Japan, UK, USA).
GATT	General Agreement on Tariffs and Trade
GEF	Global Environmental Facility
GNP	gross national product
GSP	Generalized System of Preferences
IBRD	International Bank for Reconstruction and Development (World Bank)
ICOR	Incremental Capital-Output Ratio
IDA	International Development Association (World Bank)
IDS	Institute of Development Studies (University of Sussex, UK)
IEFR	International Emergency Food Reserve
ILO	International Labour Organization
IMF	International Monetary Fund
IRA	Immediate Response Account (of the IEFR)
ISI	Import Substituting Industrialization
ITO	International Trade Organization
LDC	less-developed country
MFA	Multi-Fibre Agreement
NIC	newly-industrialized country
NIEO	new international economic order
ODA	Official Development Aid
OECD	Organisation for Economic Co-operation and Development

OPEC	Organization of Petroleum Exporting Countries
R & D	Research and Development
SAP	Structural Adjustment Programme
SDRs	special drawing rights
SUNFED	Special United Nations Fund for Economic Development
TNC	transnational corporation
UN	United Nations
UNCTAD	United Nations Conference on Trade and Development
UNDP	United Nations Development Programme
UNEDA	United Nations Economic Development Administration
UNICEF	United Nations Children's Fund
UNIDO	United Nations Industrial Development Organization
UNRRA	United Nations Relief and Rehabilitation Administration
UNRISD	United Nations Research Institute for Social Development
WFP	World Food Programme
WTO	World Trade Organization

Introduction

by D. J. Shaw

The objective of this Introduction is to provide a summary of the career and work of Hans Singer as a framework for appreciating the selection of his writings that are contained in this volume.

There are few economists in the world today who have made so many and profound contributions to the study of development economics as Hans Singer. To quote from the late Sir Alec Cairncross, who knew Singer from the days when they studied together for their PhD degrees at Cambridge in the 1930s:

> There are few of the developing countries that he has not visited and still fewer that he has not advised. He must have addressed a wider variety of academics in a wider variety of places about a wider range of subjects than any other economist, living or dead. He has moved from continent to continent, expounding, advocating, and devising strategies of economic development. His influence has been felt as much by word of mouth in the succession of countries where he has lectured as through the pile of working documents and published papers that survive like a spoor of his travels.
>
> (Cairncross, 1998, pp. 13–14)

Singer is one of that small band of pioneering development economists who have stimulated so many of the ideas that were to engage the attention of the world community for much of the last century. Now in his 91st year, his seminal contributions, not only to an understanding of the problems of developing countries, but what might be done to solve them, have been recognized widely in: six honorary doctorates; an honorary fellowship of the Institute of Social Studies in The Netherlands; the Francis Wood Memorial Prize of the Royal Statistical Society; the Alan Shawn Feinstein World Hunger Award for Research and Education; president of the New York and London chapters of the Society for International Development; president of the United Kingdom Development Studies Association; and a knighthood 'for services to economic issues'. He was included as one of the ten 'pioneers in development' in a book published in 1984 by the World Bank (Meier and Seers, 1984).

There can be few who have had five *Festschrifts* in their honour in their lifetimes (Cairncross and Puri, 1976; Clay and Shaw, 1987; Chen and Sapsford, 1997; Sapsford and Chen, 1998a; Sapsford and Chen, 1999). The list of contributors to, and the papers contained in, these volumes given an indication of the depth and breadth of Hans Singer's influence in development economics, and the respect, esteem and affection in which he is held by so many friends and colleagues, in diverse professional fields, in different parts of the world. But, as was recognized many years ago, and as emerges from his many publications – including the essays in this volume – he is 'more than an institution or an intellect or a disembodied force for good – he is a committed man with a brilliant mind and great energy harnessed to his will to serve his fellows' (*The Economist*, 1976). Throughout his long and illustrious career, he has retained a driving concern with justice, solidarity with the poor and oppressed, and, despite the many setbacks, an optimism and faith in humankind and in its ability to create humane societies and actions. He is, as Wolfgang Stolper put is, 'one of the very few people I would call truly good, *ein wahrer Mensch*' (Stolper, 1998, p. 523).

The early years, 1910–47

When searching for clues in Hans Singer's formative years for early influences that were to determine his future work, we are fortunate to have a number of autobiographical accounts, on which this introduction is based, which leave little to surmise or conjecture (Singer, 1976, 1984b, 1986, 1989, 1992a; Arestis and Sawyer, 1992; Esslinger, 1996). He was born and brought up in the Rhineland of west Germany – a member of a minority within a minority within a minority –

in a Jewish community, within a Protestant enclave in a largely Roman Catholic population. Singer recognized that identifying with groups that were oppressed or discriminated against, and with 'underdog' minorities, was strongly impressed and bred into him by early experience. As he put it, the great inflation of 1923 and the economic depression of 1930–31 turned the mind of a schoolboy and young student to the study of economic and social problems and institutions. His education was strictly classical, and interest in contemporary affairs was not much encouraged. History stopped in 1871. He got many of his economic ideas from the *Manchester Guardian Weekly*, which he read avidly 'with a sort of self-taught English'.

The influence of Schumpeter and Spiethoff

He enrolled at Bonn University on the assumption that he would study medicine and follow in his father's footsteps but determined to study economic and social problems instead. There, he quickly came under a dual influence. First, was the dominating personality of Joseph Schumpeter who opened up a new world in economics and general thinking, to Anglo-Saxon economics, to Walras and Pareto, to interdisciplinary studies, and to the history of economic thought. Above all, there was his admired masterpiece written long before, the *Theory of Economic Development*.[1]

With hindsight, Singer realized more clearly than at the time how deeply relevant many of its themes were to the development of poor people and countries (Singer, 1976, p. 5). He singled out what he regarded as two key themes. First, the great importance of technology and innovation, access to innovation, and the ability and means of linking innovation with the production process in the form of new products, or new processes, or the development of new markets. Second, the emphasis placed on the fact that development represents a disruption of familiar and traditional processes of stationary circulation, arousing resistances and hurting established interests. As Schumpeter put it, 'By development we shall understand only such changes in economic life as are not forced upon it from without but arise by its own initiative from within'. For Singer, this brought shades of self-reliance, self-sustaining growth, dependency, backwash effects and the like. He confessed that it took him many years of work in development studies before he came back to the full implications of that definition. These two great themes of Schumpeter's work now seem to him to be among the key to the problems of development in poor countries.

The second dominant influence was Arthur Spiethoff, whom Singer described as 'the embodiment of Teutonic academic punctiliousness', the chronicler in minute detail of the history of trade cycles, and the pupil and admirer of Schmoller and his 'institutionalism'. From him, Singer learned to pay attention to detail, to take an interest in history (later to emerge in his interest in historical series, land values, unemployment, terms of trade, and so on), and to study in institutions (leading to later interests in the working of international organizations and the role of the economist as adviser to governments in developing countries). Spiethoff gave Singer his first job as a research assistant, and in working on his behalf in editing the conference proceedings of the *Verein für Sozialpolitik* (the German equivalent of the Royal Economic Society), he learned how to sort out and present opposing views, and to make a coherent report out of often fragmentary and incoherent discussion (which later stood him in good stead for his work in the United Nations).[2] From Spiethoff, Singer developed an interest in the question of urban land values, which he took up as the subject of his PhD work (later to be completed at Cambridge University). This experience also merged into subsequent work on development problems, 'since the process of development is also a process of urbanization', and to have a major influence on the initial assignment of his position and work in the United Nations (see below). Singer acknowledges that Spiethoff, although a very right-wing nationalist, probably saved his life on one or two occasions by not permitting the Nazi detachments from entering the premises of the Economics Faculty at Bonn University to collect their 'opponents'.

Keynes and the Cambridge Economics School

Schumpeter, who emigrated to Harvard University in the United States before Singer completed his studies at Bonn, played a crucial role in the furtherance of Singer's academic career. The Faculty of Economics at Cambridge University in England decided to make grants available from its reserve fund to help two German refugee students, and Schumpeter wrote to Keynes recommending Singer. Austin Robinson, who was secretary of a small committee consisting of Pigou, Keynes and Clapham, recalls that Singer was selected from a 'large number' of candidates and 'How greatly he has justified our expectations' (Robinson, 1976, p. 181).[3] The Germanic academic traits that Singer brought with him from Bonn were fortified further by the unique atmosphere he found at Cambridge, with its reputation for 'thoroughness, accuracy and theoretical expertise' (Cairncross, 1993, p. 15). He was admitted to King's College at the height of the Keynesian consensus in 1934 to complete his PhD work on urban land values. Keynes was at work on his masterpiece, *The General Theory of Employment, Interest and Money*, which switched attention from the causes to the effects of changes in the level of output and, for the first time, provided a theory of demand and supply for output as a whole. The work became 'the bible of the economics profession and the politicians they advised' (Skidelsky, 1996, p. 70).

What did Singer learn from Keynes that he applied directly to his later work in development economics? Selectively, he identified six key elements. First, the macro-economic framework, interlinking consumption/savings/investments, public/private sector accounts, and the importance of thinking in real terms as well as appreciating the monetary factors involved. Second were the Keynesian values: the concept that the real resources of a country are its human resources and that the purpose of economic analysis and policy must be to prevent the waste and dissipation of those resources. Third, Keynes was the admired example of a man combining a supreme standard of intellect and theory with involvement in the problems of the day. (Singer explains that is why he found work in the United Nations so congenial and why he maintained a preference for taking the stimulus for his research work from the outside. He points out that the great majority of his published work is in response to such external stimuli and requests. He liked to feel that what he was doing helped to answer the needs of life, but also to look at these problems in the framework of more general ideas or to develop general ideas out of the analysis of specific situations).

Fourth, there is the Keynesian belief that we are in control of our own destiny, that by social and economic planning we can achieve socially agreed objectives, such as full employment or a more even distribution of wealth. (In the early days of the United Nations, when seeking approaches to the problems of developing countries, Singer found it natural that the ideas of development planning, of finding techniques and instruments of rational policy to achieve the desired objectives, should come naturally to somebody trying to follow faithfully in Keynes' footsteps). Fifth, even in a more technical sense, the Keynesian demand analysis had a great deal of application to the situations of the developing countries. Sixth, and perhaps most important of all, much of the emphasis placed in development strategies on the reduction of poverty by means of the creation of productive employment and economic growth go together, or they complement each other, instead of there being a trade-off between them. As a secondary solution, Singer considers that more attention should be given to unutilized capital capacities, partly as a result of previous import substitution policies, which makes the Keynesian strategies even more directly relevant. He also appreciates the importance of income redistribution in creating a pattern of demand in which leakages into imports, including capital imports as a result of capital-intensive technologies, are minimized – providing a 'providential coincidence' of welfare arguments in favour of increasing the incomes of the poor and the reduction of leakages preventing the application of Keynesian strategies. Subsequently, perhaps more than any other person, Singer was to advocate the value of the Keynesian consensus in solving the problems of developing countries in a number of papers that appeared over many years (for example Singer, 1984a, 1992a, 1998).

Singer also acknowledges the role that Colin Clark played as the supervisor for his PhD thesis, from whom he learned 'the tricks of national income accounting against an understanding of the Keynesian model on which it was based'. It was mainly through him that Singer maintained an interest in statistics and statistical techniques so vital for his work on his PhD thesis and his subsequent work on employment statistics and interest in development models from Harrod–Domar on. Singer completed his PhD dissertation on 'Materials for the Study of Urban Ground Rents' and was awarded his doctorate, which he took by proxy on 13 November 1936, only the third person to do so.[4] Colin Clark summarized the results of Singer's PhD work in his *National Income and Outlay* (Macmillan, 1937) and in his *Conditions of Economic Progress* (Macmillan, 1940).[5]

Early employment

Singer's first employment after Cambridge was to have a profound and lasting effect on his later work. The Pilgrim Trust was embarking upon a major enquiry into high and protracted unemployment that existed in the depressed areas of the United Kingdom under the supervision of an influential committee that included William Temple (then Archbishop of York, later Archbishop of Canterbury), with Sir William (later Lord) Beveridge (the author of the famous 'Beveridge Plan' of 1942 on social welfare) as its main adviser. Both men were to have a strong influence on Singer's future work in addition to those he met at Bonn and Cambridge. A detailed investigation into the causes and effects of unemployment was to be conducted on the basis of a sample survey in various parts of the United Kingdom. Two people had already been recruited to carry our the survey, Walter Oakeshott and David Owen. A third was required to complete the team, particularly to link the findings of the survey with macroeconomic policies and also to act as the statistician and data analyst of the group. Singer was recommended from Cambridge, presumably by Keynes who had developed a special interest in the problem of unemployment as a central part of his economic thinking.

The survey had particular characteristics that were to make a strong impression on a young economist starting out on his professional career. It was an interdisciplinary study that provided the sharpest possible reminder that economics was a social science affecting the lives of people in a direct and profound way. Far from being a desk study, the team immersed itself in the lives of the unemployed by living with them in the poor areas of the country, tracing back their life history, trying to understand their concerns, and thinking about answers to their problems. It was a team effort. By living together and continuously exchanging ideas and impressions, they learned from each other in a way that only those who have taken part on such projects can realize. (This experience was repeated later in Singer's work at the United Nations, in the work he did on the ILO (International Labor Organization) employment missions, and many other joint-projects that he did at the Institute of Development Studies.) Finally, this was not an academic study but was to lead to practical results, which was assured by the influential committee to whom the team reported. The report that was produced remains one of the best of its kind (Oakeshott, Owen and Singer, 1938). Subsequently, Singer published his work on unemployment statistics in the interim reports of the Pilgrim Trust unemployment enquiry, for which he received the Frances Wood Memorial Prize of the Royal Statistical Society, and a book on unemployment and the unemployed (Singer, 1940).

Singer's first academic posts were at the universities of Manchester and Glasgow. During this period (1938–47), he continued to apply his economic training to the problems of the day, which was to have a direct bearing on his subsequent career. While at Manchester, he repaid his earlier debt by providing material regularly to A. P. Wadsworth, editor of the *Manchester Guardian*. At the request of Keynes, who was its editor, Singer also contributed a series of 12 articles on the German war economy to *The Economic Journal* between 1940 and 1944, which he contrasted with respective developments and data for the United Kingdom (Singer, 1940–44). His account of the German measures toward wartime rationing set a new direction in the British debate on the subject. Richard Kahn, who was working as a temporary administrator in the Board of Trade at the time, took note of Singer's description and proposed a points system for the United Kingdom which was inspired by Singer's articles. This system allowed the proper planning and regulation of supply and demand for consumer goods and mitigated inflationary pressures on goods not subject to rationing due to curtailment of purchasing power under the points system (Esslinger, 1996, p. 370).

Singer's work on urban land values led to a consultant post in the United Kingdom Ministry of Town and Country Planning, where he helped to prepare compensation estimates for the nationalization of development rights in urban land under the Town and Country Planning Act 1947. He also worked with the United Nations Relief and Rehabilitation Administration (UNRRA), the United Nations refugee organization based in London. As part of his concern with unemployment problems, he became interested in the development of a social welfare state. He was an admirer of Beveridge and an ardent propagandist for his report on *Social Insurance and Allied Services* (1942). In 1943, Singer wrote in support of Beveridge's proposals (Singer, 1943a, b). Later, he was to recall that 'a partisan of the social welfare state was attracted by the thought and possibility of a global welfare state represented by the United Nations in the hopeful first days of naive utopianism' (Singer, 1984b, p. 276).

Service in the United Nations, (1947–69)

While at Glasgow University, another twist of fate was to redirect Singer's career as a development economist, this time with international dimensions. David Owen, with whom Singer had worked on the Pilgrim Trust unemployment enquiry, had been appointed to head the Economics Department at the newly created United Nations at Lake Success in the United States. He wrote to the principal of Glasgow University, Sir Hector Hetherington, requesting that either Alec Cairncross or Hans Singer might join him. Cairncross was not available and so Singer was released, provisionally on a two-year assignment that was to last 22 years.

The twist of fate went further. Singer recounted how an economist trained under Schumpeter and Keynes, born and brought up in an industrial country, who studied the problems of developed countries, and who had never set foot in a developing country, came henceforth to be absorbed by concerns of developing countries and became a 'development economist'. When Singer arrived at the UN early in 1947, Owen was away on duty and so he was welcomed by his deputy, David Weintraub, who did not know Singer. Weintraub explained the various activities that were already going on in the Economics Department, and introduced the staff undertaking them, a number of whom were well-known to Singer. He also mentioned that there was a small section dealing with the problems of under-developed countries. When Singer explained that he would like to work with any of his old friends and colleagues, Weintraub was distinctly unhappy. He had noted on Singer's *curriculum vitae* that he had worked on urban land values and at the UK Ministry of Town and Country Planning, and was therefore considered in American parlance to be a 'planning expert' and was accordingly assigned to the small developing country section. Such was the twist of fate that led to the path that Singer was to take during his long and distin-guished career in the United Nations. By the time he left the UN in 1969, the number of people dealing with the problems of developing countries had risen from three to around 3000. In reality, his original assignment was anything but restrictive. His fertile mind and fondness for grappling with practical issues and current problems, combined with the fact that the new department he joined was not rigidly structured but consisted more of a small group of individuals pursuing their chosen subjects, meant that Singer was able to take up a wide range of initiatives with equal effectiveness.

During his service in the United Nations over more than two decades, when he served as chief of the Development Section and special adviser to the UN under-secretary for Economic and Social Affairs in the initial formative years of the United Nations, Singer's pioneering work came particularly to the fore. His incisive, analytical mind, coupled with a deep and abiding concern for the well-being of poor people in developing countries, resulted in a number of significant initiatives, the benefits of which have had their impact to this day. Time and again the visions of Schumpeter and Keynes were to shine through in his work.[6] He never minded having his work set out for him by the need to prepare UN reports in response to resolutions of UN bodies, or having to write field reports, or go on missions in response to requests from various countries. His workload was phenomenal, generated by the principle that 'work gravitates to he who works'. What follows is an illustrative, summarized account of some of the main pioneering activities he undertook.

Two early initiatives, which are perhaps most known, related to: the terms of trade controversy; and attempts to establish a UN soft-financing facility. Contrary to common belief, Singer forecast a long-term deterioration in the terms of trade for primary products and in the distribution of gains between developed and developing countries in a landmark paper published in 1950 (Singer, 1950). The general policy conclusion derived from his forecast was the importance for developing countries of diversification of exports into manufactures as intensively and rapidly as possible in a process of 'industrialization'. Singer's paper fitted into the mainstream of development thinking of the time, as development and industrialization were treated as virtually synonymous (Singer, 1999). Unknown to him, Raul Prebisch (who became executive secretary of the UN Economic Commission for Latin America and later the first secretary-general of the UNCTAD secretariat) had reached similar conclusions. Singer also found a similar 'sympathetic bond' with Gunnar Myrdal who at the time was executive head of the UN Economic Commission for Europe.

The 'Prebisch–Singer thesis' was to create a growth industry in the development economics literature. Subsequent studies have largely upheld their original work leading to the conclusion that 'There can be few hypotheses in economics which have stood the test of time, not to mention the onslaught of increasingly sophisticated statistical techniques, as well as the P–S hypothesis' (Sapsford and Chen, 1998b, p. 29).[7] Apart from the 'triple alliance' (with Prebisch and Myrdal) on terms of trade, Singer's policy conclusion for import-substituting industrialization, combined with a belief in constructive government intervention and social welfare planning, derived from Keynesianism, wartime planning in the United Kingdom, and the Beveridge plan for a social welfare state. They also led to creating a strong link with India where development planning was epitomized in the first two Indian five-year plans, strengthened by personal friendship with V.K.R.V. Rao, his fellow PhD student at Cambridge.

Friendship with Rao was also to lead to the second major initiative in which Singer was involved, the attempt to establish a soft-lending multilateral financing facility at the UN to assist developing countries undertake their development programmes and to compensate for declining terms of trade and lagging import capacity, which became known as the Special United Nations Fund for Economic Development (SUNFED).[8] The attempt started in 1949 when Rao, in his capacity as chairman of the UN Sub-Committee for Economic Development, the body on which Singer served as a member of the Development Section of the UN secretariat (which even at that time had hardly more than half a dozen professionals), recommended the establishment of a United Nations Economic Development Administration (UNEDA) as a personal proposal, since quick unanimous support in the subcommittee seemed unattainable. The proposal was reproduced in a simultaneous UN secretariat report to the UN Economic and Social Council (ECOSOC), which Singer drafted (UN, 1949). The proposal combined a technical assistance element (which eventually led to the UN Expanded Programme of Technical Assistance (EPTA), the UN Special Fund and the United Nations Development Programme (UNDP)), and soft financing for 'schemes which cannot be financed from the country's own resources and for which loans cannot be asked on strictly business principles'. Special emphasis was placed on financing regional development projects which seemed particularly suitable for multilateral financing under UN auspices. The Indus River Basin problem, arising from the separation of India and Pakistan, was considered as a prototype of such regional projects.

For much of the decade of the 1950s, Singer's work centred on preparing reports on the proposal (whose name had changed to SUNFED in 1953) and working with the various rapporteurs, committees, groups and bodies concerned, as chairman of the preparatory secretariat group, and as secretary of the governmental committee. SUNFED was eventually not approved, mainly due to opposition in the United States. However, Singer and the small group of SUNFED activists felt that all their efforts – and all the abuse – over a period of eight years was not totally in vain, when the proposal was adopted by the International Bank for Reconstruction and Development (IBRD) in 1959 in the form of its soft-financing window, the International Development Association (IDA).

As part of a general compromise, Singer became strategically involved in two other major UN initiatives. The first was the establishment of a UN Special Fund for financing project studies and analysis, natural resource surveys and pilot projects on the borderland between technical assistance and investment. He was chairman of the preparatory secretariat group for the establishment of the Fund. He developed the concept of 'pre-investment' as an example of what he called the 'new pragmatism' (Singer, 1964b). He also took charge of the preparatory work for the Special Fund until the arrival of its managing director, Paul Hoffmann, a previous administrator of the Marshall Plan.[9] Singer undertook a number of assignments for the Special Fund/UNDP, and led a programming mission to Kenya, which formulated the UNDP 'country programming' procedure. The second UN initiative was the establishment of the UN World Food Programme (WFP). Singer was appointed chairman of a small group of experts that prepared a report on an expanded multilateral food aid programme that was widely acclaimed and led to the creation of WFP (FAO, 1961). Rao was a member of the group, thus emphasizing the link between food aid and the soft-financing movement (see Part V of this collection of essays).

When President Kennedy's proposal to make the 1960s a 'United Nations Development Decade' was adopted by the UN General Assembly in 1961, Singer was assigned the task of drafting the proposals for action during the decade by the UN secretary-general, U Thant (UN, 1962). Singer took the opportunity to echo a number of Schumpeterian and Keynesian themes, as well as his own, as 'new approaches' to the problems of developing countries including: the concept of national planning – for social as well as for economic development; the importance of the human factor in development, and the urgent need to mobilize human resources; tackling the problems of unemployment and underemployment; removing the obstacles to trade of the developing countries; acceptance of the principle of capital assistance to developing countries as one of the most striking expressions of international solidarity as well as enlightened self-interest; the concept of pre-investment and finance; the potentialities of modern technology and new methods of research and development for tackling the problems of developing countries; and the creation of skills through technical co-operation in the developing countries.

Among his other pioneering assignments were (the list is not complete): director of the Economic Division of the United Nations Industrial Development Organization (UNIDO) before it moved to Vienna, which included responsibility for considerable related technical assistance work and the question of appropriate technology, with its shade of Schumpeterian influence; director of the Economic Division of the newly created UN Economic Commission for Africa in Addis Ababa, Ethiopia in its formative years; association with the creation of the United Nations Research Institute for Social Development (UNRISD), which *inter alia* involved emphasis on 'social development' as a key factor in economic growth and clarification of the notion of 'human investment' (Singer, 1965, 1966), and close collaboration with UNICEF, resulting in substantial work on concerns for the well-being of children in developing countries; secretary of a group of experts and ministerial committee on African development, which led to the foundation of the African Development Bank (ADB) in Abidjan, Côte d'Ivoire, including service in ADB in its initial stages as chief economist; consultant to the ILO on the establishment and operation of its World Employment Programme; secretary of the governmental committee for the establishment of the UN Capital Fund; secretary of the UN committees on commodity trade and development planning; senior inter-regional adviser on development planning; leader of a number of UN missions, and economic adviser, to several developing countries; and member of the preparatory committee for the Stockholm Conference on the Environment and Development, the UN Expert Panel on Science and Technology, and the UN Committee on Social Planning.

One of Singer's first operational assignments was to participate in training courses for Indian and Pakistani officials in connection with the IBRD-financed Indus river-basin scheme. This was more pioneering work in providing training to national government officials in the appraisal and implementation of economic development projects as part of national development programmes (Singer, 1951), Another was detailed study of the developmental problems of north-eastern Brazil, during which he recalled his earlier work in the depressed areas of the United Kingdom. This established that the developmental problems were not only linked to recurring drought and provided a practical example of his work on the terms of trade and development financing, and the need for regional development banks (Singer 1964c, pp. 221–90).

Extra-curricular activities

Simultaneously with his work at the United Nations, Singer became a professor at the graduate faculty of the New School for Social Research in New York, and later a visiting professor at Williams College in Williamstown, Massachusetts.[10] Singer never considered this additional responsibility a great hardship since he welcomed the chance of maintaining his links with academic work, which forced him to place his thinking about development in a more systematic framework. The underlying theory of development for his course at the New School was based partly on the importance of infrastructure (which drew on the earlier work of Rosenstein–Rodan and Thomas Balogh), partly on the need for balanced growth (where he was most influenced by Ragnar Nurkse), and partly on the ideas of Gunnar Myrdal (with his emphasis on cumulative causation and vicious circles), but the main components of his lectures were on international trade problems.

This led to his pioneering conceptual work in development economics, some of which was brought together in a book in a prominent series on international development by the publisher McGraw-Hill (Singer, 1964a). The collection included what he called 'the mechanics of economic development' as applied to developing countries (Singer, 1952). His model of the process of industrialization in developing countries was based on Harrod's growth theory modified to fit the characteristics of developing countries. He added the rate of annual population increase to the *per capita* version of the Keynesian growth model to take account of the problems of over-population and of 'unlimited' labour supply. His resulting formula helped to generate different scenarios of growth for developing countries and emphasized the strategic roles of savings, capital accumulation and the capital-output ratio in development planning.[11]

He later expanded on what he called 'the seven pillars of development', based on his work in the United Nations (Singer, 1964d). These pillars included that of Science and Technology, with higher priority given to the solution of those problems which specifically concerned the poorer countries, and technology which was 'capital-saving rather than capital-using'. Another pillar was Human Investment: the crucial factor in development was not the production of wealth but rather the *capacity* (original emphasis) to produce wealth, which was inherent in people. The third pillar was Planning. The resources of developing countries were so small that they required carefully laid plans in order to make the best use of their limited resources, and to develop policies and strategies which broke the vicious circles of poverty, ignorance and disease. The real objective of planning was to create a 'plausible picture of an expanding economy', into which the public and private sectors and individuals fitted their action. But Singer emphasized that 'the plan must be realistic, the government must mean what it says, and have the capacity to see that the plan is carried out'.

Next, was the pillar of Trade. The volume of exports of developing countries had not expanded sufficiently to give them the foreign exchange they needed for their development, and the prices of their exports had continued to fall relative to the prices of their imports. Hence the importance of the pillar of Aid to maintain developmental investments in the face of unsatisfactory export earnings. The proportion of aid provided through international channels could, with advantage, be increased, and the idea of the aid consortium represented great progress. It was right that all the different sources of aid should get together with the aid-receiving countries and discuss not individual projects but the 'total picture', and the possibilities and requirements for each, especially the recipient, within the framework of this total picture. And with the tremendous surpluses emerging in the richer countries – in food, fertilizers, machinery and equipment and industrial capacity – such aid in kind was not only sensible and necessary, but 'costless, perhaps even beneficial to those rendering this aid'.

Another hopeful trend, which Singer considered should become one of the pillars of economic development, was the growth of

Technical Assistance and Pre-investment Activities. There were many *latent* (original emphasis) investment opportunities in developing countries but they had to be created and brought to a stage where productive investment could take place. Hence, the crucial importance of the 'industry' of preparing investment opportunities. Finally, there was the pillar of Regional Co-operation. Developing countries should move away from a purely national and fragmented approach to development. Many were too small to create viable economic entities and their borders had often been determined by political and diplomatic history rather than economic factors. There could be no real worldwide development unless this last pillar was in place and the developing countries tackled the job as a joint task with their neighbours.

Building these 'seven pillars of development' would not be easy. It would require time, international co-operation and a strengthening of international institutions and approaches, a new spirit of human solidarity, and, above all, a growth in intelligence, 'an understanding that a wider spread and better distribution of well-being throughout the world is in the enlightened self-interest of us all'.

This brief synthesis of Singer's work in the United Nations and related activities gives an indication of his significant, personal contribution to a number of major initiatives taken during its early, formative years. His efforts led to the establishment of important institutions and to the formulation of basic concepts and ideas which have been of considerable benefit both for a better understanding of the problems of developing countries and for implementing practical steps to assist them in their economic and social development. Each one of his ventures required long hours of work, and often team-work, negotiations, persistence and compromise, and vision on a regional or global scale, which yielded a deep sense of achievement when things went right.

When Singer left the United Nations in 1969, David Owen wrote:

> Hans is a rare being, an economist of world repute, a departmental draftsman of prodigious productivity, an inexhaustible fountain of stimulating ideas for almost all occasions (providing that economic development or the welfare of children are somehow involved) and a living proof that an international civil servant can play a creative role in the great task of changing the policies of nations.[12]

The later years

When Singer retired from the United Nations in 1969, he was appointed professorial fellow at the Institute of Development Studies (IDS), and is now also emeritus professor of economics at the University of Sussex in England. This was fortuitous. IDS, which was founded in 1966, was still in its formative years. Singer found a similar collegiate spirit in which he had flourished at Bonn and Cambridge, and a congenial environment in which to continue his prolific output.[13] In addition to making a significant contribution to the work and activities of IDS, which quickly became recognized as one of the leading institutes for development studies, he became in constant demand by governments, multilateral and bilateral and agencies and non-governmental organizations for his profound knowledge and advice. And he is remembered with respect and affection by the cohorts of students who have passed through IDS over more than three decades as a source of almost unlimited inspiration through his dedication and generosity of time. What follows is a brief sketch of some of the main activities he has undertaken in an attempts to show the extraordinary depth and breadth of his work.

Singer developed further a number of the themes and ideas that he had addressed during his period at the United Nations. One major concern was the application of science and technology for development in the developing countries. Singer chaired a small group at IDS and the Science Policy Research Unit at the University of Sussex that produced the 'Sussex Manifesto' on science and technology to developing countries during the United Nations Second Development Decade of the 1970s (Singer *et al.*, 1970) and the 'World Plan of Action' for the application of science and technology to development (UN, 1970), which starts with the premise that the developing countries must have their own scientific and technological capability not only for increasing production, but, more importantly, for improving the capacity to produce. A related concern was the need to develop appropriate technologies to provide and support employment and basic needs in developing countries (Singer, 1977).

Another continuing concern was employment. Singer, together with Dudley Seers and Richard Jolly, played a major role in the design and execution of the ILO World Employment Programme and was a consultant from its inception in 1969 (Singer, 1992b). Singer and

Jolly led an ILO employment mission to Kenya in 1971, which produced, through Singer's inspiration, the concept of 'redistribution from growth' (ILO, 1972; Seers, Jolly and Singer, 1973; Jolly and Singer, 1973; Singer and Jolly, 2000).[14] In part, this arose from the emphasis in the report of the Kenya mission on the 'working poor', rather than on unemployment in the strict sense, or even of 'disguised unemployment'. Issues of poverty reduction, income redistribution and growth were brought together in the concept. The mission proposed temporarily stabilizing the real incomes of the top 10 per cent of total incomes. The resources gained would be invested in programmes required to attain a minimum income target for the poorest rural and urban households, especially in labour-intensive, employment-oriented projects benefiting the unemployed and the working poor. By this strategy, it was suggested that the incomes of the poorest 40 per cent of the rural population, and the poorest 25 per cent of the urban population, could be increased by 50 per cent within five years and doubled within 12 years at most. This was seen as an investment strategy, channelling redistributed resources into productive investment in permanent opportunities for earning reasonable incomes, not into income transfers for consumption.

This led to a joint study by the World Bank's Development Research Centre and IDS in 1974 on not redistribution from, but with, growth (World Bank and IDS, 1974) and to its adoption as 'the signature concept of the Bank's approach to poverty alleviation' (Kapur *et al.*, 1997, Vol. I, p. 263). The change in the title of the concept (from redistribution *from* to *with* growth) was significant. Redistribution had advanced to become an integral part of the growth process, whereas in the original version of the Kenya mission report, growth was put first as essential for providing the resources for redistribution. However, the concern for equity is common to both versions, and the relation between growth and equity has remained a major feature of development economics ever since, merging more recently with the concept of human development.

Singer continued his interest on the importance of children in developing countries with a major study for the United Nations and UNICEF on *Children in the Strategy of Development* (Singer, 1972). He was later member of a team which prepared an assessment of the impact of the world recession of the 1980s on children for UNICEF (UNICEF, 1984). He wrote extensively on the debt problems of developing countries, and on structural adjustment measures, and was a constant critic of the IMF and World Bank on the measures they undertook (Singer, 1990; Sapsford and Singer, 1998). At the same time, he retained his interest in food aid and was a regular consultant for the World Food Programme, conducting extensive literature reviews that remain among the best assessments of food aid, responding to the critics of this form of aid, and co-directing seminars and training programmes for food-aid staff from bilateral, multilateral and non-governmental aid agencies (Singer *et al.*, 1987). He was also an adviser to FAO (Food and Agriculture Organization of the UN) on international agricultural adjustment and food security issues and has taken part in training programmes for FAO, UNICEF and WHO staff. And he retained a continuing interest in the role of the United Nations and reform of the UN system.

In an address on the occasion of his installation as honorary fellow of the Institute of Social Studies in The Netherlands in 1975, Singer identified as 'a task for the next twenty-five years', the reconciliation of three separate and divergent elements in the discussion on the new international economic order, which were preventing progress and contact. The first element concerned the restoration of an inter-national economic order which could do what the Bretton Woods system did so well for the industrialized countries in the 1950s and 1960s. The second element was the problem of the international disparity in income and power between countries, acutely felt by the Third World as a constant humiliation. The third element was the need to reduce world poverty, and particularly to create a situ-ation in which the world's children were no longer caught in a trap of poverty and malnutrition, failing to achieve their mental and phys-ical capabilities, and causing what he called 'a large-scale destruction of potential human capital' and calling for 'a Marshall Plan for the world's children'. Singer considered that perhaps the first basis of a happier next 25 years would be to achieve some kind of synthesis in which these three different elements were brought together. 'Then it should not be beyond the wit of mankind to find some positive solutions to the benefit of all of us'. Much of his work over the succeeding 25 years was to be within this enabling frame-work.

Collection of essays

When Tim Farmiloe, publishing director at Macmillan (now Palgrave), invited me to edit another volume of the essays of Hans Singer (a previous volume was published by Macmillan in 1975 (Cairncross and Puri, 1975)), I readily accepted for several reasons. I have deeply enjoyed the friendship and intellectual stimulation of Hans Singer for almost forty years. I was aware of his formidable contribution to development economics as both a thinker and doer but even I was amazed by the enormous range and quality of his output when I compiled a list of his publications in 1996, which ran to 424 items, including books and pamphlets, reports for the UN, other international bodies and governments, and articles and papers (Shaw, 1998). Many of his publications are as relevant today as when they were written but are difficult to access. Reprinting a selection of his works will serve to make them more available and, I hope, will stimulate renewed interest in the subjects discussed. As I am writing a biography of Hans Singer (Palgrave, forthcoming), editing this collection of his essays has helped me understand more what inspired him to take such an active interest in the subjects he addressed, and what motivated him to propose the solutions to the problems he confronted.

I worked closely with the author in selecting the essays which appear in this volume. They provide his 'perspectives' on international development co-operation with a focus on various dimensions of aid provided to developing countries, particularly through the United Nation system. The essays are grouped into five parts. The first deals with the lessons of post-war development experience. The second concerns reform of the United Nations system that is now being actively debated. The third deals with debt and debt servicing, and the fourth with structural adjustment and stabilization measures. In the final part, I have attempted, for the first time, to synthesis Hans Singer's many contributions to the international debate on food aid in which he has provided a balanced and reasoned view in place of a dialogue that has often provided more heat than light.

I am grateful to Hans Singer, who read and checked the contents of this Introduction and my synthesis of his writings on food aid, to Richard Jolly for providing me with the tapes and transcription of his interviews of Hans Singer for a history of the United Nations, and to

Hans Ulrich Esslinger for sharing with me his tribute to the work of Hans Singer. I hope the reader obtains as much pleasure in reading these essays as I have had in editing them.

Notes

1 Original version published in 1912, revised edition in 1926. Shortened and revised edition translated into English by Redvers Opie in 1934.
2 It has also helped many friends and colleagues who have sent their drafts to Singer for comment and found that nothing escaped his attention, including omitted punctuation marks and spelling mistakes.
3 Singer recalls that he received a scholarship of £150 a year, plus meals in college, which was increased to £200 in the second year. On the strength of this, he married Ilse, to whom he was already engaged and who remained his constant support and companion for 67 years until her death in March 2001.
4 I am grateful to Dr Mark Nicholls of the Department of Manuscripts and University Archives, Cambridge University Library, for this information (personal communications, 10 and 18 June 1996).
5 Singer has stressed that he also owed much to the group of students and lecturers he met at both Bonn and Cambridge who became close and life-long friends and from whom he learned his first real economics and, beyond that, attitudes to life and issues of the day. At Bonn, he particularly recalls August Loesch, who became famous as a location theorist, and Wolfgang Stolper, who emigrated to the United States, became a well-known collaborator of Paul Samuelson, and the biographer of Schumpeter. At Cambridge, his fellow PhD students included Alec Cairncross, who became chief government economic adviser during the Harold Wilson administration, master of St Peter's College, Oxford University and chancellor of Glasgow University, and V.K.R.V. Rao, from whom for the first time he learned about the problems and conditions of India, who became a leading Indian economist, director of the New Delhi Institute of Economic Growth, vice-chancellor of Delhi University, and a minister in India's federal government. Singer has also expressed a particular indebtedness to Richard Kahn, the discoverer of the 'multiplier' and someone who was so closely in touch with the germination of Keynesian thinking, for guiding his first reading and discussion toward an understanding of economics at the level and of the kind practiced in Cambridge in general and the emerging new economics of Keynes' *General Theory* in particular (see especially Singer, 1997).
6 Singer recalls that shortly after arriving at the United Nations, he paid his respects to Schumpeter at Harvard University. When he told him that his work at the UN was to be on the problems of developing countries, Schumpeter's surprised response was 'But I thought you were an economist – isn't this more a matter for anthropologist, sociologists, geographers etc.? And this from the author of the *Theory of Economic Development!*'(Singer, 1992a). Singer took Schumpeter's words as a reminder of the non-economic and interdisciplinary dimensions of the development process.

This was clearly brought home by his extensive work in developing countries and the many contacts with politicians and various interest groups and officials in national aid organizations, UN delegates and others.

7   Singer describes how this 'triple alliance', cemented by personal friendship, gave him the strength to survive the McCarthy years in the United Nations when he came under personal attack. As he put it, at the time 'to be a dissenter was also to be regarded as a subversive'.

8   A detailed account of Singer's involvement in SUNFED is given in Singer (1984b, pp. 296–303). See also Hadwen and Kaufmann (1960, chapter 5); Mason and Asher (1973, pp. 383–80); and Kapur *et al.* (1997, Vol. I, pp. 154–5, 1119–29).

9   Personal relationships were to intensify when Paul Hoffmann was later to become the first administrator of UNDP in 1965, formed through the amalgamation of the UN Special Fund and EPTA, with David Own as his associate administrator. Singer was 'thoroughly enthusiastic' about this addition to the UN family.

10   Singer describes how he owed his association with the New School for Social Research in New York to Alvin Johnson, a well-known New Dealer under the Roosevelt administration, who was president of the New School and founder of the 'University in Exile', which became the New School's graduate faculty. During the war, Johnson had written to Singer offering help to obtain a priority visa to go the United States, if needed, and a teaching post at the New School. When Singer eventually went to the UN, he visited Johnson to thank him for his kind action, whereupon Johnson said that he could no better show his gratitude than by teaching in the New School in the evenings, after his work at the UN, which Singer did throughout his stay in the United States. (Singer, 1992a, pp. 8–9).

11   The paper was included in Singer (1964a, pp. 117–32) and in a publication of contributions of 'basic significance' for the economics of underdeveloped countries (Agarwala and Singh, 1958, p. 3). In retrospect, Singer found his model showed a major weakness in that the pursuit of GNP growth through savings and investment inevitably resulted in a deepening of the dual structure in developing countries, since it applied only to a modern typically urban sector (Singer, 1981).

12   I am grateful to Richard Jolly for this quotation.

13   Paul Streeten recalls that when Singer was considered for appointment at IDS, there were voices that said that he may be too old. 'As we all know, in those three decades that have passed since, he produced more original ideas, books, articles, speeches than many others in two lifetimes' (personal communication, 23 August 1996). Since joining IDS in 1996, Singer has produced 75 books, or contributions to books, edited by him or by others, 68 reports for United Nations organizations, other international bodies and governments, 198 papers and articles, innumerable book reviews, and many letters to the editors of newpapers and journals. Many of his publications have been translated into several languages.

14   A vivid description of Singer's inspiration is given in Jolly (1998, p. 175).

References

Agarwala, A. N. and S. P. Singh (eds) (1958) *The Economics of Underdevelopment* (Delhi: Oxford University Press).

Arestis, P. and M. Sawyer (eds) (1992) 'Hans Wolfgang Singer', in *A Biographical Dictionary of Dissenting Economists* (Cheltenham: Edward Elgar, pp. 626–32).

Cairncross, A. (1993) *Austin Robinson. The Life of an Economic Adviser* (London and New York: Macmillan–now Palgrave, and St Martin's Press).

Cairncross, Sir A. (1998) 'The Influence of Trade on Economic Development', in D. Sapsford and J. Chen (1998a), pp. 12–23.

Cairncross, Sir A. and M. Puri (eds) (1975) *The Strategy of International Development. Essays in the Economics of Backwardness by H. W. Singer* (Basingstoke and London: Macmillan – now Palgrave).

Cairncross, Sir A. and M. Puri (eds) (1976) *Employment, Income Distribution and Development. Problems of the Developing Countries. Essays in Honour of H. W. Singer* (Basingstoke and London: Macmillan – now Palgrave).

Chen, J. and D. Sapsford (eds) (1997) 'Economic Development and Policy: Professor Sir Hans Singer's Contribution to Development Economics'. (Essays presented at the conference convened at the University of Innsbruck in May 1996 to celebrate his 85th birthday), *World Development*, vol. 25, no. 11, Special Section in Honour of Hans Singer, pp. 1851–957.

Clay, E. and J. Shaw (eds) (1987) *Poverty, Development and Food. Essays in Honour of H. W. Singer on his 75th Birthday* (Basingstoke and London: Macmillan – now Palgrave).

Esslinger, H. U. (1996) ' " . . . More of Keynes and Less of Milton Friedman!". Sir Hans Singer's Contribution to Economics', *Review of Political Economy*, vol. 8, no. 4, pp. 367–78.

FAO (1961) 'Expanded Program of Surplus Food Utilization. Report to the Director-General of FAO', in FAO *Development Through Food: A Strategy for Surplus Utilization*. FFHC Basic Study no. 2 (Rome: Food and Agriculture Organization of the United Nations, pp. 69–117).

Hadwen, J. G. and J. Kaufmann (1960) *How United Nations Decisions are Made* (Leyden: A. W. Sythoff).

ILO (1972) *Employment, Incomes and Equality. A Strategy for Increasing Productive Employment in Kenya* (Geneva: International Labour Organization).

Jolly, R. (1998) 'Redistribution Without Growth', in D. Sapsford and J. Chen (eds) (1998a) pp. 172–82.

Jolly, R. and H. W. Singer (1973) 'Unemployment in an African Setting. Lessons of the Employment Strategy Mission to Kenya', *International Labour Review*, vol. 107, no. 2, pp. 3–15.

Kapur, D., J. P. Lewis and R. Webb (1997) *The World Bank. Its First Half Century. Vol. I. History* (Washington, DC: The Brookings Institution).

Mason, E. S. and R. E. Asher (1973) *The World Bank Since Bretton Woods* (Washington, DC: The Brookings Institution).

Meier, G. M. and D. Seers (eds) (1984) *Pioneers in Development* (New York: Published for the World Bank by Oxford University Press).

Oakeshott, W. F., A. D. K. Owen and H. W. Singer (1938) *Men Without Work. A Report to the Pilgrim Trust* (Cambridge: Cambridge University Press).

Robinson, A. (1976) 'The Economic Development of Malthusia', in Sir A. Cairncross and M. Puri (1976), pp. 181–92).

Sapsford, D. and J. Chen (eds) (1998a) *Development Economics and Policy. The Conference Volume to Celebrate the 85th Birthday of Professor Sir H. W. Singer* (Basingstoke and London: Macmillan – now Palgrave).

Sapsford, D. and J. Chen (1998b) 'The Prebisch–Singer Terms of Trade Hypothesis: Some (Very) New Evidence', in D. Sapsford and J. Chen (eds) (1998a), pp. 27–38.

Sapsford, D. and H. W. Singer (1998) ' The IMF, the World Bank and Commodity Prices: A Case of Shifting Sands', *World Development*, vol. 26, no. 9, pp. 1653–60.

Sapsford, D. and J. Chen (eds) (1999) 'The Prebisch–Singer Thesis: A Thesis for the New Millennium' (Papers presented at the conference convened to celebrate the award to Professor Sir Hans Singer of an honorary doctoral degree of the University of Innsbruck, Austria), *Journal of International Development*, vol. 11, no. 6, pp. 843–916.

Seers, D., R. Jolly and H. W. Singer (1973) 'The Pilot Missions Under The World Employment Programme', in ILO *Strategies for Employment Promotion. Employment Research Papers.*(Geneva: International Labour Organization).

Shaw, D. J. (1998) 'Professor Sir Hans W. Singer: Academic Education and Honours, Career and Publications', in D. Sapsford and J. Chen (eds) (1998a), pp. 535–63.

Shaw D. J. (forthcoming) *H. W. Singer: The Development of a Development Economist* (Basingstoke and London: Macmillan – now Palgrave).

Singer, H. W. (1940) *Unemployment and the Unemployed* (London: King and Son).

—— (1940–44) 'The German War Economy', *The Economic Journal*, parts I–XII.

—— (1943a) *Can We Afford 'Beveridge'?* Fabian Society Research Pamphlet. (London: Victor Gollancz and Fabian Publications).

—— (1943b) Beveridge Plan Economics, *Westminster Newsletter.* Special Issue.

—— (1950) 'The Distribution of Gains Between Investing and Borrowing Countries', *American Economic Review*, vol. XL, no. 2, pp. 473–85.

—— (1951) 'Economic Development Projects as Part of National Development Programs'. *Official Proceedings of the Development Institute* (Lahore: Pakistan).

—— (1952) 'The Mechanics of Economic Development: A Quantitative Approach', *The Indian Economic Review*, vol. 1, no. 2, August, pp. 1–18.

—— (1953) 'Obstacles to Economic Development', *Social Research*, vol. 20, no. 1, pp. 19–31.

—— (1964a) *International Development: Growth and Change* (New York: McGraw-Hill).

—— (1964b) 'An Example of the New Pragmatism: Toward a Theory of Pre-investment', in H. W. Singer (1964a), pp. 18–25.

—— (1964c) 'Problems and Experience: Northeast Brazil', in Singer (1964a), pp. 221–90).

—— (1964d) *The Seven Pillars of Development*. Dean Hudson Memorial Lecture, Long Island University, 21 April.

—— (1965) 'Social Development: Key Factor in Economic Growth', *International Development Review*, March, pp. 20–36.

—— (1966) 'The Notion of Human Investment', *Review of Social Economy*, vol. XXIV, no. 1, pp. 1–14.

—— (1972) *Children in the Strategy of Development*. Executive Briefing Paper no. 6 prepared for the UN Centre for Economic and Social Information and UNICEF (New York: United Nations and United Nations Children's Fund).

—— (1976) 'Early Years (1910–1938)', in Sir A. Cairncross and M. Puri (eds), (1976), pp. 1–14.

—— (1977) *Technologies for Basic Needs* (Geneva: International Labour Organization).

—— (1981) 'Thirty Years of Changing Thought on Development Problems', in R. P. Misra and M. Honjo (eds) *Changing Perceptions of Development Problems* (Nagoya: Maruzen Asia, pp. 69–76).

—— (1984a) 'Relevance of Keynes for Developing countries', *Estudos de Economia*, vol. 4, no. 2, July–September, pp. 35–46.

—— (1984b) 'The Terms of Trade Controversy and the Evolution of Soft Financing: Early Years in the UN', in G. M. Meier and D. Seers (eds), (1984), pp. 275–303.

—— (1986) 'Some Reflections on Past Interests and Activities', *IDS Discussion Paper* no. 217 (Brighton: The Institute of Development Studies, University of Sussex).

—— (1989) 'Lessons of Post-War Development Experience: 1945–1988', *IDS Discussion Paper* no. 260 (Brighton: The Institute of Development Studies, University of Sussex).

—— (1990) 'Reading Between The Lines. Comments on the World Bank Annual Report 1989', *Development Policy Review*, vol. 8, no. 2, pp. 15–20.

—— (1992a) 'The Influence of Schumpeter and Keynes: On the Development of a Development Economist'. Paper presented at the Conference *Zur deutschsprachigen wirtschaftswissenschaftlichen Emigration nech 1933*, Universitat Hohenheim, Stuttgart, 27–29 September 1991.

—— (1992b) *Research of the World Employment Programme: Future Priorities and Selective Assessment* (Geneva: International Labour Organization).

—— (1997) 'A Former Student's Recollections of Keynes', *The Cambridge Review*, May, pp. 19–21.

—— (1998) 'Modern Relevance of Keynesianism in the Study of Development', in D. Sapsford and J. Chen (eds) (1998a), pp. 524–33.

—— (1999) 'Beyond Terms of Trade – Convergence and Divergence', in D. Sapsford and J. Chen (eds) (1999), pp. 911–16.

——, C. Cooper, R. C. Desai, C. Freeman, O. Gish, S. Hill and G. Oldham (The Sussex Group) (1970) *The Sussex Manifesto: Science and Technology to De-*

veloping Countries During The Second Development Decade. IDS Reprints 101 (Brighton: The Institute of Development Studies, University of Sussex).

——, J. Wood and T. Jennings (1987) *Food Aid: The Challenge and the Opportunity* (Oxford: Clarendon Press).

—— and R. Jolly (2000) 'Poverty, Employment and the Informal Sector: Some Reflections on the ILO Mission to Kenya', in D. Ghai (ed.), *Renewing Social and Economic Progress in Africa. Essays in Memory of Philip Ndegwa* (Basingstoke and London: Macmillan (now Palgrave), in association with the United Nations Institute for Social Development, pp. 91–101).

Skidelsky, R. (1996) *Keynes* (Oxford: Oxford University Press).

Stolper, W. F. (1998) 'Joseph A. Schumpeter: The Man and the Economist', in D. Sapsford and J. Chen (eds) (1998a), pp. 513–23.

The Economist (1976) 'Tribute to H. W. Singer', 26 June, p. 56.

UN (1949) *Methods of Financing Economic Development in the Under-Developed Countries*. Document E/1333/Rev. 1, No. 149/II (New York: United Nations).

—— (1962) *The United Nations Development Decade. Proposals for Action. Report of the Secretary-General* (New York: United Nations).

—— (1970) *Science and Technology for Development: Proposals for the Second Development Decade*. Document ST/ECA/133 (New York: United Nations, Department of Economic and Social Affairs).

UNICEF (1984) 'The Impact of the World Recession on Children', in UNICEF *The State of the World's Children*. Chapter IV (New York: Published for the United Nations Children's Fund by Oxford University Press).

World Bank and IDS (1974) *Redistribution With Growth* (New York: Published for the World Bank and The Institute of Development Studies, University of Sussex by Oxford University Press).

Part I

Post-War Development Experience

1
Lessons of Post-War Development Experience, 1945–88*

Introduction

This paper traces the development process from the creation of the Bretton Woods institutions to present-day adjustment measures: from the optimism of the post-war era to the present scenario of adjustment, retrenchment and stabilization. What were the mistakes and the success stories, and the lessons that can be drawn from them these last 40 years? The paper assesses how and why the Bretton Woods institutions fell short of their initial aims; it takes a hard look at the 'golden years' of the 1950s and 1960s; it analyses the 'debt-led' growth of the 1970s and the resulting 'lost decade' of the 1980s in Africa and Latin America. It goes on to examine the successes and failures that emerge from the history of the development process, and argues in favour of learning these lessons by resuming a policy of 'redistribution with growth' and re-establishing strong international institutions to ensure future growth in developing countries.

The story of development: differing scenarios

The story of development, the lessons of development experience, the evolution of our thinking about development – all these things (which are not exactly the same) can be written from many different angles. One could start the story with the high hopes for a Brave New

---

* Originally published as *IDS Discussion Paper* no. 260 (Brighton: Institute of Development Studies, University of Sussex, April 1989).

World at the end of the Second World War at Bretton Woods; comparing these hopes with the 'lost decade' of the 1980s, with its debt crisis, African crisis and development going into reverse – at least in Africa and Latin America. The story could then be written as one of clear deterioration, of the Brave New World of 40 years ago ending in a developmental wasteland today. But that story would certainly not be wholly true. It would not do justice to the many success stories in development, nor to the 'golden years' spanning over two decades after Bretton Woods, nor to the fact that measured by such simple but compelling indicators as expectation of life, infant mortality, technological capacity, or progress with industrialization, the Third World as a whole is markedly better off than 40 years ago.

Another possible scenario when surveying the last 40 years could be as a story of ups and downs, of problems emerging and being solved, or left unresolved, only to be replaced by other problems requiring different solutions. This would be somewhat nearer the truth than the first account. The development story is clearly a mixture of good and bad, of progress and regress, of success and failure. Indeed, it is this very mixture which leads to much confusion. Some people, institutions or schools of thought tend to pick out the failures and draw from them lessons of what should be done to redeem them or avoid them in the future. Others will be more inclined to point out successes, and base their conclusions on what should be done to extend and support them. Obviously, both approaches are justified: we should learn both from success and failure. But in practice, this polarized approach often leads to unhelpful debates with arguments based on selective anecdotal evidence. This can result in inconclusive controversies, for example whether aid is beneficial or harmful to developing countries; whether the cause of the troubles of developing countries is internal or external; whether developing countries should practise inward or outward orientation; whether developing countries should use modern capital-intensive technology or traditional labour-intensive technology, etc.

Generally, it is unhelpful to pose such questions and try to answer them in this polarized or categorical form of 'either/or'. The truth, broadly, is that the right kind of aid is good and the wrong kind bad; that inward orientation is right for certain countries, certain sectors and in certain conditions and outward orientation for other countries, sectors and conditions, while usually a selective and phased mixture of inward-oriented and outward-oriented measures is best; a selective mixture or 'blending' of modern and traditional technology is best; in the present debt crisis internal factors play a role and interact with external factors, etc. The problem is that in such polarized controversies the advocacy of either of the two alternatives often assumes the nature of a religious conviction, argued with fundamentalist passion. When one of these factions acquires ascendancy in, and control over, important institutions and governments, it can do much harm. One illustration of this is the fervent belief in planning, the possibilities of the 'big push' and 'balanced growth' and import-substituting industrialization some 40 years ago; and the perhaps even more fanatical belief in outward orientation, market power and 'getting prices right', which has succeeded today in capturing the stage in powerful international institutions and governments. One can observe that the success stories tend to be based on a cool disregard of such fundamentalism – not so much a 'search for a middle ground' as a selective use of the elements of truth contained in either of the contending doctrines.

This last point could well suggest a third scenario: one in which our approach to development problems and the lessons which we learn is simply the result of changing fashions and ideologies. If it was the Keynesian consensus 40 years ago, it is now the neo-liberal tide or 'Washington consensus' of today, and goodness knows what tomorrow. This scenario, familiar to historians, is the counterpart of the proposition that history is not a logical evolution in which events in epoch B are linked with events in the preceding epoch A and will in turn be linked with future events in epoch C; but rather that history is 'just one damn thing after another'. Yet this again does not quite seem the whole truth. There was a sense in which the belief in planning and self-reliance in the 1940s and 1950s was based on the experience of the war and the preceding Great Depression; in which the later move towards outward orientation was based on the expansion of the world economy and world trade in the 1950s and 1960s; in which the temporarily successful OPEC action of 1973 and 1979 was linked with the experience of deteriorating and unstable terms of trade; in which the debt crisis of today is linked to the OPEC action and the response of the industrial countries to this action; in which the present African crisis is linked to the historical experience of new independence and the difficulties of giving political independence a proper economic meaning and foundation. So perhaps the story of development is more than just 'one damn thing after another'; it is a story of unfolding, of one thing leading to another in a process which can be given some meaning. But the trouble seems to be one of time lags. Just as generals tend to fight the last-but-one war, so the development actors, as well as the development thinkers, seem to base their action and thought on experiences of the last-but-one decade or a last-but-one phase, only to be overwhelmed by the inappropriateness of such action and thought in the face of new events and new problems. Is it perhaps a case of a problem for every solution, rather than a solution for every problem?

This seems to come close to the truth. It can be presented pessimistically as always reacting too late and to an obsolete situation; or more optimistically as a learning process. We react – although inevitably with a time lag – to the lessons of the past. Perhaps we can also learn to speed up this learning process, to react more quickly and more relevantly to new events. Even more optimistically, we can describe the last 40 years as a journey of discovery. For example, from an earlier emphasis on physical capital accumulation we have all – planners, Keynesians, neo-liberals, structuralists or whatever we call ourselves – learnt to attribute greater importance to human capital; similarly we are all agreed – at least theoretically – to attribute more importance to reduction of poverty than to mere growth of GNP. The trouble is that while we may share in such discoveries, we still differ widely about what conclusions to draw for development policy. We all want to reduce poverty and enable people to live up to their full potential, but that does not guarantee any agreement about the policies best designed to achieve these common objectives. Instead they take their place alongside mother love and apple pie as emotional invocations. The ritual invocation of such common objectives may become a rhetorical mask. The 'human face' may become merely a face-lift for any policies which we advocate; the same may be true of the description of all types of adjustment policies as 'growth-oriented'.

The scenario which is, perhaps, the most fruitful approach to an understanding of the development story and to drawing proper lessons from it, is the one indicated by the motto from Dr Johnson which precedes the next section: 'Seldom any splendid story is wholly true'. This seems to fit the last 40 years. Compared with the pre-war and wartime situation, it *is* a 'splendid story'. The world today would be a worse place without it. Yet the splendid story that emerged was not 'wholly true'; it was incomplete, flawed and its defects carried the germ of its own destruction. Our problem, then, is to live up to the scenario of development as a learning process and create a new 'splendid story'. That, at any rate, is the angle from which we will now look at the story of development.

The high hopes of Bretton Woods and the worm in the apple

'Seldom any splendid story is wholly true'.

(Dr Johnson)

At the end of the Second World War there was clearly a unique opportunity to reshape the world international system. The old order had been swept away. There was a burning desire to learn the lessons of recent experience and avoid the errors of judgement and policies which were felt to be among the causes of the disastrous war. So, clearly, the new system created at Bretton Woods and in the UN reflected the current perceptions of the immediate pre-war and wartime experience. What were these perceptions?

First, there was the perceived need to avoid the disastrous beggar-my-neighbour policies of the 1930s when countries, dominated by traditional and classical doctrines of reliance on 'equilibrating' market mechanisms, got themselves deeper and deeper into competitive devaluations, heavy deflation, rising unemployment, and protectionism, with their terrible social and political consequences. (Perhaps this lesson now needs to be relearned.) Between 1929 and 1933 world trade declined in value by 65 per cent and in volume by 25 per cent. The belief in classical policies had been swept away by a new Keynesian consensus on active macroeconomic management by governments, with full employment set as the primary objective. In the international field, the conclusion drawn was that nationalist policies must be replaced by international rules of conduct and control by international institutions.

The 1930s had also been accompanied by a disastrous fall in primary commodity prices, and the lesson drawn by Keynes and others at the time was the need to stabilize primary commodity prices. For that purpose, it was decided at Bretton Woods that in addition to the IMF and World Bank, a third international organization was needed – the ITO, or International Trade Organization – with the dual purpose of stabilizing primary commodity prices and promoting world trade.

The wartime experience of the industrial countries had demonstrated the potential for macroeconomic planning and effective government action to maximize output, mobilize latent resources, achieve full employment, and at the same time control inflation and achieve more equal income distribution. This experience was particularly striking in the case of the UK which, in the person of Keynes, played a dominant intellectual role in the creation of the Bretton Woods system. There was a strong feeling that the same principles of planning, macroeconomic management of the economy by governments and mobilization of latent resources based on Keynesian principles, were also applicable to the problems of developing countries. These had become a more important item of world interest as a result of the emergence into independence of the countries of the Indian sub-continent and a shift in colonial policies in Africa towards preparation for independence. For many in the West, it seemed natural to extend the principles of the welfare state from the national to the international sphere, and the idea of international income transfers, including large-scale multilateral transfers centred in the UN, began to take shape.

Bretton Woods was indeed a 'splendid story'. It was an immense improvement over the situation of the 1930s; it gave us 25 'golden years' – from 1948 until the early 1970s when the Bretton Woods system broke down – as will be presently shown.

The success of the new system was not entirely due to its intrinsic value. The Marshall Plan (1948–52) had a great deal to do with creating a period over two decades when the industrial countries, through steady growth at a rate of 5 per cent or more, with full employment, little inflation and balance of payments disequilibria solved first by the Marshall Plan, then by US investment and later by a strong recovery of exports and the emerging balance of payments surpluses of Europe and Japan, provided a firm foundation (or 'engine') for the growth of production and exports in developing countries, enabling them to maintain on aggregate growth rates similar to or even higher than those of the industrial countries (although not on a per capita basis). World trade expanded even faster than GNP, and protectionist incentives were minimized.

If the Marshall Plan had demonstrated the potential effectiveness of large-scale international income transfers, the response of Europe, in presenting joint programmes and moving towards trade liberalization in the form of a common market, also seemed to demonstrate the possibility of constructive recipient policies and collaboration between donors and recipients. So, in the first days of high hopes for the Brave New World, development activists in the UN and elsewhere began to think in terms of multi-annual, large-scale aid of the Marshall type for developing countries, linked to the GNP of the industrial countries and thus increasing at the same steady rate of 5 per cent per annum or more in line with industrial countries' GNP. A target of 1 per cent of GNP then seemed to be quite modest – the USA, under the Marshall Plan, had transferred something more like 3 per cent of its GNP for four years running. While it was recognized and admitted from the beginning that development problems would be more difficult and longer term than the reconstruction of Europe and Japan, this was assumed to be offset by the strengthening of donor capacity, as the beneficiaries of the Marshall Plan would 'graduate' to large-scale donors. Moreover, the capital transfers could be partly in the form of private investment: the prevailing perception was that there should be plenty of scope for productive investment in developing countries since the marginal productivity of capital must be higher in these capital-scarce countries. However, private investment was assumed to be the junior partner to Marshall Plan-type aid (later, in the first UN Development Decade, quantified as 0.3:0.7).

Where, then, was the worm in the apple? Why did the splendid story not come wholly true? The most obvious defect was that the Bretton Woods system remained incomplete. To begin with, the International Trade Organization (ITO) which Keynes had considered to be an indispensable third pillar of the Bretton Woods system, never came into being. Although it was duly negotiated and agreed at Havana, the 'Havana Charter' was not ratified by the US Congress. This was largely a matter of time lags – by the time the ITO was ready for ratification, the climate of opinion in the USA had changed: the Roosevelt/Truman era in which 'freedom from want' had been proclaimed as a global objective, was beginning to shade into the very different McCarthy era in which the UN and all its works became 'an evil empire'. Another reason why the ITO was not ratified was the fact that commodity prices had temporarily risen, as a result first of post-war shortages and then of the Korean War, so that intervention by the ITO seemed unnecessary.

Some of the intended functions of the ITO were subsequently shifted to GATT (the General Agreement on Tariffs and Trade); but GATT was a weak version, and in some ways a perversion, of the intended ITO – a negotiating mechanism rather than an instrument of multilateral action – and did not include the vital function of commodity price stabilization. In fact, GATT emasculated the trade policy chapter in the Havana Charter, deleting not only the chapters on commodity agreements, but also those on employment, development and restrictive business practices. GATT became – and to some extent remained – very much a first world institution, and initially failed to make any allowances for the special problems of developing countries. Nor did the subsequent creation of UNCTAD in 1964 fill the gap left by the failure of the ITO; by that time the shift in economic power and relevance away from the UN was complete and the industrial countries were determined to keep UNCTAD at the level of a talking shop. However, some useful initiatives subsequently came from UNCTAD, particularly the acceptance of the GSP – the Generalized System of Preferences. In fact, this initiative was probably more useful to developing countries than all the 'trade liberalizations' under GATT which were largely offset by the growth of non-tariff restrictions outside the GATT system, including the MFA – Multi-Fibre Agreement – and the so-called 'voluntary' export restraints.

The even more far-reaching plans for commodity stabilization proposed by Keynes never had a real political chance to materialize. Keynes had proposed a world currency to be based not on gold, not on the dollar, not on sterling, not on SDRs, but on 30 primary commodities (including oil and gold); this would automatically have stabilized at least the average price of these 30 commodities. But, however ripe the situation at the end of the war was for a Brave New World, this Ultra-New World proposed by Keynes proved to be too radical; at Bretton Woods it sank without trace. Perhaps Keynes would have fought harder for it if he had known that the ITO would not come into existence, but by the time this had become clear,

Keynes was dead, and in any case, the enthusiasm for a Brave New World had largely evaporated.

The Bretton Woods system was also incomplete in that the UN, which was supposed to be another pillar of the Bretton Woods system, was never brought into action in the way initially expected. This was largely due to the adverse change in the political climate already referred to. The initial hope was that a 'special fund' should be set up in the UN to administer large-scale soft aid, more or less on Marshall Plan terms, to developing countries. This proposal, originating in the UN Sub-Commission for Economic Development in 1948, was taken up in more detail in the 1951 Report of the UN Expert Group (which included two subsequent Nobel Laureates, Arthur Lewis and Ted Schultz) on 'Measures for Economic Development'. Although the process of detailed preparations and negotiations was duly set in motion in the UN system and the statute for a 'UN Fund for Economic Development' was laboriously evolved, under the chairmanship of the subsequent UN Secretary General U Thant, the unfortunate initials of this proposed fund, i.e. UNFED, described only too well the fate awaiting this stillbirth. (When it was realized how the initials would be received, the word 'Special' was hastily put in front – but, unfortunately, the science fiction nature of the new acronym of SUNFED still provided an all too accurate description of the chances of its success.) The long opposition of the World Bank not only to involving the UN in financial aid but even to the principle of soft aid, also served to prevent this idea materializing. When, with the dawn of the more liberal Kennedy era, the chances for soft, multilateral aid became better and the World Bank dropped its opposition to it, it was clear that the Western donor countries would not be willing to channel it through the UN where the developing countries had a major say, but through the World Bank which the donors controlled. In any case, the new IDA (International Development Association) never reached dimensions remotely comparable with the Marshall Plan. At the same time, the UN received two valuable consolation prizes in the form of being allocated food aid (the World Food Programme) and technical assistance (the UNDP). In fact, the UNDP initially, before its merger with ETAP (the UN Expanded Technical Assistance Programme arising from point IV), still carried in its name of 'Special Fund', a recognition of the aborted SUNFED. But that was meagre consolation compared with the initial hopes. So the

Bretton Woods system which was meant to walk on four legs (UN, ITO, IMF and the World Bank) was hobbling along on the last two only.

Not only was the Bretton Woods structure incomplete, it was also distorted. In Keynes' original vision, and in line with his high priority for avoiding deflation and recession, he had suggested an IMF which would put adjustment pressure on balance of payments surplus countries rather than deficit countries. This was to be achieved by making it mandatory for surpluses to be held in a World Central Bank, and for these deposits of surpluses to carry a negative rate of interest (i.e. to be taxed). Although this vision is still partly reflected in the constitution of the IMF, enjoining it to put equal pressure on deficit and surplus countries, the IMF has proved utterly incapable of exerting pressure on surplus countries – neither Japan and Germany today nor OPEC in the 1970s. The pressure is now entirely concentrated on deficit countries, which are asked to 'put their house in order'; even among these the pressure is selective, and the IMF makes no significant impact on the biggest balance of payments deficit country of today – the USA. Any admonition of industrial countries, and specifically the surplus countries, to 'put their house in order' remains entirely at the rhetorical level; there is no question of conditionality or financial sanctions.

There is of course an historical explanation – to some extent an alibi – for this distortion of original intentions. The Keynesian desire to put pressure on surplus countries was based on the undesirability of deflationary pressures in times of unemployment and recession: in such conditions, the surplus country is the enemy of the world economy and should be penalized, while the deficit country is the friend of the world economy and should be supported. During the golden years of full employment this prescription, of course, was no longer appropriate; pressure on deficit countries was then justified. The trouble is that with the shift in the world situation to slow growth, unemployment and recessions after 1973, the IMF has not returned – or has not been allowed to return – to the policies originally recommended with the Great Depression of the 1930s in mind, and which now, once again, were appropriate in the light of the economic situation since 1973. In this respect the time-lag scenario previously presented would seem applicable: Keynes' proposals were made to cope with the recessionary situation of the 1930s; these proposals were then reversed to deal with the different situation of the 1950s and 1960s, but this reversal was then maintained, and indeed intensified, in a new economic climate when it was no longer appropriate.

There seems little prospect, however, that this process of 'learning, but too late' will be continued in the future. In the absence of a world central bank, world currency and global source of liquidity which can be realized or withheld – all these part of the Keynesian proposals – it is difficult to see how even in the future the Bretton Woods institutions could put effective pressure on surplus countries. It would certainly require a dramatic reform of the system in the direction suggested by Keynes. Interestingly enough, there are some faint signs of recognition of what has been lost: for example, in the case of the ITO there is the Compensatory Financing Facility and the recent addition of commodity prices to the list of IMF indicators – the beginning of a recognition that debt repayment capacity and structural adjustment capabilities are tied to terms of trade. There is again talk of developing GATT into a World Trade Organization (WTO) [which was achieved in 1994] as well as the possibility of making a reality of the embryonic Common Fund created by UNCTAD.

The golden years of the 1950s and 1960s: were they really solid gold?

The 1950s and 1960s were a period of global expansion of production and trade, one of the longest and most pronounced booms in world history, with full employment and little inflation in the industrial countries. This was a favourable environment for developing countries, including those gaining independence during that period. This was fully reflected in the statistical and aggregate picture of development, with increases in output, trade, technological capacity, acquisition of planning experience and so on. In many developing countries this period saw the rise of a middle class and the development of entrepreneurship. All the same, the approach to development, based as it was on prewar and wartime experiences and on the incomplete Bretton Woods system, and to a large extent a reflection of the progress of the industrial countries, showed certain weaknesses which were to become apparent in the course of time, and from which some lessons could be drawn. However, sometimes the actual lessons learnt were based on 'yesterday', i.e. they came too late to be appropriate to newly changed circumstances.

Some of the characteristic approaches to development during the golden years have already been mentioned. To begin with there was a heavy and almost exclusive emphasis on physical capital accumulation. The Keynesian consensus ruled supreme, and the neo-Keynesian development model, embodied in the Harrod–Domar formula, emphasized capital accumulation as the source of growth, with the capital/output ratio in the denominator of the formula being taken more or less as constant. This emphasis on physical capital accumulation also drew support from Russian planning and its apparent successes. This virtually exclusive emphasis was perhaps most clearly expressed by Maurice Dobb lecturing to the Delhi School of Economics in 1951:

> The largest single factor governing productivity in a country is its richness or poorness in capital instruments of production. And I think that we shall not go far wrong if we treat capital accumulation, in the sense of a growth in the stock of capital instruments – a growth that is simultaneously qualitative and quantitative – as the crux of the process of economic development.

This emphasis on capital accumulation was almost universally shared: it was also clearly embodied in the approach underlying the previously mentioned proposals of the UN experts in 1951. Subsequently, and in the light of experience, it was found that the 'capital/output ratio' can be a very troublesome factor. It may have an obstinate tendency to remain unfavourable, i.e. high, or even to rise; it is largely governed by 'human' factors such as education, skill, training, health, nutrition and so on not explicit in the Harrod–Domar model; and much of the physical capital accumulation, at least in the earlier stages, is of the infrastructure type, with high capital/output ratios and long maturity periods needed for a full return. Moreover, contrary to the optimistic belief, based on external economies and the theory of balanced growth, that capital/output ratios would rapidly decline as investment expands, other factors may intervene in the opposite direction: for example, increased investment may outrun the technical and administrative capacity of a country to design, implement and operate efficient development projects. The smaller size and lack of economies of scale could also be relevant for developing countries. So the initial equation of development with physical capital accumulation led to increasing problems and was increasingly questioned as the golden years went on.

A more mature synthesis later emerged in which physical and human capital formation were seen as necessary, but neither alone sufficient, and emphasis was laid on their interaction. Familiarity with physical capital and its operation will help to develop human skills, just as educated and skilled labour will improve the operation of physical capital and suggest lines of technical progress.

Emphasis on physical capital accumulation was linked with optimism regarding the domestic capacity of developing countries and their governments to mobilize domestic savings and investment, and an equally optimistic belief that this might be supplemented by large foreign aid injections on the precedent of the Marshall Plan. Domestic capital accumulation was to be promoted by utilization of surplus labour, especially in agriculture, and utilization of the potential of 'disguised unemployment'. Such confidence that domestic savings and investment could be rapidly increased was not entirely misplaced. In fact, domestic savings and investment ratios in most developing countries increased quite rapidly and soon reached and exceeded the rather modest initial targets set for them (which in turn were based on optimistic assumptions for capital/output ratios). However, it turned out that quite often the source of the increased domestic savings and investment was not so much the mobilization of latent surplus labour (which would have been a factor making for an egalitarian pattern of development), but rather an emerging inequality of income distribution and a squeezing of the agricultural sector (making for an inegalitarian pattern of development and long-term problems with demand for manufactured goods).

As for the hoped-for Marshall-type flow of external resources which was supposed to supplement domestic savings and prevent balance of payments difficulties, this failed to materialize. The failure of an attempt at a Marshall Plan under UN auspices, in the name of SUNFED, has already been described. In any case, it is doubtful whether an injection of the Marshall Plan type, whether bilateral or multilateral, would have had the same effect in developing countries as in Europe. The lesson of the Marshall Plan was that such injections are most effective where the recipients come forward with their own proposals and agree in advance on the division and use of the external funds; where the recipients are willing to use the funds as the basis for increased co-operation among themselves; where there is already the human basis in terms of skill, experience and education; and where there is a high degree of technological capacity among the recipients. None of these conditions would have been present in a Marshall Plan for the developing countries during the golden period. Perhaps today the preconditions would be better, but the sad fact is that a Marshall Plan today would not be devoted so much to development as to solving the debt crisis and to damage limitation from the setbacks of the 1980s.

The type of external resource which did, in fact, flow in excess of expectations was private capital. The target for the First Development Decade of the 1960s was for aid to constitute 70 per cent of the total inflow, more than double the private inflow. However, the situation was more or less reversed. This substitution of private capital for official aid at concessional terms had obvious implications for future balances of payments: the seeds of the future debt problem were sown. Moreover, in so far as much of this private inflow represented direct investment by multinational corporations, often in the form of subsidiaries, some of the growth of the golden years inevitably acquired an exogenous, and often enclave, character rather than representing truly national capacity. Towards the end of the period, debates developed around whether the transfer of technology connected with such direct foreign investment was a valuable bonus of such investment and had national demonstration effects; or whether, on the contrary, it introduced inappropriate technology, stifled local enterprise and technology and encouraged a brain drain from developing countries. It also meant that some of the rents accruing to protected import-substituting industries were expatriated as profits of foreign subsidiaries, with strain on the balance of payments, thus nullifying the saving of foreign exchange through import substitution. But the same also applied to more export-oriented types of industrialization. In so far as the exports came from foreign subsidiaries, the degree of retention of the foreign exchange earned from exports was clearly reduced. The share of foreign subsidiaries in exports of NICs (newly industrialized countries) towards the end of the golden era was estimated at 15–30 per cent for South Korea, 40–50 per cent for Brazil, 25–30 per cent for Mexico and 70–85 per cent for Singapore.

Another reason (apart from excessive expectations of aid inflows) why insufficient attention was often paid to possible balance of payments constraints was that at the beginning of the golden years commodity prices were buoyant, with a peak in 1951 at the time of the Korean War. Also, many developing countries had accumulated important foreign exchange reserves during the war which could be gradually drawn upon. This happy situation did not last however: terms of trade and relative prices of primary commodities deteriorated quite sharply during the golden years, resuming their declining prewar trend. This took quite a lot of steam out of the great savings and investment effort; development turned out to be an uphill struggle, and the possibility of 'immiserizing growth' began to raise its ugly head. The single-gap neo-Keynesian formula which made growth dependent only on the rate of investment began to be replaced by 'dual gap' theories of development where the balance of payments appeared as a separate and often dominant constraining factor. Thus, for balance of payments reasons, success in raising domestic savings rates could turn sour in that the potential savings capacity could not be fully utilized for lack of foreign exchange. Here, the failure of aid to reach the modest targets set, let alone the dimensions of a 'Marshall Plan', came increasingly to be felt as a constraining factor.

Another consequence of the poor experience with primary commodity prices during the period immediately before the war was a certain export pessimism which contrasted sharply with domestic optimism. This export pessimism led to emphasis on industrialization as the most obvious diversification out of primary commodities – not just any kind of industrialization but that with an emphasis on import substitution. As far as reliance on exports of primary commodities was concerned, this pessimism was largely justified by events: in spite of unprecedented expansion in the industrial countries, the terms of trade for primary commodities fell by over 25 per cent between 1951 and 1965 and volume also expanded much less than might have been expected. Where the pessimism proved to be unjustified, however, was in being extended to all exports. This was based partly on the pre-war experience of recession in the industrial countries and shrinking world trade, and partly on a belief that exports of manufactures were largely beyond the reach of developing countries. The first assumption turned out to be quite false: in contrast to the pre-war shrinkage, world trade bounced ahead at rates considerably exceeding even the high growth rates of industrial countries. But the second assumption was largely justified at the time: in the early 1950s it was very difficult to visualize the rapid expansion of exports of manufacturers from the NICs, India, Brazil and other developing countries beginning in the 1960s. Much of the infrastructure needed for export industries was simply not there; such industries would have lacked the foundation of a domestic market which still had to be created by planning for balanced growth. With the benefit of hindsight and in the light of experience, we can now say that developing countries did not pay sufficient attention during the golden years to the possibilities of export substitution rather than import substitution, i.e. moving from exports of primary commodities into exports of manufactured goods. As a corollary, not enough attention was paid by many developing countries to the need to keep the import-substituting industries efficient so that they could rapidly develop into export industries. In fact, the methods adopted to establish import-substituting industries were often directly hostile to the development of efficiency as a basis for subsequent exports.

There is a long list of factors now recognized as creating such a danger of inefficient import substitution. This list would include rent seeking rather than efficiency as a basis of profits in protected import-substituting industries; encouragement of foreign penetration of the economy, leading to the elimination of local producers and preventing indigenous learning processes; a tendency to adopt imported capital-intensive technologies; concentration on items of luxury consumption of the type previously imported; and absence of sufficient vertical deepening of the import-substituting industries, in particular a failure to develop local capital goods industries.

Such a catalogue of sins is fashionable today as a basis for arguing that industrialization should have been more 'export led' or 'outward oriented' from the beginning. However, one should be careful before drawing this particular lesson from the experience of the 1950s and 1960s. To begin with, when exports of manufacturers did start in a promising way in the 1960s, they were often based on industries originally developed as import substitutes, or at any rate for the domestic market; many of the export industries were only possible on the basis of previous infrastructure investment in transport, education, and so on. The technological capacity for successful export competition in manufactures had to be built up by industrial experience gained from industrialization for the domestic market.

Moreover, even today it can be shown that 'outward orientation' works better as a recipe for middle-income countries than for low-income countries – and in the 1950s practically all developing countries were still in the category of what are now considered to be low-income countries. There is a clear danger that the lesson of 'outward orientation' will be learned in a less favourable international climate than during the golden years and then become counter-productive. There is also a fallacy of composition in jumping from the success stories of some countries in exporting manufactures to the conclusion that all or most developing countries could have followed the same strategies with the same results.

The emphasis on industrialization was right (within limits to be discussed) and the emphasis on substitution, i.e. substituting manufactured goods for primary commodities, was also right. But the possibilities of export substitution were underrated. Although this did not prevent a vigorous participation of developing countries as a whole in world trade in manufactures at a later stage, it did mean that when the time came, this participation was concentrated on a relatively small number of developing countries.

Probably the most important weakness of the import-substituting industrialization strategy was that it did not really substitute for imports. Due to the lack of vertical integration, it shifted imports from finished products to inputs of intermediate and capital goods, saving very little foreign exchange in the process. However, the same objection can also be raised about the later export-led success stories, like South Korea and the other East Asian 'tigers': the net value added by exports was often only a small fraction of the statistical export value, with a high proportion of the exports being offset by imports of necessary inputs to produce these exports. The chief difference, however, was that whereas import substitution tended to run out of steam when the simpler and final-stage imports had been substituted, in the case of export-led growth, the import content of the exports was steadily reduced in the case of the tigers and also of some of the Latin American countries (as happened before in Japan), so that the net value added represented by a given value of exports was steadily increased. However, it must remain an open question to what extent this difference is due to the superiority of outward orientation over inward orientation, or to what extent it is due to the fact that both import substitution and export promotion were handled with greater efficiency in the case of the successful countries, helped by third factors such as standards of education, promotion of indigenous technology, administrative efficiency of the government, entrepreneurial culture, labour discipline and so on. There must be a presumption that such third factors were important, because in most of the outward-oriented success stories one will also find that the import-substitution industries developed to a high level of efficiency (many of them becoming export industries) and that these outward-oriented countries relied heavily on import substitution in the earlier stages and continue to do so with proper selectivity. Proper selectivity, overall efficiency, proper timing and phasing, the ability to 'pick winners' seemed to be more important elements of successful development than any so-called inward or outward orientation.

The neo-classical 'new orthodoxy' has revived the myth of the passive state. The active developmental state supposedly just regards growth by creating widespread inefficiencies, stifling enterprise and preventing market signals from functioning. Governments should move towards limiting their role to ensuring 'sound money' and 'getting the prices right'. Yet the success stories belie such an interpretation. The East Asian NICs, and especially South Korea, have had extensive state intervention throughout their development in industrial planning, infrastructure, training, finance and labour relations, with subsidization of some industries and protection of others. As Amartya Sen has commented: 'If this is the free market, then Walras's auctioneer can surely be seen as going around with a government white paper in one hand and a whip in the other.' This is not to deny the importance of private sector dynamism, but the strategic role of the state was crucial. It is not the size of the state that is the real issue, but rather its roles and effectiveness. In practice this is acknowledged by many neo-classical economists.

In any case, much of the import-substituting and inward-looking nature of the early industrialization was the almost inevitable result of the political situation. This was clearly true in countries like India. The independence struggle had been intimately mixed up with protection against the imports from industrial countries destroying local and traditional industries: Gandhi's spinning wheel and boycott of textile imports from Lancashire are symbolic. The linkage between national independence and inward-looking industrialization was also due to the political perception that national independence and sovereignty are meaningless without a measure of industrialization and self-sufficiency. This perception was to be repeated in the 1960s in the newly independent African countries with economically even more unsatisfactory results, because of the absence of many preconditions for successful industrialization compared with Asia or Latin America. If this process of import-substituting industrialization is looked at as a political necessity, much of the criticism of the process as being economically inferior loses in relevance.

The emphasis on physical capital accumulation as the 'crux' of development also led, in due course, to a tolerance for income inequalities and the persistence of poverty. This took the form either of a belief that growth was sooner or later bound to 'trickle down' and spread to the poor, or even more strongly, that increased income inequalities were a necessary price to pay for the time being until the luxury of welfare could be afforded from an enlarged cake of production. During this period of the 1950s and 1960s Kuznets's famous 'inverted U-curve' played a big role, and seemed to show that in the earlier stages of development, income inequalities increased until a turning point was reached – presumably at middle-income levels, perhaps after the 'take-off stage' identified by Rostow – when income distribution would become more equal again, and poverty would rapidly recede under the dual impact of a larger cake and a more equal income distribution. The same idea of a turning point away from inequality towards greater equality and welfare was also inherent in the Arthur Lewis model of development with surplus labour, which was very influential during this period. As the golden years went on, however, the existence of such a turning point at a reasonably early development stage became more and more doubtful. There seemed little sign either of trickle down or of a turning point in most of the developing countries. Hence, new strategies of 'redistribution with growth', and more directly employment- and poverty-targeted approaches, came to the fore, as will be described in the next section.

The Arthur Lewis model was also indicative of another weakness in the type of development prevalent during the golden years, namely a comparative neglect of agriculture. In this model, and much related thinking, the main function of agriculture was to provide rural surplus labour as the cannon fodder of industrialization (reminiscent of what happened in the pioneer days of the Industrial Revolution in Great Britain), to provide a market for industrial goods and to provide the raw materials for processing by the prominent textile, leather and other industries. This passive or negative role ascribed to agriculture was never very convincing: how could agriculture provide a market for industrial goods unless rural incomes were raised? How could agriculture release surplus labour unless productivity was increased? How could growth trickle down to the poor when the great mass of the poor lived in rural areas? These and similar questions were not clearly faced, let alone answered.

There were several reasons for this blind spot in the early industrialization drive. One was the justified pessimism about relative prices of primary and agricultural products, which was perhaps too unthinkingly extended from the international to the domestic arena. There was also a strong belief (derived from classical credentials) that technical progress in agriculture would always be much slower and more difficult than in industry. This belief has proved unjustified, as shown by the tremendous increases in agricultural productivity in North America, Europe and the Far East, where technical progress in agriculture proved to be at least as fast as in industry, as well as the green revolution in some parts of the Third World.

Another reason was more political: an 'urban bias' injected into development policies by the disproportionate political influence of the urban minority compared with the rural majority. The opposite 'rural bias' in the agricultural policies followed in North America, Europe and Japan provided yet another reason for comparative neglect of agriculture in developing countries: it reduced international food prices, making imports easier and more tempting. It also made available during this period of surplus massive US food aid, enabling governments so inclined to justify low investment priorities for national food production. However, all the very large recipients of food aid during the 1950s and early 1960s, such as India, South Korea, Israel and Greece, eventually managed to use the resources provided by massive aid, including food aid, to provide the infrastructure investment for their own green revolutions. In this they followed in the footsteps of Western Europe and Japan, who also very quickly graduated out of the massive food aid provided by the Marshall Plan into becoming substantial surplus producers with strong 'rural bias' policies.

Overvalued exchange rates, often typical of countries engaged in import-substituting industrialization, work to the disadvantage not only of export industries but more particularly of agriculture, both by reducing exports and facilitating competing imports. So, in the total picture of relative neglect of agriculture, it was not surprising that the heavy net agricultural exports of developing countries began to fade as the period went on and net food exports were steadily converted into net food imports (although the agricultural policies of the richer countries had as much – or more – to do with this than the policies of developing countries).

Yet another phenomenon became apparent towards the second golden decade which served to take off some of the gilt, and was subsequently to become a source of great trouble and worry. This was an increasing divergence among developing countries. Growth turned out to be distinctly faster and easier among the middle-income countries than among the low-income countries. This remains true even when the circular nature of this relationship is taken into account, i.e. that faster growth pushes countries into the middle-income category while slower growth condemns countries to stay in the low-income category. Thus, during the last five years of the period (1965–70), the per capita income of middle-income countries, growing at 3.8 per cent per annum, increased almost twice as fast as the low-income countries, at 2.2 per cent. In fact, the middle-income developing countries grew slightly faster than the industrial market economies, even in per capita terms. It was the low-income countries which were beginning to fall behind. Thus, the gap opening up during that period was not so much between North and South, but rather between the upper- and middle-income countries on the one hand, and the low-income countries on the other. The sub-category of what later came to be known as 'least developed countries' began to emerge, and so did a geographical concentration of this sub-category among the then very recently independent countries of sub-Saharan Africa. 'Marginalization' and the 'economic underclass' crept into the development agenda.

Another worrying feature of the golden years was the fact that in spite of rapid growth, increasing inflationary pressures and an international environment which should have been very favourable to primary commodity prices, they obstinately refused to improve relative to the price of manufactures imported by developing countries.

Again, the least developed countries were the worst sufferers since they depended almost entirely on exports of primary products and, in the case of many African countries, on a single primary product. This seemed to reveal a structurally persistent weakness boding ill in the event of the kind of deterioration in the international climate which was to follow. Also, the suspicion arose, based on the emerging evidence of the 1960s, that even those developing countries which had engaged in successful export substitution of simple manufactures, typically textiles, shoes, processed primary products and so on, for primary exports did not seem to escape the threat of adverse terms of trade. An uneven distribution of gains from international trade was beginning to be seen to be not just a matter of different types of commodities but also of different types of countries, different degrees of technological power and different types of labour markets.

To sum up the experience of the golden years: the favourable growth experience, particularly for the middle-income countries, had certainly demonstrated the possibility of economic growth. This was more important than it might seem, since initially considerable doubt existed, both among politicians and economists, as to whether economic growth was not 'naturally' limited to *homo economicus* – economic man as existing in the industrial countries of the temperate zone. Newly independent countries in particular were viewed rather sceptically as to their growth possibilities. So this demonstration of the golden years of growth feasibility was no mean achievement; at any rate, the voices doubting the possibility of growth outside the sacred circle of the North were no longer heard towards the end of the period. Moreover, understanding of development problems had increased considerably during the period: the simple view of growth as a type of vending machine suggested by a superficial reading of the Harrod–Domar formula, i.e. that you put in more savings and investment and you pull out more growth, had given way to an understanding that even growth, let alone development, is a much more complex process, and that in particular it involves factors relating to human rather than physical capital. So in this respect it was particularly important that the golden years showed rapid progress, not only in physical investment rates, but also in such indicators of human capital formation as spreading literacy and education, elimination of a number of diseases, and reduced mortality rates, including infant mortality rates. This progress in human indicators could be shown to be only tenuously related to GNP growth, illustrating both the limitations of 'trickle down' and the possibility of development along alternative routes.

But since all this encouraging progress was made in a period of rapid growth in the industrial countries and a situation in these countries, as a result of full employment and the Keynesian consensus, extremely favourable to trade liberalization, it was not clear during the golden years to what extent the growth achieved was dependent on the existence of an 'engine of growth' outside the control of the developing countries themselves. This was to be tested when the favourable international climate was drastically changed in the early years of the following decade of the 1970s, signifying the end of the golden years period. It was then that the lack of an internal dynamism in many countries, due often to neglect of agriculture and of indigenous technological capacity, became painfully apparent.

The 1970s: growth maintained? The illusion of debt-led growth

The decade of the 1970s saw the breakdown and disintegration of the Bretton Woods system. The best date to attach to the end of Bretton Woods is probably 15 August 1971 when President Nixon suspended the free convertibility of the US dollar into gold at the fixed rate agreed at Bretton Woods. This ended the era of fixed exchange rates and destroyed the foundations of even the truncated Bretton Woods which had emerged. The breakdown of the system was more immediately connected with the emerging payment imbalances between the industrial countries, but also with increasing concerns with 'overheating' of their economies and a consequent displacement of full employment by control of inflation as a priority objective. Thus the engine of growth which had supported the developing countries during the golden era began to stutter and then violently change gear. But the event which most marked the 1970s and gave a disarrayed international system its final ominous push was the assertion of oil power by OPEC in 1973–74, with the decade suitably ending with a second assertion of oil power in 1979–80. This provided an opportunity for broader assertion of commodity power and for fundamental shifts in international economic relations; in the event, however, this opportunity was not realized.

So here again we can speak of 'a splendid story not wholly true'. The splendid part of the story was that if we simply look at growth rates, the developing countries as a whole, and even the oil-importing developing countries, proved quite capable of continuing their growth rates even in the face of reduced growth and serious recessions in the industrial countries. In fact, contrary to what happened during the preceding two decades, the gap in per capita income between the developing countries and the industrial market economies narrowed rather than widened during 1970–81, at least in relative terms.

A mixed picture

The maintenance of growth during this period is, however, subject to some qualification. The growth rate of GDP for all developing economies, excepting the high-income oil exporters, receded from the high rate of 6 per cent per annum which it had reached during 1965–70, the last five golden years, to 5.2 per cent in 1971–80, although this was still higher than the average figure for the preceding two decades. The serious exception was sub-Saharan Africa, where the 1971–80 growth rate not only fell much more heavily (from 4.8 to 3.3 per cent), but was lower than at any period during 1950–70. In per capita terms, growth in sub-Saharan Africa was virtually wiped out; 16 out of 41 African countries showed absolute declines. This phenomenon of development in reverse, then still confined to half of sub-Saharan Africa, was to become more widespread in the 1980s. In the three worst cases of declines of over 4 per cent per annum (Angola, Chad and Uganda), this reversal was associated with civil wars, and could thus still be ascribed to 'extra-economic' causes. At the other extreme, the Middle East and North Africa, benefiting directly or indirectly from high oil prices, achieved new growth records, well beyond the level of the two preceding decades, and the East Asia and Pacific region maintained the very high growth rate of 8 per cent which it had achieved in the preceding five years. But Latin America and South Asia shared the African decline, although less drastically: both these regions, accounting for most of the population of developing countries (outside China), more or less returned to the growth rates of the earlier part of the two golden decades.

There was also vigorous progress in the competitive position of developing countries in world trade in manufactures. While absolute levels of imports of manufactures by industrial countries were held down by their slower growth and protectionist measures, the share of developing countries in their total markets and in their total imports increased, although from low levels (from 1.7 per cent of the total market share in 1970 to 3.4 per cent in 1979), with all classes of manufactured goods sharing in the increase. The increase in the share of developing countries in total trade of manufactured goods from 13.5 per cent in 1970 to 16.5 per cent in 1979 was, however, entirely concentrated on Far Eastern countries; Latin America and other regions failed to participate in this increase. Both shares in industrial country and world markets are still quite small and should leave room for further expansion is the light of new comparative advantages, always with the important proviso that protectionist measures in the industrialized countries do not prevent this.

Moreover, the maintained growth of GDP is subject to some doubt concerning the D (for 'domestic'), and this applies specifically to the growth of manufactured exports. We have already seen that during the golden years the expected preponderance of aid and official development assistance over private investment had been reversed. During the 1970s aid from Western countries continued to stagnate and dwindle, well-below the modest UN target, while private capital continued to flow strongly, supported both by the maintained 'credit-worthiness' of developing countries bolstered by commercial bank lending of recycled OPEC surpluses, and also by the revolution of communications which made internationalization of operations much easier. As a result, by the mid-1970s in Latin America and Africa, typically 40–50 per cent of manufacturing industry was controlled by foreign firms (in some countries 60–70 per cent). In Asia this share was typically lower (India and South Korea 10–15 per cent) although in some Asian countries the share reached or exceeded 40–50 per cent. In the light of the high share of foreign firms in manufacturing in Latin America and Africa, the conventional warning against an 'enclave' character of foreign investment appears ironical; it was domestic manufacturing control which was beginning to look like an enclave. It was equally ironic that industrialization had been recommended as a way of 'de-linking' from an unequal world economy; in fact, it was leading to firmer integration.

Thus, the cherished aim of industrialization as a means of strengthening national independence had been widely missed. The real growth factor in the 1970s, apart from some oil exporters, had come from neither the industrial nor the developing countries, but from the TNCs (transnational corporations). The typical sales value of the large TNCs had become equal to or higher than the total GDP even of many larger and better-off developing countries. (Exxon, for example, has a sales value equivalent to the GDP of Argentina or Nigeria, close to South Korea, more than twice the GDP of Egypt or Pakistan, and almost four times that of Chile or Peru.) Even the last in ranking of the 20 largest TNCs had sales equal to the GDP of Morocco. To a TNC, investment in any given developing country is usually a small, often marginal, part of its total operations and easily fungible; while to a developing country the operation would be an important, and perhaps technologically indispensable, part of its manufacturing capacity – a situation clearly not making for an equal bargaining position. Competition among TNCs helps to balance the scales, but may be offset, or more than offset, by competition among LDCs (less-developed countries) for the money and technology of the TNCs.

The data for the import-purchasing power of total exports by developing countries also seem to tell a 'splendid story', but once again further analysis shows it to be not wholly true. In the aggregate, this increased faster between 1970 and 1980 than for industrial countries, but the following points should be borne in mind:

- 1980 represented a peak year for oil export values, and much of this favourable differential had been lost by 1983; for developing countries other than major oil exporters the purchasing power of exports increased more slowly than in industrial countries;
- the aggregate figures do not take into account the more rapid increase in population in developing countries; on a per capita basis the comparison would be less favourable;
- the least developed countries actually showed an absolute decline in the purchasing power of their exports by over 13 per cent;
- even among the remaining countries, the favourable differential was entirely confined to exporters of manufactures; the other countries fell behind the industrial countries, in relative terms.

Another apparent achievement of the 1970s was that the successful assertion of producer power in the case of oil interrupted the deteriorating trend in terms of trade of developing countries as a whole for all primary commodities taken as a whole; though of course, the oil-importing countries had a very different story of sharp deterioration to tell. But taking the developing countries as a whole, the improvement in terms of trade through high oil prices shifted financial surpluses and financial power strongly in the direction of the Third World. This raised great hopes of using this newly found power for the establishment of a new international economic order (NIEO). It also raised the possibility of creating an indigenous dynamic of development within the Third World itself, and the prospect of using the new financial power for the creation of indigenous technological capacity. The sad part of the story is that this opportunity was lost, and the NIEO ran into the sands. Worse, the way the oil surpluses were recycled through EURO dollars and the commercial banks of the industrial countries, as well as the new non-Keynesian deflationary response of the industrial countries, together ensured that the net outcome would be adverse to the Third World. Not only was the opportunity lost, but it turned into a trap: the term 'debt trap' which became current in the 1980s is an apt description of what happened.

But we are concerned here not so much with the history of this decade as with the lessons of experience that were drawn for development policy and for development thinking during this time. In the first place, there was a growing disillusionment with growth as a necessary and sufficient development objective. This was not in any way due to a slowing of actual growth in the course of the golden years. Quite on the contrary, the growth rate of developing countries speeded up from 4.2 per cent in 1950–60 to 5.1 per cent in 1960–65 and 6.0 per cent in 1965–70. Even the growth rate of the low-income countries taken as a whole speeded up during the period, although less than in the middle-income countries, as well as starting from a lower level, so that the gap between the two groups widened over the two decades. Rather, the disillusionment was due to increasing evidence that rapid growth of GNP could be combined with growing unemployment and underemployment, increasing poverty, and often also greater inequality of income distribution. At the same time, the industrial countries also became disillusioned with growth, although for rather different reasons, since in their experience growth led to inflationary pressures and balance of payments trouble. For the developing countries the shift in objectives from simple growth initially took two forms: one was the establishment of employment as an overriding objective; the other was a shift to redistribution.

The new employment priority

The shift to an emphasis on employment was based on evidence of increasing unemployment and underemployment, both in urban and rural areas. The social and political tensions and pressures thus created were seen to undermine the foundations of continued growth so that there was a need for a new approach. Although there was much talk at that time of a 'dethronement of GNP', this is not a very good description of what happened. Growth continued to be regarded as a necessary condition for development, but was no longer accepted as a sufficient condition. Employment creation was not seen as an alternative to growth, but as a proper instrument of growth which would produce not only growth in itself but also a pattern of growth conducive to more equal income distribution, less poverty, more social contentment and less political unrest. In development analysis, this shift to employment objectives was typified by the move from the Arthur Lewis model, in which the surplus labour released from agriculture was assumed to be more or less fully absorbed by the growing urban industries, to the Harris–Todaro model. Under the Harris–Todaro model the drift to the towns would be far in excess of available employment opportunities; the gap between rural subsistence incomes and wages in the modern industrial urban sector would attract job seekers from the rural areas in a multiple ratio equal to the income gap. If modern urban sector wages are three times rural incomes, one-third of the chance of a job would be sufficient to attract a migrant from the rural areas; hence there would be three job seekers for each available job and two-thirds of them would remain unemployed or condemned to make a living as well as they could in the informal sector. This model seemed to correspond much better to reality than the Arthur Lewis model.

The shift to employment as a main objective was quite logically accompanied by particular emphasis on the need for employment-intensive technologies; so this also became the era of a search for and emphasis on 'appropriate' technologies. Moreover, since small-scale production is normally more employment-intensive than large-scale production, it also became the era of 'small is beautiful'. Equally logically, with employment moving to the centre as the crux of development, such 'human capital' aspects as training, skills, health and other factors in productivity were now given increased weight, compared with physical capital accumulation.

In institutional terms, the new emphasis on employment placed the International Labour Organization (ILO) in the centre of development policy, particularly through its newly organized World Employment Programme. The ILO employment missions, first with 'pilot missions' to Colombia, Sri Lanka and Kenya and subsequently many other countries, had a considerable impact on policy and thinking. This was true in particular of the Kenya Employment Mission, which also marked the transition from an emphasis on employment to an emphasis on the need for a more direct attack on poverty, by pointing out that the so-called unemployment or underemployment in developing countries was a misnomer. In fact, most of the so-called unemployed or underemployed were working quite hard to earn a living; the real problem was their low income levels. They were the 'working poor' rather than the 'unemployed'. The Kenya Mission also drew attention to the potential of the informal sector as a source for the labour-intensive and appropriate technology needs, rather than an undesirable residual as it appeared in the Harris-Todaro model.

The new 'employment-oriented strategy' had some obvious limitations. The idea of labour-intensive small-scale appropriate technology conflicted with the desire for industrialization and modernization; the creation of 'appropriate technology' required a technological capacity in some ways even greater than that required for the earlier growth-oriented investment pattern. The latter could to a large extent be imported or imitated, whereas the appropriate technology would have to be newly created. Ironically, under the Harris–Todaro model, the creation of more employment would only intensify the urban unemployment problem, since for every new job there would be several migrants as long as rural surplus labour was available. Reliance on employment-oriented strategy also conflicted with the increasing role of direct foreign investors and multinational corporations. Also, employment could not deal with the poverty groups not capable of employment: those too old to work, too ill, crippled, broken families, orphaned children, and so on. Employment to provide an income does not solve the problem of access to health, education, clean water, sanitation, and so on – all services which relate to public action rather than employment.

Yet in spite of such limitations, the employment orientation had a valid and lasting impact. It emphasized not only the contribution to production which employment could provide, but also the sense of participation and self-respect which improved earning capacity from employment could bring: the issue of human rights as a development objective emerged at this stage. Employment emphasis was especially useful in the agricultural sector, where the basis for an appropriate technology already existed, and it became increasingly realized that the small-scale farmer was more productive in terms of output per acre than the large farmer, and also was quite capable of responding to economic incentives.

Employment creation in the rural sector also became the key to agricultural improvement through public works schemes, particularly during the slack agricultural seasons, and in times of drought or other emergencies. It was discovered that not only emergencies but also persistent poverty were due not so much to a lack of food available, but rather to a breakdown in the 'entitlement' mechanism for obtaining access to food and other essentials of life. Employment, either for an income or directly paid in food, was perhaps the most obvious way of creating such entitlements.

An employment-oriented development policy also provided an essential bridge between the growth-oriented strategy emphasizing 'productive' investment, and a subsequent poverty orientation which could be accused of shifting to 'unproductive' activities such as redistribution, provision of social services subsidies and direct income support. Employment creation was at the same time clearly productive and yet naturally targeted so as to achieve greater equality of income distribution and produce a better trickle-down effect on the poor than mere growth by itself. Nobody could accuse an employment-oriented strategy of playing 'zero-sum games'.

Where employment creation seemed most successful, as in the case of the East Asian 'tigers', it was because it was nurtured both by a high degree of literacy, education, skill and willingness to train in the labour force, and a rapid development of general technological capacity (rather than a specific 'appropriate technology') which enabled them to remain internationally competitive in labour-intensive lines of export even with rising real wages, and to maintain an equal income distribution. It was such factors, rather than concentration on employment creation as such, which made for expansion of employment – in other words, employment was more of a result than an objective or instrument of policy.

The redistribution priority

The other shift in development strategy during the earlier part of the 1970s, apart from the emphasis on employment objectives, was greater concern with income distribution, or 'Redistribution With Growth' (RWG). This was, of course, linked to employment-oriented strategies: an increase in employment would normally also improve the equality of income distribution, particularly if it related to agriculture, the informal sector and was based on labour-intensive technologies, as proposed. So it is not surprising that the RWG strategy emerged from the Kenya Employment Mission Report, which contained a chapter entitled 'Redistribution From Growth'. The subtle shift from redistribution *from* growth to redistribution *with* growth added an important new element. Redistribution from growth put growth first and then suggested the use of the resources created by growth for deliberate distributive measures, rather than waiting for 'trickle down'. This policy, which could be described as 'incremental income distribution', was put forward as having the great advantage of making redistribution politically more acceptable, since it would come out of additional resources and nobody would be absolutely worse off. This aspect of growth first and redistribution afterwards from the resources created by growth was always a worrying weakness, since it disregarded the possibility, perhaps likelihood, that the policies needed to promote growth might be incompatible with redistributive policies (and vice versa), and hence that one might undermine the other.

The shift to redistribution with growth emphasized the simultaneity and complementarity of redistribution and growth: it was part of the greater emphasis on human capital, with a denial of a trade-off between distribution and growth, and instead an assertion of the compatibility and complementarity of the two. A number of development analysts went one step further and advocated redistribution *before* growth. An important argument for this was that Japanese and Korean growth, for example, owed both its intensity and egalitarian character to the fact that through land reform, heavy investment in education and health, and so on, physical and human capital assets were fairly equally distributed before the growth process started. It was argued that in this way growth not only had a more solid and sustainable foundation, but would also assume a pattern which was favourable for sustained equality and poverty reduction.

The shift in thinking away from growth towards employment and redistribution in the early 1970s found a particularly ready echo in the World Bank which at that time (the McNamara period) had a liberal phase (in the sense of Keynesian/progressive) in sharp contrast to its subsequent domination by monetarist and neo-liberal views (this time in the Chicago sense). The World Bank became a lead agency in advocating RWG strategies, emphasizing the importance of human capital investment and helping to promote directly poverty-oriented 'basic needs strategies'. One indication of the compatibility of these strategies with growth was that the World Bank's rate of return on its projects did not suffer in this period.

This shift also had implications for approaches to development planning. The original stress on GNP growth focuses attention on macroeconomic planning, which indeed was developed in close parallel with implementing GNP targets. This is less true of employment targets. Clearly there is no single homogeneous employment problem; the problem of the unemployed school leaver, for example, is rather different from that of the small farmer without access to water. So an employment emphasis paves the way for a less aggregated and more dispersed view of planning. This is even more true as we move to poverty and basic needs objectives. The character of the different poverty groups is even more diverse and heterogeneous than the different employment problems. Moreover, the nature of poverty problems may vary even among neighbouring villages, or among urban households living close to each other in the same town. Thus poverty-oriented planning and the provision of basic requirements for population groups now lacking them are by their very nature, and almost by definition, a highly decentralized affair. Local planning as well as local participation, particularly on the part of those directly affected by the lack of basic requirements, are naturally moving into the foreground of the picture. Community development, rather than central planning, seems the natural principal tool of a basic needs-oriented development strategy.

Perhaps ironically, this particular implication of RWG/basic needs strategies, in moving away from the centralized macroeconomic planning associated with GNP growth to looser and more decentralized approaches, was to fit in well with criticism of centralized planning coming from quite a different direction during the tide of neo-liberal counter-revolution characteristic of the 1980s.

The lower growth rate and re-emergence of unemployment in the industrial countries almost inevitably meant an increase in their protectionism. The attempts by GATT to reduce tariffs and liberalize trade were more than offset by increased non-tariff barriers, 'voluntary' export restraints, further tightening up of agricultural policies with inevitable protectionist consequences, and other ways of evading the spirit – if not the letter – of GATT. These non-tariff barriers applied with greater severity to developing countries than to North–North trade, and affected about a quarter of their total exports. The protectionist measures already introduced against an export thrust from a limited number of developing countries give some indication of the industrialized countries' possible response if a more wide-spread competitive export expansion were attempted.

In addition to rising protectionism, the abandonment of fixed, or at any rate stable, exchange rates in favour of floating rates introduced new elements of uncertainty into the international trade prospects of developing countries. Under normal circumstances such uncertainty would have been an argument for greater inward orientation, reliance on import substitution and expansion of trade of developing countries among themselves. If this did not happen to any significant degree, it was largely because the pressures on import capacity deriving from industrial countries' protectionism and from trade uncertainties were swamped by the readiness, indeed the passionate keenness, of commercial banks in the big financial centres to offer loans, initially at low or negative real rates of interest. This made it relatively easy to maintain imports, even in the face of more precarious export prospects and uncertainties. The temptation for developing countries to avoid timely adjustment to the less favourable climate of the 1970s by relying on 'easy money' from the commercial banks, offered not only readily but without conditions, proved too much to resist. This overall picture did not apply equally to all developing countries; the four East Asian tigers, for example, showed their remarkable capacity for adjustment by absorbing high oil prices, increasing protectionist barriers for their exports and countering exchange rate uncertainties by raising productivity, keeping real wages low and demonstrating a strong planning capacity in picking winners. Moreover, they did this with less reliance on commercial bank loans than the Latin American countries.

Another factor which maintained the growth of countries like South Korea, but also a number of other developing countries, was the spill-over effect of OPEC surpluses. OPEC aid and investment programmes were developed, although aid was highly concentrated in Middle Eastern countries and investment often channelled through the financial institutions of industrial countries. But additional exports to oil exporters, the export of labour to these countries resulting in significant remittances back to the developing home countries, as well as the procurement of construction and other contracts in oil-rich countries, all helped to maintain growth. Although this was a more solid basis than borrowing from commercial banks, in that it did not result in an increased debt burden, it also turned out to be a somewhat precarious and temporary source of development finance, dependent on the continuance of the large OPEC surpluses. It was still 'dependent development', although from the point of view of the Third World as a whole it could be considered as a better approach to self-reliance. But in the event, the OPEC engine of growth proved as temporary as the Keynesian growth of the industrial countries during the golden years had been, and the opportunities it offered were not taken. Instead of laying new foundations for sustainable growth in the 1980s, the OPEC engine merely served to replace the failing other engine and postpone the impact of its failure.

The breakdown of Bretton Woods – divergent perceptions

The nature of the 1970s as a period of illusionary debt-led growth raises a number of issues which contain important lessons for the future. The initial collapse of the Bretton Woods system in 1971 and the subsequent failure of the industrial countries to co-ordinate their own exchange rate and other policies, together with the shock in 1973–74 of the first large rise in oil prices, clearly led to quite different perceptions on the part of the industrial and developing countries respectively. The industrial countries at first assumed that the crisis was merely a temporary phenomenon, no doubt a serious hiccup in the progress of the two previous decades but one that could be dealt with through existing institutions, largely by way of normal lending operations of their own commercial banks recycling OPEC surpluses. Meanwhile, the rapid growth with full employment of the golden years might have to be abandoned in favour of slower growth, unemployment and recessionary periods. But at a time when prevailing politics and ideologies were beginning to swing to the right, and the fight against inflation became a chief objective, this price seemed worth paying. In the event the basic assumption that the shift in financial power relations towards developing countries, or at least towards OPEC countries, could be counteracted by the industrial countries turned out to be justified. This perception on the part of the industrial countries further implied that any later debt repayment phase could be easily handled in traditional ways through the resumed growth in the 1980s which was confidently expected, and/ or through continued lending and capital transfers. It took the second big rise in oil prices in 1979–80 to shake this view.

On the part of the developing countries there was a different perception. It was felt that the shift in financial power and the successful assertion of commodity power represented a permanent and fundamental break with the past, both necessitating and making possible a new international economic order. The developing countries felt strong enough to confront the industrial countries with programmes and demands for such an order. They underestimated the ability of the industrial countries to absorb the shocks of the early 1970s within the framework of the existing order and institutions, and also their readiness to abandon the Keynesian full employment consensus of the 1950s and 1960s. The lesson of the past had been that it took a crisis of the dimensions of the recession of the 1930s and the World War to create the preconditions for a completely new international order, and even then (as we have seen) there was in the end hesitation and difficulty in adopting wholly new and radical ideas. The developing countries assumed that the upheavals of 1971 and 1973–74 constituted a similar crisis offering a similar opportunity.

In the event, the breakdown of Bretton Woods in 1971 and the assertion of oil power in 1973–74 constituted a crisis sufficient to terminate the progress of the golden years, but not to create a consensus for a new order. By the time the second big oil shock came at the end of the decade, the world system had adjusted to running at a slower rate, and the industrial countries had brought into play their technological capacity to reduce the impact of high oil prices by energy substitution and by changing the volume and pattern of their production, stepping up exploration and new supplies, and so on. Thus, although the recession following the second oil shock was at least as severe as the one after the first oil shock, it once again failed to reach the dimensions required for a consensus on a need for fundamental changes.

With the benefit of hindsight, the developing countries, rather than relying on a perceived fundamental power shift and confronting the industrial countries with a programme for a new order, could have chosen two other strategies. One was to use their new financial power for the creation of a separate international system, at the same time additional to, and partially de-linked from, North–South relations. This was, of course, the route of extended South–South co-operation for which there was in any case plenty of economic scope and justification. Another strategy was to use the power shift which had undoubtedly occurred in the early 1970s to press for more piecemeal concessions and modifications of the battered Bretton Woods system – perhaps restoring some of the missing pieces discussed above – in the hope of inducing the industrial countries to return to the Keynesian consensus of high growth rates and full employment which had stood the developing countries in good stead.

The lesson of events of the 1970s for the developing countries was that assertion of commodity power without control of financial institutions, and not backed up by technological power, is empty and temporary. The same failure was also demonstrated for the assertion of power by individual countries or groups of producers without a system of full collaboration within the Third World as a whole.

The 1980s: the lost decade – development in reverse?

The idea of the 1980s as a decade 'lost' for development could be described as 'a sad story not wholly true'. It is not wholly true most obviously in the geographical sense: the decade may be 'lost' for Latin America, Africa and also the oil exporters (at least compared with the position they achieved in the 1970s) but it is not true of Asia. Given the demographic and economic importance of Asia, it is not clear which is the exception and which is the rule! But for the other three categories mentioned, to speak of a 'lost' decade may be an understatement; for sub-Saharan Africa, in particular, the 1980s became a disastrous decade, and this sub-continent rapidly acquired the character of a marginalized fourth world, increasingly recognized as requiring special action and special criteria. The other true part of this sad story is that the decade was 'lost' to development in that attention shifted to debt settlement, stabilization, adjustment, structural change, liberalization, and so on – often at the expense of everything that had previously been understood as development, whether growth, employment, redistribution, basic needs or reduction of poverty. This shift was associated with the ascent of neo-liberal ideologies, a shift in decision making on development strategy to creditors, donors and international financial institutions, and within the Bretton Woods system from the World Bank, which had traditionally stood for development, to the IMF which had come to stand for 'stabilization'. Perhaps the most symbolic development was the World Bank's shift out of exclusive project lending – previously put forward as the soundest form of development assistance – to balance of payments support in the form of structural adjustment lending and the establishment of a largely IMF-determined 'cross-conditionality' for World Bank action.

The geographical separation between Asia, where development continued, and the rest of the developing world where it was 'lost', had already been foreshadowed in the 1970s. In that period (1969–78) the export volume of Asia (without the Middle East) had increased faster than import volume (10.8 per cent per annum against 8.6 per cent), thus simultaneously constraining debt accumulation and strengthening repayment capacity, while in sub-Saharan Africa and Latin America export volumes increased much slower than import volumes, with the opposite effect. In sub-Saharan Africa, export volume increased by only 1.4 per cent per annum, less than the rate of population increase; even an increase in import volume three times higher at 4.1 per cent was barely sufficient to maintain per capita imports. In Latin America also, import volumes grew over three times more than export volumes (6.4 per cent against 1.7 per cent). The roots of a debt crisis were thus clearly planted in Latin America and Africa, rather than Asia.

For these countries, the 1980s proved a time of rude awakening from the illusionary growth of the 1970s. Over the five years 1982–86 the cumulative percentage falls in per capita GNP totalled 16.5 per cent for sub-Saharan Africa, 9.7 per cent for the highly indebted countries and 11.5 per cent for oil exporters. For all these categories of developing countries this amounted to a major reversal of development, not just a 'lost decade'. The share of industry in GDP in developing countries, which had increased during 1965–80 to that of the industrial market economies, fell back, and by 1986 was again below that of the industrial countries; it was the developing, not the industrial economies which 'de-industrialized'. In sub-Saharan Africa, de-industrialization was precipitous and brought the share of industry below what it had been in 1970; industrial output declined absolutely by 2.3 per cent per annum during the first half of the decade. There were also absolute declines in the highly indebted countries and the high-income oil exporters. Investment ratios generally declined for practically all categories of developing countries; in the aggregate, the fall from 26.9 per cent of GDP in 1980 to 23.5 per cent in 1986 brought the ratio below the 1973 level; again the cuts in the ratio were sharpest in sub-Saharan Africa and in the highly indebted countries; thus again the focus of development reversal emerges clearly. The terms of trade of developing countries as a whole deteriorated during 1981–86 by a cumulative percentage of 13.9 (but 34.1 for sub-Saharan Africa and 17.3 for the highly indebted countries). The only thing that seemed to be vigorously increasing for many categories of developing countries was their outstanding debt, with debt service reaching 4.3 per cent of GNP and absorbing 19.7 per cent of exports (as much as 29.6 per cent in sub-Saharan Africa and 27.8 per cent in the highly indebted countries). External debts in 1987 exceeded three years' exports for both sub-Saharan Africa and the 15 heavily indebted countries. The main exception of Asia must be re-emphasized. The overall performance of low-income countries was held up by the remarkable progress of China and India, which dominate this category, and exporters of manufactures were buttressed by the success stories of the East and South-East Asian NICs. Predictably, during the decade much debate centred around the lessons from Asian successes and the ways in which they could be transplanted to Africa and other parts of the developing world.

The 1980s opened with a strong recession which represented a culminating point of the contest between commodity power on the one hand, and technological and financial power on the other. Commodity power was represented by the second quadrupling of oil prices in 1979–80, while the technological and financial power of the industrial countries was represented by their capacity to reduce the oil content of production, to step up oil exploration and substitution for oil, and to reduce the demand for oil further by accepting or even welcoming a recession which would reduce inflation as well as the demand for oil. In this contest, technological/financial power proved to be stronger than commodity power, all the more so since the industrial countries had had the chance of adjusting to higher oil prices seven years earlier, when they first quadrupled in 1973–74.

For the oil-importing developing countries the constellation of circumstances could not have been worse. These were:

- reduced import volumes by the developing countries with recession and protectionism interacting in the same direction;
- highly unfavourable terms of trade, as a result both of high oil prices and a deterioration of other commodity prices in relation to their manufactured imports from industrial countries (the latter increased by high energy costs);
- a reduction and, later, virtual cessation of commercial bank lending and a rise in real interest rates so that debt burdens were increased both through lower export earnings and higher service payments simultaneously;
- a strong appreciation of the dollar in the early years of the decade resulting from the high rates of interest;
- spreading 'aid fatigue' among industrial countries due to both the recession and the spread of monetarist neo-liberal ideologies.

The shortcomings of the Bretton Woods system in providing no mechanism for the industrial countries and the balance of payments surplus countries to recover made themselves strongly felt. All these circumstances conspired to make the 1980s a lost decade for development. It was a sign of the times that even under such conditions it could be seriously debated whether the internal policies of developing countries, rather than external circumstances, were responsible for their difficulties.

Yet just at a time when the international climate became so disastrously hostile to development, the bastions of financial power in the industrial countries and in the leading financial institutions were captured by a neo-liberal ideology which preached all-out 'outward orientation' and 'market orientation' as the secret of successful development. If the 1950s and 1960s could be said to have displayed a time-lagged misplaced trade pessimism based on prewar experience, so the 1980s could be said to be dominated by a doctrinal and time-lagged trade optimism based on the trade expansion of the 1950s and 1960s and the subsequent illusionary maintenance of developing country imports in the 1970s. The crucial difference, however, was that the inward-oriented industrialization policies of the 1950s and 1960s were almost certainly justified as a necessary foundation for a subsequent successful outward orientation in a favourable economic climate; whereas the policies now impressed on developing countries under the name of outward orientation were intended not to lay the foundations for subsequent sustainable growth (although that was their supposed purpose), but rather to permit payment of their debts.

Here again there was a tragic time lag. Adjustment and restructuring for the purpose of repaying debts – or rather of keeping debts within more manageable limits – would have been an appropriate requirement for the 1970s. The maintenance of import capacity at the expense of balance of payments deficits and increasing indebtedness could have been justified only if the policies of the developing countries had then been firmly directed towards using the borrowed capital to build up a firm position in tradables permitting a discharge of debt service. Given the inability of industrial countries to prevent the slowed-down growth and sporadic recessions of the 1970s, or even their willingness to repeat such recessions and accept unemployment as part of their fight against inflation and OPEC power, the developing countries during the 1970s would have had to rely as much, or more, on import substitution than on export promotion. That at least would be an overall judgement, without excluding the possibility of specific countries finding their place in a pattern of a gradual increase in the capacity of a number of developing countries to export manufactures of a genuinely national character, i.e. other than as a result of relocation and internationalization of production on the part of the transnational corporations.

To the extent that this did not happen, there is an element of truth in holding the domestic policies of developing countries responsible for some of the troubles of the 1980s. This, however, is subject to some significant qualifications: at the time, in the 1970s, when exhortations to restructure in preparation for debt settlement would have been appropriate, not much was heard in this direction from those now in a position not only to advise but to impose such policies. Instead, the developing countries were encouraged to borrow without conditionality or much control of the use of the borrowed resources. Moreover, the type of internal policy that would have been needed in the 1970s was not the type of structural adjustment advocated in the 1980s. There is no evidence that the rise in real interest rates and the severe global recession of the early 1980s was foreseen at the time of low or negative rates in the 1970s.

The policies now impressed upon developing countries under the signs of restructuring, adjustment, retrenchment, stabilization and so on are justified on the grounds that they are necessary to 'lay the foundations of subsequent sustainable growth'. Leaving aside the question of symmetrical adjustment required from industrial, creditor and balance of payments surplus countries, this approach disregards one of the basic insights of the early development period of the 1950s. Much thinking prevalent then had been based on a view of development and growth as a process of 'cumulative causation', or a system of (beneficial or vicious) circles or spirals. The vicious circle of poverty, for example, was well-established: poor people are poor because they are undernourished or illiterate, and they are undernourished and illiterate because they are poor. In the same way, poor countries are poor because they have low savings and investment and they have low savings and investment because they are poor. In the strategy of balanced growth, the vicious circle took the form of treating the failure of section A to grow as due to the failure of other sectors B, C, D, and so on to grow and supply both the inputs and demand for sector A; the same is true of sector B, which fails to grow because sector A fails to grow. In the 'stages of growth' paradigm developed by Rostow this took the form of saying that the earlier stages of assembling the preconditions for growth are very difficult, but once the various elements have been assembled and can mutually complement each other, everything will fall into place and the economy can take off.

The present doctrine of neo-liberal adjustment is in danger of disregarding all this. It holds that one can temporarily deflate, arrest growth, reduce government expenditures, reduce expenditures on physical and human investments and so on, while at the same time gathering strength for a new and, it is hoped, more sustainable period of growth and development. This disregards the possibility that each cutback may make it more difficult to resume future growth from such a weakened basis. The picture of a 'slippery slope' may be more appropriate than the picture of *reculer pour mieux sauter* (stepping back to gain room for a forward jump) which underlies the neo-liberal approach to adjustment. Yet this possibility is not sufficiently considered or guarded against in the climate of the 1980s.

Yet the neo-liberal critics of earlier development policies deserve to be listened to seriously. It had become apparent to the developing countries themselves that a regime of overvalued exchange rates carried dangers of inefficient allocation, rent seeking, capital flight and so on; that prices and markets have a role to play in the efficient allocation of resources and are often better instruments than administrative regulation or controls; that over-expansion of the government sector might conceivably suppress latent entrepreneurial sources in the private sector which could be released by less regulation; that planning machinery can easily become overcentralized at the expense of local initiative and popular participation; that trade liberalization can be to the advantage of developing countries themselves; that proper price incentives to farmers can be a useful tool for stimulating domestic food production when they can be combined with other measures of a more structural character which are also needed; that industrialization which is at the expense of agriculture can be self-defeating, and should be replaced by a type of development in which agricultural development and industrialization can mutually support each other; that policies should not be excessively 'urban biased'; that subsidies and other measures targeted at lower-income groups often have a way of failing to reach the poorest and sometimes benefit the better-off instead; that public services no less than the private sector should be governed by principles of efficiency and low-cost services, etc. All this long list of insights (which could easily be further extended) had already emerged from previous developments, and there is no need to create a neo-liberal counter-revolution for discovering them. All the same, in so far as the critics of previous strategies have kept on hammering away at these and other shortcomings, they have rendered a useful service. But they have rendered no service by combining these insights with an abandonment of development objectives for the sake of adjustment; by being indifferent to the social impact or 'human face' aspects of the policies they propose; by a failure to put equivalent pressure on surplus countries as well as deficit countries, or on high-income deficit countries as well as poorer deficit countries; by applying doctrines on the value of free markets developed in different circumstances to other circumstances where the assumed conditions simply do not exist; by elevating discharge of debt service to an ultimate objective and allowing it to displace the old consensus objectives of growth, employment, redistribution and basic needs.

The insistence on structural adjustment as a precondition for new development is justified on the grounds that it is not a policy imposed by the international financial institutions and big industrial governments, but rather an inescapable necessity, given the 'facts of life' – these being slower growth in the industrial countries, failure of industrial countries to co-ordinate balance of payments and exchange rate policies, protectionism, the overhanging debt burden, weakness of commodity prices and so on. This is an argument which is obviously true as far as it goes. Given an international climate so unfavourable to development, the developing countries have no choice but to adjust themselves to it and if necessary cut back their ambitions, and they must try as much as possible to make a virtue of necessity. However, the argument leaves scope for two substantial doubts. First, in the spirit of Bretton Woods and numerous UN resolutions and other proclamations as well as under their own constitutions, it should be the duty of the international financial institutions as well as governments not simply to accept the unfavourable international climate and expect the developing countries to adjust to it, but rather to change and improve it. Second, even if the unfavourable climate is taken as given, it does not follow that the only or even the best form of adjustment is in the nature of 'stabilization', which tends to become a code word for retrenchment. Are there not more expansionary forms of adjustment available? In particular, adjustment through intensified trade and other forms of economic cooperation between developing countries is not included in the adjustment packages now presented. Moreover, the country-by-country approach in which individual, although in essence very similar, packages are imposed country by country seems designed, by its very nature, to set developing countries against each other, for example in trying to expand exports simultaneously. This can be self-defeating due to the fallacy of composition and the possibility of immiserizing growth. The route through increased co-operation among developing countries would often seem more hopeful, but it is not taken up in the dominant neo-liberal approach.

The potential for trade between developing countries remains largely untapped. Expanded South–South trade can be treated as a partial de-linking from the slowed-down rate of growth of the industrial countries no longer acting as an efficient engine of growth, as Arthur Lewis did in his Nobel Prize lecture of 1980. Alternatively, expanded South–South trade can also be supported by those in favour of closer international integration as a stepping stone towards fuller integration on more equal terms. This debate is as fruitless or inconclusive as the question whether a half-filled glass of water is 'half full' or 'half empty'! South–South trade is not the only method open to developing countries to maintain their own growth in a less favourable international climate; other methods include the export-led route in securing a greater share of domestic markets in industrial countries, or successful import substitution, or the development of internal dynamism based on increased technological capacity so as to create a domestic engine of growth to replace the faltering external engine. The latter would almost certainly be required in any case, even for a successful implementation of the other methods of export promotion, import substitution or increased South–South trade. South–South trade in turn can be helpful in creating technological dynamism, and also in providing a basis for improved exports to industrial countries as well as efficient import substitution.

At present only around a quarter of LDC exports go to other developing countries. Thus a given percentage fall in exports to industrial countries would require a three-fold proportionate increase in South–South trade to compensate. However, the heavy taxation of normal export proceeds for debt payment puts a strong premium on unorthodox methods of trade expansion through barter trade, countertrade and so on; South–South trade could play an especially important role in promoting such unorthodox methods of trade expansion.

What is striking is the self-assurance and disregard of institutional specificities with which the neo-liberal recipe is applied by its advocates, in the face of much previous experience, much professional doubt and obvious economic, social and political realities. In this respect, it resembles more a brand of religious fundamentalism than a school of thought. Perhaps this also explains the surprising ease with which this counter-revolution has captured the commanding heights in the dominant countries and institutions. The severe depression of the early 1980s was sufficient to produce fundamental changes, if not in the actual international order then at least in thinking about development. But it is difficult to believe that this shift in thinking will be more lasting than some of the earlier shifts described. Like the other changes in thinking which come and go, and yet leave some of their insights behind, the 'adjustment' period and the neo-liberal religion may have passed its peak in the mid-1980s. There is an increasingly visible wish now, at the beginning of the 1990s, to return to the business of development, which remains a global priority. There is now more doubt about the social, political and environmental consequences of adjustment policies; less self-confidence in the neo-liberal conditionality as against the judgement of LDC governments and many practitioners; less assertion of the doctrine that development is constrained by domestic mismanagement to the exclusion of external factors.

Both physical investment and human capital formation have received serious setbacks during this phase, when concern with development and growth has been largely displaced by adjustment and stabilization. The decline in investment in low-income economies other than China and India, and among major debtor countries and oil exporters, has been described at the beginning of this essay. Similarly, human capital has been run down alarmingly. As documented by the UNICEF studies on *Adjustment with a Human Face* and *The Impact of the World Recession on Children* the cuts in government expenditures have affected the welfare of poorer people and particularly women and children disproportionately; the measures taken under the neo-liberal prescription for adjustment, such as abolition of food subsidies, devaluation, trade liberalization, privatization and so on, have contributed to greater inequalities of income distribution, with the well-to-do in a better position to protect their interests. The resulting deteriorating indicators of child nutrition, child health and schooling, as well as the rise of child mortality – the ultimate indicator – are particularly ominous since their impact on development is bound to be felt for at least a generation. It is difficult to see how this can possibly be described as 'laying the foundations for subsequent substainable growth'.

It is not only growth which has gone into reverse, at least in Africa and Latin America, but also the basic needs strategies of the late 1970s and redistribution (with or without growth), together with the increase in the savings and investment rations. Thus it may be said that all the previous approaches and recipes for development have been submerged by the new orthodoxy of primacy for coming to terms with the debt crisis, and of conforming to the deterioration of the international climate since the early 1970s.

As the 1980s drew to a close and the broad decline of investment, physical and human, and widespread reversal of development has become apparent, resistance to the neo-liberal counter-revolution has increased. It is now accepted that:

- adjustment has not been sufficiently 'growth-oriented';
- adjustment must be given a more 'human face';
- more external resources are needed to smooth the process of adjustment and make it politically possible;
- adjustment must be made less harsh and stretched out over a longer period;
- some element of debt relief is inevitable as part of the adjustment process;
- the reverse transfers of capital from developing to industrial countries, including even to the international financial institutions, are counter-productive and perverse as well as reverse;
- the neo-liberal recipe is of doubtful validity in an unfavourable economic climate and when applied to low-income countries with difficult structural problems;
- a common ideology (neo-liberal in this case) results in adjustment programmes which are much too similar – almost identical – between different countries and which fail to take sufficient account of country-specific features;
- adjustment must become more symmetrical between debtor and creditor countries, surplus and deficit countries and also between

LDC deficit/debtor countries and key currency deficit/debtor countries like the USA.

The adjustment problems which many of the developing countries have faced in the 1980s are unique in their abruptness and cumulative impact. The problem is at least three-fold: first, to adjust to a growth rate of industrial countries which has now been set for 15 years at a 'good year' maximum standard of 3 per cent per annum instead of 5 to 6 per cent of the golden years, and this with interruptions by recessions, without any apparent sign of a return to former growth rates. Second, to deal with the steep deterioration in terms of trade for primary commodity exporters (now also including the oil exporters) which brought commodity prices in 1987 to their lowest real level since the 1930s, leaving a major cumulative deterioration by over 40 per cent in terms of trade since 1979. Third, there is the cessation of capital inflows and their replacement by a reverse transfer of capital – some of this represented by the capital flight almost inevitably connected with the adjustment plight of developing countries and representing one way in which the well-to-do can protect themselves.

To put this in concrete and broad quantitative terms: developing countries' export earnings are by now perhaps 25–30 per cent lower than they would be if the industrial countries had maintained earlier growth rates and continued trade liberalization. A further tax of perhaps another 30 per cent is put on export earnings as a result of deteriorating terms of trade reducing the import capacity represented by export earnings. Yet another 30 per cent or so represents a tax on export earnings as a result of debt service commitments. For the large number of developing countries simultaneously affected by all three factors, the cumulative tax on export earnings and import capacity represented would be of the total order of around 60–70 per cent, amounting to a real collapse of export earnings available for the financing of developmental imports.

Admittedly, not all countries are simultaneously and equally affected by all three factors; the 25–30 per cent tax on export earnings for debt service in particular is often unsustainable, and leads to reschedulings and increasingly also to measures of debt relief. It is difficult to translate this into the golden years' metaphor of the 'take-off'; the more appropriate metaphor now would be the aborted take-off with heavy damage to the machine which may take quite some time to repair, or even the crash landing. For those parts of the developing world where development has been reversed in the 1980s, perhaps the 1990s will have to be a 'decade of rehabilitation', aided, it is hoped, by a better international climate and a truly international structural adjustment in global relations.

Summing up the experience of the last two decades, we can now see that in some senses all those involved seemed to act rationally in their own interests: the OPEC members in raising the price of oil; the international banks in lending the deposited receipts to then fast-growing third world economies – the very term 'developing countries' suggested a potential for rapid growth. For the developing countries, the chance to borrow funds at low or negative real rates of interest, without conditionality, was too good to miss.

The lack of any appropriate international institutions prevented proper co-ordination of this process. Any desire amongst OPEC members to channel their resources into development projects was heavily circumscribed by a lack of appropriate development agencies. Depositing their funds with commercial banks ensured that they went predominantly to the middle-income developing countries. Furthermore this meant that they flowed in a haphazard way determined by short-term outlooks, rather than a longer-term assessment of LDCs' needs and absorptive capacities that an effective international institution might have provided.

The failings of this process are now all too apparent; in its own way it is a striking example of the severe shortcomings of leaving the distribution of development funds to the free market. Just at the time when the institutions – actual and projected – of Bretton Woods were most needed, they were either disintegrating or surrendering to an ideology which made them agents of retrenchment rather than development – a new policy of NRNG (neither redistribution nor growth), of adjustment without a human face. The 'decade of rehabilitation' will also have to apply to the international system and to international institutions. Some of this rehabilitation will have to consist of retrieving earlier insights and initiatives which we have lost; another part will have to consist of new insights and initiatives. Fortunately, the signs are that the need for this rehabilitation is now too obvious to be disregarded. The road of the 1990s may lead us away from NRNG through AWHF (adjustment with a human face) to a resumed RWG (redistribution with growth) and on to a real Bretton Woods – which is where we came in.

This essay, dealing with general problems rather than those of specific countries, has inevitably put much weight on the international environment which is largely common to developing countries, rather than domestic policies and domestic governance. There is a lively debate whether the external or internal factors are more important. This is really a non-question which cannot be answered in this form – certainly not in any quantitative sense. In this debate, the developing countries tend to emphasize the importance of external factors while the industrial countries put heavy emphasis on domestic governance.

Those who proclaim the dominant importance of domestic factors point to the very divergent records of different developing countries, even though they are faced with the same or similar international environment. They also argue that the developing countries must take the international environment given as a 'fact of life', and that hence it is fruitless for them to keep on moaning about the international environment. The counter-argument emphasizes that the international environment is not a given 'fact of life' to which developing countries must unilaterally adjust, and that institutions like the IMF, World Bank, and United Nations were created to change the external 'facts of life'. Moreover – so the counter-argument continues – if some developing countries manage to do well in spite of an unfavourable external environment, this means that others will be prevented from doing so (the fallacy of composition); whereas in a favourable environment developing countries could move forward together as they roughly did in the golden age.

We shall come back to this debate in the next essay. There is clearly merit on both sides of the argument; that sustainable development will involve both action on the international front as well as improved domestic governance.

2
The 1990s: On to Fortune or Bound in Miseries?*

> There is a tide in the affairs of men
> Which, taken at the flood, leads on to fortune;
> Omitted, all the voyage of their life
> Is bound in shallows and in miseries.
>
> (William Shakespeare, *Julius Caesar*)

In the last essay, we looked at global and domestic development policies since 1945 and the lessons which emerge. What conclusions can we draw for the decade ahead? We have described the 1980s as a lost decade for a large part of the Third World, especially Africa and Latin America. At the time of writing, the problems which have caused the troubles of the lost decade are still largely with us. The debt crisis has been contained but not resolved; commodity prices are even lower – in fact the lowest since the Great Depression of the 1930s – and terms of trade for developing countries have become even more unfavourable. Moreover, the growth rate of industrial countries has remained sluggish and ambitions for the next decade are limited to a 2–3 per cent growth target, not enough to restore the industrial countries as the engines of growth of the world economy which they were during the golden age; there is still no sign of effective macroeconomic global management; and there is no genuine demo-cratically shared global consensus for North–South co-operation.

---

* Originally published in H. W. Singer and Sumit Roy (1993) *Economic Progress and Prospects in the Third World: Lessons of Development Experience since 1945* (Aldershot, UK and Brookfield, USA: Edward Elgar, pp. 169–80).

But it is not all a tale of woe. There are bright spots: East and Southeast Asia is one such bright spot; the large-scale perverse capital transfers out of developing countries show signs of disappearing and private capital flows show some signs of reviving. All the same, the best that we can realistically hope for is that the 1990s will become a decade of rehabilitation, of repairing the ravages of the 1980s to enable us to resume in the next century the growth path of the previous decades – and this time, it is hoped, more solidly based than the debt-led growth of the 1970s.

Even this limited objective presents a formidable task. The first thing to realize is the tremendous devastation which the ten years of the debt crisis (dating it from the Mexican moratorium in 1982) have wrought upon the developing countries. Compared with where they would have been had they continued the GDP growth rate of 1965–80, the developing countries have lost income during the past decade as follows: low-income countries other than China and India 35 per cent of GDP; lower middle-income countries 39 per cent, upper middle-income countries 23 per cent; sub-Saharan Africa 40 per cent; Latin America and the Caribbean 45 per cent; the severely indebted countries also 45 per cent. These would be the jumps in income required to bring the Third World back to the 1965–80 growth line. In manufacturing – still the flagship of economic development – the cumulative setbacks have been even more severe: 32 per cent for the low-income countries other than India and China; 53 per cent for the lower middle-income countries; no less than 85 per cent for sub-Saharan Africa; 57 per cent for Latin America and the Caribbean. Only the upper middle-income countries have managed to keep this cumulative loss to a relatively modest level of 10 per cent.

Not all of this economic devastation (compared with 1965–80) is due to the debt crisis. The industrialized OECD countries have also had their set-backs but with a cumulative setback of 7 per cent for GDP and only 4 per cent for manufacturing these setbacks seem minimal compared with those of the Third World and could easily be made up in the next ten years by better economic management on behalf of the G7 and by restoring the growth objective to a more equal place relative to control of inflation – more of Keynes and less of Milton Friedman!

By contrast, to return the third world countries during the next decade back to the 1965–80 line, so as to make up for the cumulative loss during the 1980s, would require nothing less than a miracle. GDP of low-income countries would have to grow by 8.5 per cent per annum; lower middle-income countries by 9.4 per cent per annum; upper middle-income countries by 7.9 per cent per annum; sub-Saharan Africa by 8.8 per cent per annum; Latin America and the Caribbean by 10.5 per cent per annum; and the severely indebted countries also by 10.5 per cent per annum. Failing a big sustained Marshall Plan fed from the 'peace dividend' (see below), the task is impossible (except perhaps for the upper middle-income countries). The only reasonable conclusion is that if we ever at any point in the future are to get back to the interrupted 1965–80 line, it will take very much longer than a decade. The job may have to be spread out over 30–40 years at least. So we will be walking in the shadow of the debt crisis for a generation or more, even if the debts were wiped out tomorrow. It will be a long run and 'in the long run we are all dead'.

In spite of the much-vaunted 'outward orientation' achieved during the 1980s, it is true even in the case of trade that arrears have to be made up. The rate of growth of exports of low-income countries other than China and India fell from 5.9 per cent per annum in 1965–80 to 0.5 per cent in 1980–88; their exports would have to increase by no less than 11.3 per cent per annum to come back again to the 1965–80 growth line. For sub-Saharan Africa the figures are even worse. In the case of the lower middle-income countries, the impact of outward orientation on export volume has been minimal, from growth at 5.8 per cent in 1965–80 to 6.0 per cent in 1980–88. It is only in the case of upper middle-income countries and of Latin America that there has been a visible shift to outward orientation reflected in the volume of exports. And these figures relate to the *volume* of exports and therefore do not reflect the deterioration of terms of trade which has occurred not only for the primary commodity exports but also for the manufactured exports of developing countries. Nor do they show the import strangulation – directly related to the cuts in investment already noted. The volume of imports of low-income countries other than China and India has *fallen* at the rate of 3.2 per cent in the 1980s after rising by 4.5 per cent per annum in 1965–80. They would have to rise by no less than 12.2 per cent per annum in the next decade to make up for this shortfall. For the severely indebted countries as a whole, as well as for Latin America and the Caribbean and for sub-Saharan Africa, this downward shift and shortfall is even greater.

It is noteworthy that, while the OECD members also showed a drop in their growth of exports (some of it explained by the import strangulation in developing countries), they were able to increase the growth rate in the volume of their imports (from 4.2 per cent to 5.1 per cent), largely due to their improved terms of trade – the counterpart of the deteriorated terms of trade of third world countries.

As against this, the neo-liberal counter-revolutionaries which today control many of the strategic development positions will argue that this is a false calculation based on excessively static assumptions. They argue that many developing countries have improved the quality of their policies through structural adjustment programmes and thus 'laid the foundations for subsequent sustainable growth', in a favourite phrase of this school. In this picture of the world, the past decade was a period of necessary consolidation, of *reculer pour mieux sauter.* Perhaps so; only the future can tell. If this view is correct, and if the third world countries are really in better shape now for subsequent growth, then perhaps catching up with the 1965–80 line is not impossible, at least gradually in the course of time. The potential of the peace dividend, if constructively used for development, will be discussed later in this essay.

But there is also the opposite view, that is, that what has happened in the past decade, far from 'laying the foundations of subsequent growth' has done exactly the opposite: it has *destroyed* the foundations for subsequent growth. This view can find support from the particularly heavy decline of investment in the indebted countries and third world countries generally. Investment has declined even more than GNP, i.e. it has declined as a proportion of GNP. Physical capital investment is not the only – perhaps not the main – source of growth, but it is an important determinant of future growth. Gross domestic investment in the severely indebted countries, after growing by 8.4 per cent per annum in 1965–80, has over the past decade *declined* by 3.1 per cent per annum. This is a swing, in the direction of decline, of 11.5 per cent, or no less than 65 per cent cumulatively by the end of the decade. This means that the volume of investment in these countries over the next decade would have to be almost treble that of the last decade in order to bring it back to the 1965–80 line. The corresponding figures for sub-Saharan Africa and for Latin America are equally bad or worse. Thus I think there is another scenario, at least as plausible as that of 'laying the foundations of subsequent growth'. That is the scenario, first introduced into development economics by Gunnar Myrdal, of cumulative processes and vicious circles leading countries into a poverty trap.

In any case, scepticism about our having 'laid the foundations of subsequent growth' does not depend on belief in physical capital investment, Harrod–Domar, ICOR (Incremental Capital-Output Ratio) and all that. The picture is no different if we talk about human capital. The proportion of central government expenditure spent on education has fallen from 20.5 per cent to 9.0 per cent in low-income countries; from 17.5 per cent to 13.3 per cent in lower middle-income countries; from 15.4 per cent to 11.0 per cent in Latin America and the Caribbean; and from 15.6 per cent to 10.8 per cent in the severely indebted countries. There are similar declines in health expenditures as a proportion of government expenditure from 5.5 per cent to 2.8 per cent in low-income countries; 5.7 per cent to 4.0 per cent in lower middle-income countries and from 5.9 per cent to 4.4 per cent in the severely indebted countries. Again it will take many years before such a cumulative shortfall can be made up. All this does not look like laying the foundations for growth in terms of the human resource basis.

Third world poverty has increased in absolute numbers although not as a proportion of world population. The current best estimate is that over 1.1 billion people, or 33 per cent of their population, live in poverty; and more than half of them in 'extreme poverty'. Thus more people than ever are exposed to the vicious circles of poverty or 'poverty trap'. The amount of human capital destroyed in the process is incalculable. Part of this may be amenable by market processes and economic 'empowerment' of the poor, but not even the most ardent neo-liberal would deny the need for complementary state action to provide opportunities and safety nets for the poor. The World Bank itself, in its 1990 *World Development Report*, with poverty as its main theme, has opened the new decade with an impressive argument for such a 'balanced' or 'double-track' approach, combining labour-intensive growth with social safety nets – back to the Redistribution with Growth strategy of the 1970s? Growth policies are more sustainable if they are simultaneously accompanied by poverty alleviation. Poverty alleviation in turn is more sustainable, or only sustainable, if additional resources are available from domestic growth or external sources. On this at least a genuine consensus could perhaps be emerging. But the study of India, the country with the largest single number of poor, illustrates the obstacles standing in the way of an effective policy of poverty reduction and Nigeria presents an example of increased inequality and poverty.

So there is some reason to be sceptical about the view that the third world economies are now 'leaner and fitter' to face the decade ahead beyond the debt crisis. They are certainly leaner but whether they are fitter remains to be seen. It is probably true in the case of much of Asia, but probably untrue in the case of Africa, Latin America, and the Middle East.

But it seems not very useful to dream in terms of statistical scenarios for a return to paradise lost. Nor is it productive to sit down wearing sackcloth and sprinkling ashes on our heads, wailing about the setbacks and failures of the past. Far better to accept the setbacks of the lost decade as water under the bridge and ask ourselves: Where do we go from here? How can we do better in the future?

Economic projections are notoriously tricky and our record as forecasters is very patchy to say the least. World Bank projections, whether on commodity prices, growth rates or the results of structural adjustment programmes, have proved chronically over-optimistic and had to be repeatedly revised downward. As a result the World Bank, and all of us, have become more humble about our projections and hedge them with careful assumptions. As Galbraith has said: 'there is nothing wrong with making projections as long as you leave the future out of it'. There is practically no area, from the 'peace dividend', financial flows, the Uruguay Round, oil prices, future technologies, and so on where you could not make plausible optimistic assumptions about the impact on developing countries or equally plausible pessimistic assumptions.

For example, technology may work as much against developing countries as in their favour. It is true that biotechnology, improved health technology, globalization of production due to improved communications technology, and so on may benefit them. But increased replacement of natural raw materials, increased importance of high skills rather than cheap labour, closer integration of R & D with production will operate against them. Nobody can be sure today where the balance will lie. The only thing we can say with confidence is that countries with good technology policies could gain by maximizing the advantages and minimizing the disadvantages, and vice versa. The Indian experience showed the tremendous effect of improved agricultural technology in creating a green revolution, but also its limitations in respect of equitable distribution and poverty reduction.

This last statement can be generalized also for other areas beyond technology. The 1990s could be a decade of great opportunities – especially if we manage to learn from errors of the past – but it also continues one of great dangers lurking for developing countries. The end of the Cold War – assuming that it has finally ended – is a good example: the much-talked-about peace dividend could release new resources for development. Even if it only resulted in an achievement of the theoretically accepted aid level of 0.7 per cent of donor countries' GNP, this would mean an extra $60 billion a year or more and, if the switch out of military expenditures were to increase the growth rate of the OECD countries by only half of 1 per cent, that, transferred to financing development, would add a further yearly $90 billion (all at 1992 prices). Add to this the resources that could be released by reducing military expenditures within the developing countries themselves – and assuming that all these additional resources were productively invested at reasonable returns – it would not be difficult to construct a hopeful scenario, even a new golden age. On the other hand, the end of the Cold War could equally well lead to a large-scale diversion of resources towards Eastern Europe and the former USSR and the dying away of interest in aid or other forms of development support. That danger of diversion may be strengthened by political factors: the developing countries will no longer be able to manoeuvre for support from West or East in order to 'keep them on our side' or stop them from joining 'the other side'. While up to now the developing countries had to compete 'only' with the USA for the world's limited savings, now they will have to compete not only with the USA – assuming that the US balance of payments deficit will continue – but also with the vast, almost limitless, needs of the former 'second world'.

In fact, as a consequence of the end of the Cold War, we can be fairly certain that the old categories of a first, second and third world will become obsolete in the 1990s. We will still have the first world, the opulent Western industrial OECD countries. We will then have a new second world of less opulent industrial countries in which most of the old second world will be joined by many Asian countries, perhaps including China, but also by Mexico, Chile, Venezuela and others. There will be a reduced Third World which would include the periphery of the former second world and those developing countries which manage a measure of rehabilitation and recovery from the 1980s. Finally there will be a fourth world, increasingly marginalized, of countries (mainly in sub-Saharan Africa) where the vicious circles set in motion by the ravages of the 1980s and of ultra-neo-liberal methods of curing them prove to be too powerful for rehabilitation.

In the light of so many uncertainties, any projections and the assumptions underlying the models on which they are based will reflect the beliefs and wishes of the projectors more than anything else. We are on somewhat safer ground when we turn to the development policies and strategies which are likely to emerge and which may help to cope with such a highly uncertain external environment.

A return to pragmatism

At the end of the previous essay, we referred to the somewhat unproductive debate as to whether domestic policies are more or less important than external factors and described this as 'a non-question'. There is some hope that this debate will recede in the coming decade or at any rate take more productive forms. Good policies are clearly easier to formulate and above all to implement in a favourable economic environment, particularly one associated with capital inflows and agreed debt reduction. The two must go hand in hand; the Bretton Woods institutions in particular need to adopt the more symmetrical approach visualized at Bretton Woods, that is to put equal pressure on the powerful and surplus countries which shape the external environment and on the poorer and deficit countries which must improve their policies.

It is hoped that this could be linked with a general return from ideology back to pragmatism. Ideology has dominated both sides of the development debate in the 1980s: on the part of the industrial countries and the institutions which they dominate, this has taken the form of proclaiming not only the dominant importance of so-called good governance but also the detailed prescriptions of what constitutes it. On the part of the developing countries it has taken the form of hammering away at the need for a new international economic order even though in the 1980s this has been

done in a less confrontational style against a background of awareness of their weaknesses. A major reform in particular can be hoped
for from any such growing consensus on the need for simultaneous
and symmetrical action on the external and internal fronts. First of
all, the stabilization and structural adjustment agreements under the
auspices of the IMF and World Bank which determine the policies of
so many developing countries today must be shaped much less on a
country-by-country basis and much more within the framework of
global commodity markets, global trade expansion, and global debt
relief policies.

It is a debatable point whether the presently dominant neo-liberal
ideology is bound to shift emphasis away from general economics to
specific and diverse characteristics of individual developing countries
or not. The basic tenet of the neo-liberal approach is that there are
general economic principles, for example, concerning markets,
prices, incentives, and so on which are universal and can be applied
to all countries. There is clearly a danger that those with the perceived knowledge of the universally valid economic principles should
then fail to modify their application to individual countries sufficiently to take account of their diverse individual circumstances.
That indeed is a criticism frequently made in connection with the
IMF/World Bank-promoted stabilization and structural adjustment
programmes. But this need not necessarily be so. Even if there are
universally valid principles, it is still perfectly possible, in their application to individual countries in specific situations, to adapt and
modify them to suit different kinds of political, economic, social
and administrative realities. It is to the willingness of such adaptation
and modification that we must look for the better balance between
ideology and pragmatism here suggested. If this is not only theoretically admitted but also practised, in the end the difference between
the neo-liberal approach and more structuralist and institutional
approaches may turn out to be bridgeable and lead to a real consensus.

A second reform proposal arising from this is that the programmes
themselves must be formulated in a much broader negotiating
framework than the present largely financial setting. The sectors
and interests concerned with the real economy and with different
social and economic groups should be much more directly involved.
This will also help to make the programmes more country-specific

and move them away from their present ideologically-based uniformity. As explained in the previous essay, the agreements shaped during the 1980s were at the same time too country-specific (in the sense of blinkered country-by-country negotiations) and yet not country-specific enough (in the sense of being too uniform and giving insufficient consideration to the great variety, indeed uniqueness, of political, economic and social factors in each country).

Quite apart from the end of the Cold War and the potential of the peace dividend, the increasing importance of environmental considerations could be another favourable factor, another silver lining to the generally cloudy outlook for the 1990s. The co-operation of the developing countries is indispensable in protecting the ozone layer, rainforests, endangered species, exhaustible energy resources, and so on of our globe. Even beyond this, there is an increasing realization of the connection between world poverty and environmental deterioration. It is not impossible to visualize that an enlightened new global environmental priority would include poverty alleviation in developing countries as an essential ingredient. The danger here is – once again a cloud to the silver lining – that the richer countries may seek protection of the environment at the expense of the poorer countries – the potential conflicts over logging and agricultural settlement in the rainforest areas are already apparent today. It will be a task for the 1990s to make the environment into an opportunity for world development and to eliminate the inherent risk that it might become an impediment. Opportunities abound, but so also do the risks of such opportunities being lost through policy failure.

Another silver lining with a cloud attached to it is the emerging formation of three major regional blocs among the industrial countries. A North American bloc may well offer great opportunities not just to Mexico but also to other Latin American countries if they can secure better access to North American markets, North American technology, North American capital, and perhaps even North American labour markets. Similarly the East Asian and South-east Asian developing countries could benefit from access to Japanese markets, technology and capital. This creates a special responsibility for the European Community – likely to be further expanded in the course of the decade – to provide similar opportunities for Africa well beyond the present very limited benefits of association.

Where then is the cloud attached to this silver lining? These regional blocs could either be stepping stones towards a free multi-lateral trading system or they could become 'fortresses', blocking a global multilateral system. It is very much in the interests of developing countries that the former alternative should materialize. Much of this will be decided in the earlier part of the decade, with the GATT Uruguay Round hanging in the balance at the moment of writing. A liberalized multilateral trading system would also provide a better basis than regional blocs for the long-delayed development of South–South trade. Given its present low level, inexplicable on purely economic grounds, there should be considerable upward potential by creating the financial and institutional basis for expanded South–South trade. This is also in the interests of the industrial countries and it should not be beyond the wit of economic statesmanship to find non-confrontational solutions to fill this conspicuous gap in the network of world trade.

A large-scale inflow of capital from the big industrial centres could well help to restore growth and improve the outlook for the 1990s but at the same time carry with it the seeds of a new debt crisis and a new debt trap in the more remote future. Admittedly, the newly incurred debts would not be in the form of fixed commitments but in the form of repatriated profits and dividends. But in its balance of payments impact, and in creating a need for structural adjustment, this new debt problem might not be too dissimilar from the debt crisis of the 1980s.

The previous essay discussed gaps and distortions in the Bretton Woods system. There is also much talk now of a revitalization of the UN. So far this has centred largely, although not exclusively, on the peace-keeping and peace-making responsibilities of the UN, follow-ing upon its role in the Gulf War, Namibia, Cambodia, El Salvador and so on. But there is also discussion about an enhanced role in disarmament, protection of the environment, and disaster relief. Furthermore, following upon the UNICEF Report on *Adjustment with a Human Face* and the UNDP *Human Development Reports*, there is a new emerging paradigm of a division of labour within the UN system between the Bretton Woods institutions and the rest of the UN system. Under this paradigm, anything to do with economics, finance and growth would be within the domain of the IMF and World Bank while the UN would look after human resources, poverty alleviation and social sectors, in addition to the environment and disaster relief. Superficially, this looks like a neat and tidy division which would give the UN a more important role than it has had in the past and which would reflect the comparative advantages of two types of organization.

Yet it is essentially an untenable and undesirable division. To begin with, it would require that the functions given to the UN shouldreceive the same financial and political support now reserved for the Bretton Woods institutions. Otherwise there would be a danger of the functions allocated to the UN being swept under the table and dying of neglect. Hence, to make this division workable, the UN would have to be given much larger and dependable sources of finance, possibly through new sources of international taxation. Given such a financial strengthening of the UN, the proposed division might be workable, but it is far from clear that this precondition is realized by those advocating the new paradigm.

Second – and perhaps more important – such things as prevention of disasters, as distinct from mere relief, protecting the environment, alleviating poverty, supporting refugees and so on are too much intermixed with economic growth, debt relief, employment creation, and the like to confine these functions to a humanitarian category and divide them from economics and finance.

Finally, this arrangement would leave unsolved the urgent need for better and more democratic macroeconomic global governance. It is clear that the G5 or G7 is neither effective nor democratic and the Bretton Woods institutions are little more than reflections of the G5 or G7 – as evidenced by the distribution of voting power. In the original vision of a new international order after 1945, this function was to be centred in the UN and specifically in its Economic and Social Council, supported by a multilateral soft aid programme administered by the UN. In the previous essay we described how this initial vision failed to materialize. A true revitalization of the UN would oblige us to look at the UN Charter and the 1945 vision once again. No doubt the world has changed since 1945 and the different elements of this vision would have to be combined in different ways than was then proposed. But in one form or other a more effective and more democratic system of global management is essential, and there seems no candidate in the field other than the UN.

The experience of developing countries vividly illustrate the difficulties of combining growth and equity objectives. All governments of developing countries as well as those advising them are rhetorically in favour both of growth and of equity and declare their wish and intention to combine them. But in practice this turns out to be extremely difficult. Growth tends to go hand in hand with increased efficiency and increased efficiency often means less employment and less employment means more poverty. Similarly, emphasis on equity and poverty reduction all too often means increased taxation or more inflation or otherwise reduced incentives for the productive sector of the economy and thus may reduce growth. Again it is easy theoretically and on paper to point out ways in which growth and equity could be made to work together: growth could and should be labour-intensive and thus increase employment, and poverty programmes could be of a kind to increase production by providing productive assets and employment for the poor; but once again all this is more easily said than done.

The equity element in the growth/equity combination encounters the further difficulty of targeting poverty reduction programmes effectively on the intended beneficiaries. Almost by definition, the neediest and most vulnerable groups are also the ones most difficult to reach by public action, especially by public action emanating from a central government. It is here that the question of decentralization to regional and local levels and the involvement of non-governmental organizations and the community itself emerges as a problem awaiting progress in the 1990s. This is the principle of 'subsidiarity' now increasingly emphasized in the development discussion.

More generally, although closely related to the problem of growth with equity, there is emerging from the case studies the crucial role of human capital. The decade of the 1990s opened with the annual splendid *Human Development Reports* of the United Nations Development Programme. The strengthening of human capital is clearly the long-run answer to the quest for an effective combination of equity and growth. This is not to deny the role of physical investment but its creation as well as its efficiency are increasingly seen as products of human capital formation. For this reason the setbacks during the lost decade of the 1980s in human as well as physical capital formation described earlier are particularly worrying. The 'human face', not only for structural adjustment programmes but also for development generally, is not a humanitarian luxury but an economic necessity. It is not least for these reasons that the undue weakness of the UN and its associated agencies and the corresponding undue preponderance of the financial Bretton Woods institutions should be corrected. To create a more balanced and restructured set of international institutions is one of the many tasks facing us in the 1990s and beyond.

Part II
Reform of the United Nations

3
The Bretton Woods System: Historical Perspectives[*]

Keynes' vision of an international economic system rested on four pillars: global economic management, a development finance mechanism, an international trading organization, and an aid programme. This essay traces the background of the vision and assesses what has developed in reality in the past five decades. The reality has veered from the original ideas, with key decisions on global economic and financial matters being made by a few major countries, rather than within a truly multilateral process.

It is customary to date the origin of the Bretton Woods system back to 1942 when Keynes, and his associates in London, prepared the three famous memoranda on the International Clearing Union, on Commodity Buffer Stocks, and on plans for Relief and Reconstruction. To these three memoranda we may add the Beveridge Report which appeared in the same year, 1942. Keynes had taken a great interest in the Beveridge Report and this model of a national social welfare state was readily capable of international extension and application.

However, in this historical perspective we may well go a little further back. The Great Depression of the 1930s had shown that in the absence of multilateral agreements and multilateral institutions

---

* This paper was originally prepared for North-South Roundtable meetings of the Society for International Development on 'The United Nations and the Bretton Woods Institutions: New Challenges for the 21st Century', which were held in New York in April 1993 and subsequently at Bretton Woods, New Hampshire, USA (where the original Bretton Woods conference was held in 1944) in September 1993. It was published in *Third World Economics*, no. 71, August 1993, pp. 13–18.

the economic system was in danger of degenerating into beggar-my-neighbour policies leading to general immiserization. The World Economic Conference of 1931 had been a first attempt to create an international economic order to prevent this from continuing. Although this attempt ended in failure, the ideas then brought forward had continued to reverberate in Keynes' mind. His vision underlying the 1942 documents was governed by the overarching principle of 'never again!' – never again back to the conditions of the 1930s which were seen as having brought about not only mass misery and mass unemployment but also Hitlerism and war. Also never again a failure like that of the 1931 World Economic Conference.

We may then move forward to 1940. Hitler was triumphant and his Minister of Economics and President of the Reichbank, Walter Funk, proclaimed in Berlin a 'new order' under which Europe with its colonies and indeed the world would be unified under German leadership. This was treated as a big propaganda item by the Germans and the British Minister of Information, worried about the propaganda effect of Funk's new order, asked Keynes to prepare a broadcast to counteract and discredit the German propaganda. At that point Keynes became convinced that the most effective counter-move would be to prepare a valid counter-proposal rather than attack Funk's 'fraudulent offer' as he called it. From then on, Keynes' mind turned to such a constructive counter-proposal, that is, to counter Funk's fraudulent new order with a genuine new international system. In that sense, the Bretton Woods system can be considered as a case of good coming out of evil.

The structure envisaged by Keynes, arising from his belief in the possibility and sustainability of full employment through active government policy – later expanded by Harrod and Domar to full employment growth – and embodied in the 1942 memoranda rested on four pillars.

The first pillar: global economic management

The first pillar was that of global macroeconomic monetary and financial management. The original bold idea was of a world central bank which would maintain full employment equilibrium and provide the liquidity required for this purpose by expanding the supply of bancor (his proposed world currency). This would mainly serve to finance the balance of payments deficit countries: quite logically, the balance of payments deficit countries were to be supported; they were the 'good boys' who created additional net employment in the rest of the world.

By contrast, the balance of payments surplus countries were the 'bad boys' exporting unemployment to the rest of the world. In fact, at one stage Keynes proposed an international tax on balance of payments surpluses at the rate of 1per cent a month, partly to finance the deficits, partly to finance international commodity buffer stocks, and partly to give an incentive to balance of payments surplus countries to reduce their surpluses by following more expansive policies. While this is an over-simplified picture of 1942 thinking, there is sufficient truth in it to bring home to us the startling contrast to the current orthodoxy when balance of payments equilibrium or surpluses are considered to be the result of virtue and deficits are a symptom of vice.

Even in 1942, in his Proposals for an International Clearing Union, when ideas of a world currency and world central bank were beginning to recede, Keynes had written: 'We need a system possessed of an internal stabilising mechanism, by which pressure is exercised on any country whose balance of payments with the rest of the world is departing from equilibrium in *either direction*, so as to prevent movements which must create for its neighbours an equal but opposite want of balance' (note that the emphasis on the underlined words is in Keynes' own Proposals).

Some traces of this original vision are still visible today in the somewhat shadowy so-called 'surveillance' of industrial countries by the IMF, as well as demands that structural adjustment enforced by the Bretton Woods institutions should be more 'symmetrical'. In essence, however, the task of global macroeconomic management has been removed from the multilateral system and is now undertaken – in theory at least – by the G5 and G7, in combination with the 'privatised liquidity creation' through the commercial banks.

Keynes had already given a great deal of thought to what emerged as one of the key controversies surrounding the IMF, that is the question of conditionality. He objected to a 'grandmotherly' Fund. Today the Fund as well as the Bank have become worse than grandmotherly – grandmothers are supposed to have a human face! When he had to accept the idea of conditionality, he did so on the basis and assumption of a very large Fund. He proposed a Fund equal to half of annual world imports and on that basis was willing to concede conditionality. The American side (Harry Dexter White) proposed a much smaller Fund – one-sixth of annual world imports – and on that basis was ready to relax the criteria for conditionality. In the upshot what we got instead of a trade-off between size of the Fund and degree of conditionality was the worst of all possible worlds – a small Fund with tough conditionality. Today's Fund is only 2 per cent of annual world imports, perhaps the difference between Keynes' originally proposed 50 per cent and the actual 2 per cent is a measure of the degree to which our vision of international economic management has shrunk.

The second pillar: the World Bank

The second pillar was what ultimately emerged as the World Bank, or International Bank for Reconstruction and Development. The historical origin of this lies in the proposed European Reconstruction Fund – a natural answer to Funk. In the 1942 relevant memorandum this had developed into an investment fund for relief and reconstruction – hence the often-quoted statement that originally the IMF was supposed to be a bank (i.e. a world central bank), while the World Bank was supposed to be a fund (i.e. the investment fund proposed in 1942).

The reconstruction task proved to be less important for the new institution than was visualized in 1942, partly because of the Marshall Plan and the large US loan to the UK negotiated by Keynes towards the end of his life, and partly because some of the intended functions were taken over by the newly-created UN Relief and Rehabilitation Administration (UNRRA).

On the other hand, the development function for poor countries was given additional emphasis at Bretton Woods as a result of the presence of delegations from these countries (mainly Latin American but also including an Anglo-Indian delegation in the transition to independence). Originally in 1942 not much attention had been paid to development problems. Most of the countries involved, especially the Latin American countries, were assumed to do quite well during the war as a result of high prices and high demand for their raw materials, and also the protection afforded to their nascent industries as a result of reduced competition from the belligerent industrial countries. In fact Argentina emerged at the end of the war as one of the richest countries in the world in terms of per capita GNP.

Most of the rest of the Third World had not yet emerged into independence and was not considered to be in urgent need of external support. Many like India were accumulating large external surpluses – the sterling balances – and the problem seemed to be more one of help for the UK in clearing these sterling balances than of external aid for India.

It is fair to say that originally the British side – in other words Keynes – was much more interested in the Fund then in the Bank. By contrast, the preparatory moves on the US side had been much more centred on what became the Bank. The first major move in US thinking about the post-war International Order was the commissioned report of a study group of the US Council of Foreign Relations (led by Jacob Viner and Alvin Hansen). This proposed an International Development Board to study and prepare development projects throughout the world. The shape of a future project-oriented World Bank can be clearly seen to emerge from this report.

Given this initial concentration of the British side on the Fund or International Clearing Union and the US initial concentration on the Bank, it is somewhat ironic that at Bretton Woods itself it was the Americans (in the person of Harry Dexter White) who chaired and organized the discussions on the Fund in Commission I, while the British (in the person of Keynes) chaired the discussions on the Bank in Commission II.

By that time, in 1944, the work in the US Treasury on the Fund had, of course, strongly developed, while Keynes' interest in the Bank had steadily increased. However, perhaps even more important in his thinking was the establishment of an international organization to stabilize primary commodity prices. That was the third pillar of the system he envisaged to which we will turn later.

The World Bank was set up on a project basis without a mandate to make lending conditional on the overall macroeconomic policies of the recipient government, nor even on its general micro or supply-side policies. However, in so far as more general policies or quality of governance affected the rate of return from projects, this was of course a legitimate factor in World Bank lending; so it entered in this indirect way. The limitation to project lending was not thought to be a serious constraint. It was assumed that, given the scarcity of capital in poorer countries, the marginal productivity of capital there must be high; it was also assumed that there must be an abundance of potential high-yielding projects only waiting to be designed, financed and implemented. Why then did the Bank move into programme lending and adopt policy conditionality?

There are a number of reasons which may be listed as follows:

1 While the Bank acquired tremendous and unchallenged competence in project design, project analysis, cost-benefit calculations, monitoring of projects, and so on, this very competence was acquired at the expense of devoting considerable staff resources to these functions. This meant that the total volume of lending which could be 'pushed out' while maintaining this high quality of project work was rather limited. When Mr McNamara became President of the Bank – who had been used to handling much larger budgets as US Secretary of Defence – he understandably was impatient with the small sums pushed out by the project-based system. He wanted to continue to play a larger part on the world scene than that, and the addition of programme lending seemed to open a door to such a larger role.

2 The academic analysts had pointed out at an early stage that there was a fallacy involved in project lending.[1] If the project was in fact a high-yielding top-priority project it would be carried out with the government's own resources. The World Bank financing would then merely set free government resources which would go into another marginal – and possibly low-yielding – project. Thus in effect the Bank's money would serve to finance projects which it had not examined and was not even aware of. This principle of 'fungibility' would thus provide an obvious argument for examining the overall investment programme of the government, to make sure that the marginal projects were still sound and creditworthy. Mr McNamara readily adopted this academic fig leaf for his ambitions!

3 It became increasingly clear that the success of individual projects depended as much (or more) on the efficiency of policies and institutions in the recipient countries than on the design of the project itself. This became particularly clear as the Bank adopted objectives such as poverty alleviation and moved into social sectors such as health, education and so on.[2]

4 The shift to programme lending was also related to a marked shift in power and self-confidence between recipient governments and

the World Bank. In the earlier period, the governments were supposed to be the Platonic guardians and best judges of national interests and the World Bank, a UN organization, designed to serve them. As late as 1971, in his David Owen Memorial Lecture on *The Evolution of Foreign Aid*, Arthur Lewis took it for granted that there could be no policy conditionality in foreign aid since the developing countries would consider this as an infringement of their sovereignty and would never accept it.[3] More recently, there has been a remarkable reversal of this relationship: now the governments are depicted as centres of corruption, policy failures, rent-seeking, ignorance and so on while the Bank has acquired a self-confident position of being in possession of the Holy Grail of good policies and an ability to sort out the 'good boys' from the 'bad boys'. The debt burden has also been instrumental in reducing the power and bargaining status of the recipient governments while enhancing that of the Bank. It has also helped to give the Bank a focus and target for structural adjustment, that is, to achieve a balance of payments position enabling them to service debts. All this while strengthening the Bank's position *vis-à-vis* the governments, has weakened its position *vis-à-vis* the Fund which has the unquestioned mandate to concern itself with government policies which the Bank lacks.

The third pillar: an international trading organization

The third pillar was the International Trade Organization (ITO). Keynes had been a long-term advocate of stabilizing primary commodity prices, particularly in his article on 'The Policy of Government Storage of Food-Stuffs and Raw Materials' in *The Economic Journal* 1938. Predictably he incorporated this idea in his proposals for Bretton Woods, linking it in an early version with his proposed International Clearing Union by suggesting a world currency based not on the dollar, gold, bancor or Special Drawing Rights (SDRs), but on the average price of 30 primary commodities (including gold and oil). This would automatically have stabilized the average price of these commodities without ruling out fluctuations of individual commodity prices. The main idea was to prevent the collapse of primary commodity prices which had been a marked feature – and in Keynes' view a contributory factor – of the Great Depression of the 1930s.

Such bold ideas cut little ice with Henry Morgenthau, the Secretary of the US Treasury, and in fact were quickly subdued even in the London preparatory group. What remained was the proposal to set up an ITO which would have among other objectives that of stabilising primary commodity prices by buffer stocks, commodity agreements and direct intervention. The establishment of the ITO was firmly decided at Bretton Woods and when Keynes left the conference with everybody standing up in his honour and singing 'For he's a jolly good fellow', it was in the firm belief that the achievements of Bretton Woods included the creation of this favourite brain-child of his.

Alas the ITO was never created. Although it was quite smoothly negotiated in Havana and accepted there by all concerned, the mood in the US Congress by the time it was presented for ratification had begun to swing against the UN and international institutions. The internationalist Roosevelt/Truman era was coming to an end and the McCarthy era was beginning to cast its shadows. The ITO charter was not brought to the US Congress in time to catch the favourable tide. By the time it was brought to the US Congress, ratification had become hopeless and the ITO was abandoned even without a vote. The other countries were all set to ratify but had waited for the US Congress to ratify first. Thus the Bretton Woods system was incomplete from the beginning, lacking its intended third pillar. GATT did not fill the gap since it had no functions relating to the stabilization of commodity prices or regulation of commodity markets.

One can engage in a number of counter-factual speculations. If Keynes had suspected that ITO would not be created, would he still have advocated acceptance of the agreement concerning the Bank and the Fund? We do not know – by the time it was clear that the ITO would not be established Keynes was dead. My own guess is to answer this hypothetical question with a 'no' – but there is no way of proving it (or for that matter of disproving it). Another counter-factual speculation is that if the real price of oil – together with practically all other primary commodities – had not deteriorated from the 1950s to 1973, would the OPEC countries still have engaged in their dramatic quadrupling of oil prices in 1973 and then again multiplied in 1979? It is often forgotten that the 1973 action did little more than restore the real price of oil in terms of manufactures to what it had been before. Without the OPEC action in 1973 the Bretton Woods system might not have collapsed and might have recovered from the abandonment of the fixed exchange rate between gold and dollar by President Nixon in 1971. Also, if the non-oil primary commodity prices had been maintained and stabilized between the 1950s and 1973, the rise in oil prices would not have created the balance of payments crisis and subsequent debt crisis among the developing countries. Yet another speculation: if the Havana ITO Charter had been brought more speedily to Congress for ratification and had been more firmly supported by the US Administration, the ITO might well have come into existence. History as it might have been is always a fascinating business.

The fourth pillar: a UN aid programme

The fourth pillar of the system was meant to be a soft aid programme linked more directly with the United Nations. It is noteworthy that the first draft proposal for the World Bank prepared at the US Treasury under the direction of Harry Dexter White was entitled 'A Bank for Reconstruction and Development of the United and Associated Nations'. At that time, of course, it was still visualized that the two Bretton Woods institutions would be a firm and integral part of the United Nations system which had still to be created during the year or two following upon Bretton Woods. Indeed, legally and technically, the Fund and Bank are specialized agencies of the United Nations and their guidance by the UN General Assembly and UN Economic and Social Council are still embodied in their respective charters – but we all know what the reality is. Today, the Secretary-General of the United Nations is not even allowed to address the annual meetings of the Fund and Bank!

The aid programme within the United Nations was meant to be different from World Bank lending in being on a grant or highly concessional basis, and also not limited to a project basis. The attempt to create such a mechanism within the United Nations centred around the proposal for UNEDA (United Nations Economic Development Administration). This was originally proposed by V.K.R.V. Rao in his capacity as Chairman of the UN Sub-Commission for Economic Development and in a simultaneous UN Secretariat Report on *Methods of Financing Economic Development in Underdeveloped Countries.*

This was then continued in the negotiations for SUNFED (Special United Nations Fund for Economic Development). In the uncongenial climate for the UN of the early and mid-fifties, this – like the ITO – was doomed to failure. SUNFED remained UNFED – its original and unfortunate acronym.[4]

However, in the happier climate of the late fifties and early sixties (the Kennedy era), there was at least a partially satisfactory outcome. The soft aid fund was created, but it was attached to the Bank rather than to the United Nations, in the form of International Development Association (IDA).

The United Nations obtained two valuable consolation prizes: the UNDP (technical assistance had always been a strong feature of UNEDA and SUNFED) and the World Food Programme. While this 'Grand Compromise' of 1959–61 was more satisfactory than could have been hoped for some years earlier, it laid the foundation for an unfortunate division between financial aid on the one hand and food aid and technical assistance on the other hand.

It also helped to confirm an even broader cleavage: the UN was not to be trusted with the 'hard' instruments of development such as finance and macroeconomic policy-making that was to be the preserve of the Bretton Woods institutions with their system of weighted voting and firm control by the Western industrial countries. The UN was to be put in charge of the 'soft' instruments, such as food aid, technical assistance, children, women, social policy, and more recently the environment. We will not here discuss the justification and viability of such a division of functions.[5] All this would not matter too much if there were really a unified UN system – this remains a 'hope' for the future.

Thus, in overview, the original vision of a system resting on four pillars has remained unfulfilled. Some pillars are missing altogether, and some are constructed in a way quite different from the original plans. All the same, the system proved an immense benefit to the world for the 25 years or so until its collapse in 1971 and 1973. Our task is to recreate a genuine system with the same vision as that shown in 1942. It would not of course be the same system: times have changed and we should have learnt some lessons from past experience; but all the same, the original ideas have still much to teach us if we can only recapture the spirit of 1942.

Notes

1   See H.W. Singer: 'External Aid: For Plans or Projects?', *Economic Journal*, vol. LXXV, September 1965, pp. 539–45.

2   This point has been quite recently emphasized by the World Bank's Portfolio Management Task Force: *Effective Implementation; Key to Development Impact* (the Wapenhans Report), World Bank, 1992. In this report an increasing percentage of unsatisfactory results over the last decade was attributed to a failure to appreciate the importance of policy and institutional factors in determining the rate of return on projects. The report did not make the point – at least not explicitly – that this deterioration could also have something to do with the diversion of attention and staff resources to structural adjustment lending in the service of debt collection.

3   Sir W Arthur Lewis, *The Evolution of Foreign Aid*, University College Cardiff, 1971.

4   For further details see H.W. Singer 'The Terms of Trade Controversy and the Evolution of Soft Financing: Early Years in the UN', in *Pioneers in Development*, edited by Gerald M. Meier and Dudley Seers, A World Bank Publication published for the World Bank by Oxford University Press, 1984, pp. 273–303.

5   See *International Governance* by Paul Streeten, Louis Emmerij and Carlos Fortin, with an introduction by H.W. Singer, IDS Silver Jubilee Papers nos 1, 2 and 3, Institute of Development Studies, 1992.

4
Revitalizing the United Nations: Five Proposals[*]

Relations between the Bretton Woods institutions and the UN

This question is specifically referred to in the General Assembly resolution requesting the Secretary-General to submit his report on an *Agenda for Development* and also in the draft report itself. It clearly has important institutional implications and is likely to be an important area of discussion during the coming years.

Legally the IMF and World Bank are specialized agencies of the UN and their Terms of Agreement provide for guidance by the UN General Assembly and ECOSOC. However this has clearly become unrealistic. The current practice of distinguishing a 'Bretton Woods system' from the UN system, although legally incorrect, reflects reality. The main reason why the financially powerful countries have shifted their support to the Bretton Woods (BW) system, and why their support for the UN system has eroded, lies in the different voting methods governing the two systems. The Bretton Woods system is essentially based on the principle of one dollar one vote – voting proportionate to financial support – whereas the UN system is based on one country one vote. This gives the financially powerful countries control of the Bretton Woods institutions which they

* Originally published in H. W. Singer and R. Jolly (eds) (1995) 'Fifty Years On: The UN and Economic and Social Development', *IDS Bulletin*, vol. 26, no. 4, October, pp. 35–40.

therefore consider as 'their own'. The UN system, after the first few years, now has a built-in majority of developing countries.

The preference for the BW system is rationalized on the grounds that these institutions are more effective and have recruited more skilled and competent staff. But, to the extent that this is true, it may be taken as a consequence of lack of support and lack of resources for the UN system. This creates a vicious circle: alleged lack of competence leads to withholding of resources which in turn makes it more difficult to recruit and keep competent staff or undertake effective action which will then be taken as a reason – or pretext – to withhold resources. By contrast, the BW system can be said to benefit from a benevolent circle.

We must assume that the unequal distribution of support and resources between the two systems will continue as long as this difference in voting systems persists. It is therefore suggested that thought be given to ways of moving the two voting systems closer together, i.e. moving the BW voting system in the direction of the UN system, while moving the UN system in the direction of the BW system. It is realized that the UN system of one country one vote is embodied in the UN Charter and greatly treasured by the developing countries. But what is suggested here is not a unilateral abandonment of this voting system but a package: what the developing countries lose in the UN they would gain in the BW institutions. But the main point is that a rapprochement of the two voting systems would induce the financially powerful countries to distribute their support and resources more evenly.

It is often claimed that the UN voting system is 'more democratic' than the BW system, but this is not entirely clear. The system of one country one vote gives equal voting powers to very large countries and to tiny countries, and thus discriminates against people in the larger countries. The UN Charter begins with the words: 'We the peoples...', not 'We the countries' or 'We the governments...'

There are some precedents for voting systems which represent a compromise or combination of the UN and BW systems. One example is in the Global Environmental Facility (GEF); another example is the proposed voting system in the World Trade Organization (WTO). In both these cases, the essential feature is a requirement that a majority both of member countries and of financial contributions is required. While this carries a danger of more frequent stalemates, it emphasizes the need for compromise between North and South and should give all concerned confidence that their interests are safeguarded.

It may seem Utopian to propose such a far-reaching change involving changes in the Charter and Terms of Agreements of the various institutions. However, the suggestion is put forward in the belief that without a change in the direction here proposed the present unsatisfactory distribution of support and the erosion of UN support is likely to continue.

Meanwhile, a number of smaller and readily implementable suggestions can be made to mitigate the erosion of the status of the UN in relation to the BW institutions. It is clearly an anomaly that while the President of the World Bank and Managing Director of the IMF address the ECOSOC there is no reciprocity: the Secretary-General is not represented at the annual meetings of the World Bank and IMF and does not bring the views of the UN to the attention of the Directors of the Bank and Fund. There is no reason why the Secretary-General or President of ECOSOC should not be the voice of the UN heard at the annual meetings of the Bank and Fund and why in the documentation for these meetings the UN should not bring relevant decisions of the General Assembly and ECOSOC to the attention of the Directors. Moreover, the Bank and Fund might well be requested to submit an annual report to the General Assembly and ECOSOC to explain what attention they have paid to the resolutions of the General Assembly and ECOSOC, in accordance with their Terms of Agreement. The present speeches by the President and Managing Director to ECOSOC do not fulfil this function – they are more in the nature of expressing their views about the current situation and action required. There is no reason why they should not continue to have this opportunity, but it is suggested that the UN should have the same opportunity at the annual meetings of the Bank and Fund.

What is said above about the Bank and Fund would equally apply in future to the World Trade Organization.

A new integration of peace and development

The old dichotomy of emergency (largely connected with conflict today) and development becomes more and more questionable. The roots of conflict are not only military and political (within the mandate of the Security Council), but also (and more fundamentally) economic and social. This raises questions of preventive action (already touched upon in UN Secretary-General Boutros-Gali's *Agenda for Peace*) and of the proposal to create an Economic Security Council contained in the 1994 issue of the UNDP *Human Development Report* and possible alternatives.

The proposal for an Economic Security Council would raise difficult questions. Since it would create a new principal organ of the UN, it would require a change in the Charter. It would also raise questions of size and membership (although such questions might have to be faced anyway in connection with the present Security Council). Presumably there would be no veto in an Economic Security Council. Given the difficulties of creating an entirely new organ, perhaps priority should be given to considering alternatives. The simplest alternative would be to extend the mandate of the present Security Council to deal with 'threats to peace' also preventively and in the form of economic and social emergencies – before they erupt into actual military conflict. In fact this may not need a new mandate at all, but could be treated as a clarification of the present mandate – in that case it would not need any legal change. However it may be considered that such an extended mandate should not be subject to the present veto and non-military (not-yet military) threats to peace might be dealt with by a separate committee of the Security Council – a parallel to the present Military Committee.

The other alternative – also discussed in the *Human Development Report 1994* – would be to strengthen the capacity of ECOSOC to deal with such non-military threats to peace. For this purpose a special new high-level segment of ECOSOC could be created, with smaller membership than the present ECOSOC, and meeting in continuous session with periodic high-level meetings.

Whatever solution is adopted there is now a consensus that there is a gap to be filled. *Agenda for Peace* has drawn attention to the opportunities and need for preventive action in the case of tensions (often triggered by economic and social emergencies) which can be foreseen to carry acute dangers of military conflict. There is also a present gap in dealing with the other end of the development/emergency continuum. The question of reconstruction and rehabilitation after conflict should also be tackled by an Economic Security Council or whatever alternative is preferred. This may involve new relations with the Bretton Woods institutions, especially the World Bank. As indicated by its official title – International Bank for Reconstruction and Development – the World Bank was expected to be strongly involved in post-war reconstruction. In the event, this function did not develop, largely as a result of being overtaken by the Marshall Plan, and then withered away as a result of preoccupation of the World Bank first with specific development projects and later with structural adjustment programmes and debt collection. Perhaps the time has come to restore the reconstruction functions of the World Bank in close collaboration with whatever UN mechanism carries out the functions proposed for the Economic Security Council.

A special concern of the Economic Security Council (or its alternatives) should be the question of food security. The abolition of the UN World Food Council has created a gap and the problem is further accentuated by the GATT Agreement and the creation of the WTO. By general consensus, this will lead to a rise in international food prices and a reduction in food surpluses. Thus the need for food aid or other forms of providing food security for poor food-importing countries, especially in Africa, will increase, while at the same time the cost to donors of giving food aid will increase and surpluses will diminish, thus reducing the willingness to give food aid. This creates a situation calling for international vigilance and action which should be the concern of the UN in collaboration with the new WTO. Among the actions required would be the activation and enlargement of the International Emergency Food Reserve, including the pre-positioning of food stocks in danger spots in advance of actual conflict.

The need for global economic management

In the original Bretton Woods proposals global economic management was assumed to be in the United Nations (General Assembly and ECOSOC). Although at the time of Bretton Woods the UN did not yet exist (being created a year later at San Francisco) its creation had already been announced and the broad outlines of its organization were under negotiation. This impending arrangement was also reflected in the Terms of Agreement of the IMF and World Bank which made them specialized agencies of the UN and provided for guidance by the General Assembly and ECOSOC. The IMF was visualized, with much larger resources than actually materialized, as a powerful instrument of dealing with financial, monetary, and balance of payments disequilibria, with an overriding objective of full employment, and with many of the functions of a world central bank. The World Bank was established on a project basis and not visualized as being involved with macroeconomic policies or structural adjustment problems.

In the event today, whatever macroeconomic global management exists has been moved out of the multilateral system altogether and is now in the hands of the G7. This cannot be acceptable as a satisfactory solution of the problem: the G7 represents little more than 10 per cent of mankind and even with the possible future addition of Russia it would still only represent a small minority. Moreover it is clear that the G7 – quite apart from insufficient attention being paid to the implications of macroeconomic measures for the rest of humankind, especially the developing countries – has not even proved able to promote satisfactory coordination among the 7. There is now spreading acceptance of the fact that global economic management must be made more democratic and moved back in some way, and to some extent, to the multilateral framework visualized at Bretton Woods and San Francisco.

Simple measures have been proposed which would not directly involve the UN institutionally although they would be clearly welcome to the UN. The principal such measure is an enlargement of the G7 to make it more representative and effective, and to include such developing countries as Brazil (for Latin America), Nigeria (for Africa), India (for Asia) and Eastern Europe, perhaps on a rotating basis. The inclusion of Russia is already on the agenda.

There are however other proposals which would concern the UN more directly. One suggestion would be for the Secretary-General, or his appointed representative, to participate in the discussions of the G7, more or less as a spokesman for the majority of humankind now excluded and as a guardian of their interests. Another proposal is for the UN Secretariat to be involved in the preparation of documentation and agendas for the meetings of the G7, with a view to drawing attention to neglected areas, urgent problems, and particularly problems concerning the developing countries (such as the debt problem, deteriorating terms of trade, etc.). Mr Sutherland, the then Director General of GATT, in a letter to the *Financial Times* (7 June 1994) has proposed that the new WTO, jointly with the World Bank and IMF, should 'evolve a single coherent statement on issues of economic concern for the G7. It may be suggested that this would be a proper task for the UN (which need not exclude submissions by the IMF, World Bank or WTO, and should certainly involve consultation and collaboration with these institutions). The restoration of the objectives of growth and full employment, as well as the newly prominent objective of poverty reduction, should be the special task for the UN to keep in the forefront of the G7 discussions. The implementation of decisions at the World Social Summit (Copenhagen, 1995) should be brought by the UN to the agenda of the G7 and firmly kept there. The creation of an Economic Security Council (or the alternatives suggested above) would in itself serve to bring global co-ordination back to the multilateral forum where it was intended to be, at least in the area at the cutting edge of development and emergency.

Strengthening the resources of the UN

As previously explained, the question of resources is closely intertwined with questions of political support and competence. In the case of the UN this intertwined complex threatens to take the form of a vicious circle. This circle could be broken by reviving political support from powerful countries, perhaps at the price of a change in the UN voting system. Another way of breaking the vicious circle is by giving the UN independent resources which would enable it to tackle the problems for which it has responsibility more effectively and promptly (and perhaps in doing so then elicit further support and contributions, thus breaking the vicious circle). In this connection, the possibility of providing resources for the UN from some form of international taxation is increasingly raised and is now firmly on the international agenda.

Various forms of international taxation have been mooted. Perhaps a leading candidate for consideration is the proposal for a tax on international currency transactions. This has been supported most recently by the Nobel Laureate, James Tobin, in the *Human Development Report 1994*. Given the current huge volume of foreign exchange transactions, a very small tax rate would yield a large revenue – for example a tax of 0.05 per cent would yield $150 billion a year. Such a tax rate would be too small to deter genuine trade or capital movements, but it would have the merit – in addition to providing resources for international purposes – to deter disruptive speculative movements and to restore greater autonomy both to national monetary policy-makers and also to the IMF. This could be expected to result in greater weight being given to economic fundamentals and less to personal enrichment by functionless gambling. Other international taxes have been proposed including taxes on air travel, exploitation of common resources such as the Arctic Seas, etc. A system of tradable permits for pollution would also lend itself well to help to finance international purposes, including the UN (although the basic purpose of such proposals is to provide funds to compensate victims of pollution). This last proposal of tradable permits has the advantage of applying market principles ('the polluter pays'), thus helping to 'get prices right' by internalizing the cost of pollution. Given the present support for market orientation in important quarters, this idea should have some appeal and deserves serious consideration.

The idea of international taxation is by no means new. In his original memoranda in preparation for the Bretton Woods Conference, Keynes had proposed a tax on balance of trade or balance of payments surpluses, at the rate of 1 per cent a month. His idea was that this would be an inducement to surplus countries to increase their imports thus helping in the achievement of the full employment objective. At the same time, the yield from this tax would provide resources for deficit countries enabling them to maintain their imports, further contributing to full employment. At the time, this proposal vanished without a trace, but the present recurrence of unemployment, balance of payments disequilibria, and the need for finding resources for international purposes might serve to revive interest in this proposal.

Even without such novel instruments, UN resources could of course be increased if member countries paid contributions more promptly, and if international commitments such as the 0.7 per cent aid target, commitments as a result of the Rio Conference resolutions, contributions to the International Emergency Food Reserve, etc., were more fully and more promptly discharged. This would require concerted action by the contributors since otherwise we would face a 'prisoners dilemma' situation, with each country waiting for the others to contribute.

There are also other latent international resources which could be activated and used for the benefit of international action, specifically of UN action. There is the power, unused since 1981, to issue Special Drawing Rights (SDRs) through the IMF. The Managing Director of the IMF is himself on record as advocating an issue of SDRs to the extent of $36 billion. If part of this issue could be reserved for international purposes, or alternatively if the richer member countries of the IMF could forego their quota of SDRs for the benefit of the UN or for other agreed international purposes, the problem of resources would be that much nearer to a solution. Similarly, there is latent international capital available in the gold reserves held by the IMF – the sale of some of these reserves is also increasingly suggested. Ultimately this comes back to the question of political will. Once the principle of international taxation or tapping of latent international resources is accepted, the detailed forms of such taxation or mobilization should be amenable to international agreement.

Specific roles for the UN

The present role of the UN system in the narrower sense – excluding the Bretton Woods system – is now often defined as looking after the 'soft' parts of development: social factors, poverty reduction, employment, vulnerable groups, women, children, refugees, war victims, health, and so on, while the Bretton Woods system would look after the 'hard' facts of development, that is, money, finance, trade, as well as macroeconomic policies, dealing with debt problems, and so on. Such a division of labour between 'hard' and 'soft' areas is also mentioned in the Secretary-General's Report on an *Agenda for Development*. There would be a great deal of scepticism among development professionals about such a division of development issues into 'hard' and 'soft' issues. Moreover, the implication that the hard issues are more important and the real core of development and require greater competence to deal with is out of tune with more recent insights into the development process. These recent insights tend to place increasing emphasis on human capital and human resources – presumably in the soft area – as distinct from physical investment and financial resources presumed to be in the hard area. From that point of view, the UN system could be quite satisfied with responsibility for the allegedly soft part of development, provided that both parts were taken equally seriously and equally supported with resources. That however is not the case. Insofar as the soft parts of development – poverty reduction, health, education, and so on – are taken as seriously as they should be, they are then undertaken by the Bretton Woods institutions which command the necessary support and resources and are presumed to have competence derived from their experience of dealing with the hard parts of development.

A good example is the field of technical assistance. Under the 'Kennedy Compromise' of around 1960, soft financial aid was allocated to the World Bank (IDA) while technical assistance and food aid were allocated to the UN (UNDP and WFP). The UNDP was supposed to be the chief funding agency and co-ordinating agency for technical assistance throughout the UN system. Yet today the World Bank gives as much or more technical assistance than the UNDP and the IMF is rapidly expanding its technical assistance operations without having to rely on funding from the UNDP. In an effort to restore the role of the UNDP, attention is now focused on enhancing the role of the UNDP resident representatives to that of UN co-ordinators or even UN ambassadors. Similarly, there is a parallel effort to place the technical assistance activities of UN agencies into a country-programming framework, devised and negotiated by the UNDP. All such proposals may improve the efficiency and coherence of UN technical assistance and enhance the role of the UNDP, but they do not solve the problem of relationship with the Bretton Woods system. To give the UNDP or UN representative the enhanced role aimed at, the suggestion may be made that the UN co-ordinator should take part in the discussion of stabilization and structural adjustment programmes; perhaps representatives of specialized agencies should also participate. Some of these programmes have a crucial impact say on agriculture and health, and presumably the field officers of the FAO and WHO have more concrete country knowledge and competence than Washington-based macro-economists. (Similarly on the governments' side, one would wish for these negotiations not to be limited to ministries of finance and central bank officials but to include representatives of the ministries of agriculture, health and so on – but that is a matter for governments rather than the UN system.)

In pursuit of this greater co-ordination of technical assistance and operational programmes by the UN at the country level it has been proposed that all these programmes (UNDP, WFP, UNICEF, HCR, etc.) should be merged into a single institution. However, this proposal ought to be resisted. It could make matters worse by depriving UN operations even of some of the support which they now enjoy. Organizations like WFP, UNICEF, and others have established a clear identity of their own; their concrete purposes attract both political and financial support and they have backing in public opinion which in the long run may influence governments of contributing countries. It would be counterproductive to throw all this away by a merger into one large omnibus institution without the distinctive identity and distinctive appeal of the present agencies.

Part III

Debt and Debt Servicing

5

The Debt Issue – A Historical Perspective[*]

The debt issue has a history. More immediately, it goes back to the large financial surpluses of oil producing countries upon the two explosions of oil prices in 1973 and 1979. These oil surpluses flowed into the commercial banks of the United States, the United Kingdom, Switzerland and other industrial countries. Other scenarios would have been possible: the surplus could have been used to establish a financial basis for extended South–South trade, considering that the OPEC countries thought of themselves as members of the Third World; or they could have gone into supplies of cheap oil for developing countries; or directly into real estate or other fixed investments, and so on. But, by and large, they went into commercial banks and since at that time in the 1970s the industrial countries, taken as a whole, did not have balance of payments deficits, the money was available to be 'recycled' into developing countries. This helped them to maintain their growth rate, in spite of deteriorating terms of trade as a result of higher oil prices and also in spite of the reduced growth rate of industrial countries. At that time, during the 1970s, this seemed a viable system and everyone, World Bank, IMF, OPEC governments, OECD governments and commercial banks, were patting themselves on the back and congratulating themselves on how well the world financial system was coping.

So, as a first move, we can trace back the debt problem to the rising oil prices, but this would not be very perceptive. One essential factor

---

* Originally published in *Oeconomic*, Erasmus University, Rotterdam, The Netherlands, 1989, pp. 10–11.

was the reaction of the industrial countries to the rising oil prices by adopting restrictive domestic policies, reducing demand and slowing down their growth rate (and with it the growth rate of world trade) from the 5–6 per cent of the 1960s to some 2.5 per cent in the 15 years since 1974. We could go even further back and trace the origin of the debt crisis to the weakness of the new international economic order which was established after the last war, at Bretton Woods. The original plans included an organization to stabilize prices, including the price of oil, or even to create a world currency based on primary commodities, including gold and oil, rather than gold, dollars or sterling. If this had been implemented, we would not have had the high volatility in the price of oil and other primary commodities. Nor would we have had the collapse of primary commodity prices in the 1980s, which has been such an important factor in making the debt burden impossible to carry for the developing countries.

So an historical perspective could tell us that the debt issue is part and parcel of the total picture of post-war development experience.

The present situation, by general consent, has become untenable, at least for these highly indebted countries – mainly in Latin America – who would owe their debts mainly to commercial banks at floating rates of interest. Three factors have come together to make their situation untenable – we can picture them as successive and cumulative taxes on their export earnings. In particular, there are three such cumulative taxes:

1 the slowdown in the growth rate of industrial countries and their restrictive policies, including protectionist policies, have reduced the exports of developing countries much below what they otherwise would have been;
2 the deterioration in their terms of trade, affecting mainly, but not exclusively, their primary exports, have reduced the buying power of their exports and hence their capacity to import goods to support their development;
3 the rising interest rates from a negative real figure (that is, relative to inflation) in the 1970s to something like 15–20 per cent today has magnified the debt burden to a degree unforseen when the debt was incurred.

We can picture this process as that of a successive tax on the export earnings of some 25 per cent or so – first, a 25 per cent tax on account of reduced growth in the world economy, then a 25 per cent tax on the remainder as a result of deteriorating terms of trade, and then another 25 per cent tax on the remainder on account of high interest rates. No wonder that with the triple blow of such taxation of export earnings the currently fashionable receipt of advising developing countries to be more 'outward oriented', meets with some difficulties!

The market has long expressed its sceptism about full debt repayment in the 'secondary market', where debt certificates of developing countries are traded with heavy discounts. The commercial banks have by now made provision in their balance sheets against losses due to non-payment of their claims; the government of creditor countries have taken measures to reduce or cancel their own claims, particularly those on the very poor countries of Africa; professional opinion has long come around to the conviction that some degree or method of debt reduction of debt forgiveness is inevitable. The Baker plan of 1985 was a first hesitant step in this direction; the Brady plan of 1989 is a second – although still hesitant – step. But the direction in which things are moving has become unmistakable. The question is whether we can find a way to solve these problems without conflict and as part of the world plan to promote growth and prosperity, or whether the problems will be solved by prolonging the miseries of the 'lost decade' of the 1980s.

6
Debt Pressures, Adjustment Policies and Deterioration of Terms of Trade for Developing Countries (with Special Reference to Latin America)*

I Overview

The Prebisch–Singer (P–S) hypothesis suggested that, contrary to classical teaching, the terms of trade of primary products in international trade – and hence the terms of trade of countries more dependent on export of primary products than their trade partners – would tend to deteriorate rather than improve. From the beginning this hypothesis had two elements, initially not clearly distinguished. The first element related to the characteristics of primary *commodities* (inelastic demand, liability to substitution, and so on), whereas the second element related to the characteristics of primary producing *countries* (surplus labour leading to high supply elasticity, weak labour organization leading to low wages, and so forth) compared with their industrialized trade partners (strong trade unions, technology leadership leading to monopoly rents, etc.).

The first of these two elements relating to barter terms of trade of primary products was hotly debated, mainly in statistical rather than

* Originally published as 'The Relationship between Debt Pressures, Adjustment Policies and Deterioration of the Terms of Trade for Developing Countries (with Special Reference to Latin America)', *Institute of Social Studies Working Papers Series*, no. 59 (The Hague: Institute of Social Studies, 1989).

analytical terms, but this debate has now died down. At least for this present decade there is little dispute that the P–S hypothesis has a better projection record than most other economic projections (including the commodity projections of the World Bank and the IMF). But the essence of the P–S hypothesis was always in the second element which should have led to debates on income terms of trade and factoral terms of trade rather than barter terms of trade (as emphasized by Spraos, 1980). This second element of P–S which also emphasized the greater scope for technical progress in industry compared with primary production, has analytically led to the development of theories of unequal exchange and dependency, and in policy terms to strategies of ISI (import-substituting industrialization) leading on to ESI (export-substituting industrialization), that is, substituting manufactured for primary exports.

This essay deals with both aspects, but in the new context of debt. This new context affects both elements of P–S. It will be shown that both barter terms of trade and factoral terms of trade are closely interwoven with pressures arising from debt payments. In particular we maintain that in addition to the resource burden there is an additional transfer burden of debt payment in the form of deteriorating terms of trade. This is also the position which was maintained in the debate over German post-First World War reparations by Keynes (based on John Stuart Mill), but contested by Ohlin (based on Ricardo). We also argue that not only is there a transfer burden but that in fact it forms a very important dimension of the debt problem. In relation to the second element of P–S, it is argued that diversification or shifts into manufactured exports under debt pressure do not provide a satisfactory escape from the transfer burden but in fact form a part of it. This emerges particularly in relation to factoral terms of trade. Thus the debt situation unleashes forces which tend to make for immiserizing growth in the Periphery and for widening income gaps between the Centre and the Periphery.

II

The debt situation and the terms of trade problem are deeply entangled with each other in a process of mutual causation – much more so than is usually realized. The rise in indebtedness can be attributed to changes in terms of trade in various ways:

(a) Historically, the debt crisis can be attributed to the failure at Bretton Woods to embody commodity price stabilization in the new Bretton Woods system as Keynes had intended. In addition to the World Bank and IMF, the Bretton Woods system was to have included an International Trade Organization (ITO), with the main function of stabilizing and maintaining primary commodity prices. Even further, Keynes had imagined a world currency based on 30 primary commodities including gold and oil; this would have prevented first the fall in real oil prices between 1948 and 1973, and then their abrupt rise in 1973 and 1979 (as well as their subsequent fall). The Bretton Woods system was also to include a system of soft aid under UN auspices, as well as automatic liquidity for deficit countries provided by the IMF as well as pressure on surplus countries – in fact, taxation of their surpluses. The fact that the Bretton Woods system remained incomplete contains the germ of the current debt crisis. Only very minor attempts were made to replace the yawning gaps in the system; these include the creation of GATT, of IDA in 1960, compensatory financial mechanisms in the IMF even later, and so on. But these remained very weak and ineffective mechanisms often perverted to serve quite different, sometimes opposite, purposes from those intended. Thus GATT became more an instrument for legitimizing trade barriers, and the IMF and World Bank (which stood on the sidelines while the debts accumulated or even applauded the 'efficient recycling' of surpluses) have now become agencies for debt collecting rather than suppliers of liquidity for deficit countries. The present debt burden is a legacy of the incompleteness and perversion of the Bretton Woods system in the area of commodities and commodity prices.

(b) More immediately, the debt crisis goes at least partly back to the rapid increases in oil prices in 1973 and 1979, resulting in enormous OPEC surpluses which were then recycled through the commercial banks in the USA, Europe and Japan. Thus the unfavourable terms of trade of the oil-importing countries were one of the immediate causes of their debt accumulation, especially after 1975/76 when the temporary boom in primary commodities other than oil collapsed. In the oil-exporting countries such as Venezuela and Mexico, the causation and role of terms of trade in debt accumulation was obviously different. But even there terms of trade played a vital although indirect role: the favourable terms of trade and financial surpluses engendered a growth and investment optimism for the future which seemed to make debt accumulation safe (on the assumption of continuing high prices for oil); at the same time it made these countries particularly creditworthy in the judgment of the commercial banks so that they were even more beleaguered by the banks to accept loans than the oil-importing countries. For developing countries as a whole, according to calculations by Cline, of the total debt accumulation of $500 billion between 1973 and 1982, about $260 billion were directly attributable to increased costs of oil (Cline, 1985).

(c) The debt burden has predictably been added to by an additional 'transfer burden' in the form of pressure on terms of trade. 'Predictably', because we have been there before – at the end of the First World War when the Treaty of Versailles imposed heavy 'reparations' on Germany. At that time, Keynes (based on John Stuart Mill) demonstrated that there was a secondary burden in the form of worsened terms of trade, on top of the primary burden of mobilizing and transferring savings at the expense of domestic investment. The case made by Keynes was later supported, in different ways, by Pigou, Harry Johnson and Samuelson, but opposed by Ohlin (based on Ricardo). Today, the Latin American countries in paying *their* reparations (debt service) demonstrate the validity of Keynes's views: apart from negative ('reverse') transfer of capital there is the invisible, but connected, additional burden of terms of trade deterioration due to 'desperation exports'. The association between the German First World War reparations and the hyper-inflation of 1922–23 was more than accidental; it contains warnings for today's debtor and creditor countries – we have been there before! Irving Fisher wrote in support of Keynes in *Econometrica* (1933):

> The liquidation of debts cannot keep up with the fall in prices which it causes. In that case, the liquidation defeats itself. While it diminishes the number of dollars owed, it may not do so as fast as it increases the value of each dollar owed…then we have the great paradox: *The more debtors pay the more they owe.*

Mutatis mutandis, translating from the deflation of the early thirties to the inflation of the eighties, these words seem a prophetic forecast of the current debt trap. In fact, the debt burden (representing, as it does, a tax on export earnings and a reduction of import capacity), amounts to a deterioration of terms of trade – of income terms of trade rather than barter terms of trade – in all but name. When Raul Prebisch wrote of vulnerability of the Periphery to deteriorating terms of trade and a widening gap *vis-à-vis* the Centre, he could have written of the Debtors *vis-à-vis* the Creditors, and his warnings against reliance on exports of primary products could be extended to warnings against falling into a debt trap (at least of the type characteristic of the 'Potemkin years' of the 1970s).

The effects of such multiple taxation of export earnings can be readily illustrated. If we just take three sources (triple taxation): debt service represents a 30 per cent tax on export earnings in Latin America today, terms of trade deterioration over the decade is at least 20 per cent, and loss of exports due to the slowed-down growth of the industrial countries cumulatively for 1980–88 compared with the 'Golden Years' of 1950–73 is another 20 per cent. Successive cuts of 30, 20 and 20 per cent will result in a total cut of 55 per cent or over one-half of export earnings. This means that less than half the potential export earnings are available for the financing of development imports.

(d) The worsening terms of trade for primary products after 1975 have been a major contributory factor in the present dimensions of the debt problem. Of the total accumulation of debt by Latin American countries of $179 billion between 1980 and 1988, the cumulative loss due to deterioration of terms of trade for non-oil countries accounted for $75 billion or 42 per cent. It also represented over half of the total negative transfer of resources since 1982 (of $146 billion). Similarly, of the total increase of $66 billion in the current account deficit of non-oil developing countries in 1981 compared with 1978, terms of trade deterioration accounted for $21 billion (32 per cent), more than the rise in oil prices (27 per cent) and almost as much as net interest payments (36 per cent). These calculations are based on the difference between actual export earnings and export earnings as they would have been if terms of trade had remained constant and assuming all other things, particularly export volume, had remained the same (that is, assuming zero price elasticity of demand). This overstates the loss to the extent that the volume of exports was greater at the worsened unit values than it would have been without the deterioration.

For the non-oil Latin American countries (excluding Ecuador, Mexico, Trinidad and Venezuela), over the seven years 1980–86 the average deterioration in terms of trade was 19 per cent, equivalent cumulatively to the loss of 16 months (1 year and four months) of exports. This compares with average net resource transfers during the 1982–86 period of 25 per cent of total exports of goods and services. Thus, for the non-oil Latin American countries the 'tax' on export earnings due to terms of trade deterioration was comparable in magnitude at 19 per cent to the 'tax' represented by net resource transfers at 25 per cent. In terms of the old Mill–Keynes versus Ricardo-Ohlin controversy, there was an additional transfer burden in addition to the resource loss (as argued by Mill and Keynes). Moreover, the resource loss would have been reduced from 25 per cent to 20 per cent if conjecturally calculated on the higher exports undiminished by terms of trade losses; this would virtually equalize the two burdens. Conjectural as this calculation is, it serves to emphasize the size of the burden of deteriorating terms of trade.

Within this contribution of deteriorating terms of trade to debt accumulation, the main factor clearly was in relation to deteriorating terms of trade for exports of primary products. However it is not often realized that the recent deterioration in terms of trade also applies to trade in manufactures. The period 1975–88 saw the share of manufactures in Latin American exports increase from 12 to 19 per cent. This shift from primary exports to manufactured exports mitigated but did not eliminate the role of deteriorating terms of trade in debt accumulation. The neglected subject of terms of trade in manufactures will be considered in more detail in a later part of this essay.

In the world economy as a whole, real commodity prices fell during the current decade (1980–87) by an average of 23 per cent, compared with the previous decade of 1970–79 and also the decade 1960–69 (these two comparisons are identical since there was no change between 1960–69 and 1970–79). This average decline of 23 per cent per annum during 1980–87 adds up to a cumulative decline or cumulative loss over the eight-year period of 185 per cent of primary exports earnings. In other words, almost two full years of primary export earnings were lost as a result of the decline in real commodity prices.

Another way of picturing the contribution of deteriorating terms of trade and resulting shortfalls of export earnings on debt accumulation is as follows:[1]

During 1980–85 the average debt service ratio of developing countries (debt service as percentage of total exports) increased from 12.5 per cent to 20.1 per cent. Of this total increase in the debt service ratio of 7.6 percentage points, loss in export earnings accounted for 1.1 percentage points, that is some 15 per cent of the total increase in the debt service ratio. In addition to volume factors due to slowdown of growth in the industrial countries, trade obstacles, and so on, the decline in commodity prices obviously played a major role in this 15 per cent contribution to the increase in the debt service ratio through loss of export earnings.

In some Latin American countries the fall in commodity prices had a much bigger effect in raising the debt service ratio than the average of 1.1 percentage points. For example, the figure for Bolivia is 12.9 percentage points; Chile 12.1 percentage points; Peru 6.1 percentage points.

Taking Latin America as a whole the contribution of losses in export earnings to the increase in the debt service ratio is almost twice as large as for all developing countries (2.0 percentage points compared with 1.1 percentage points), and its relative contribution is 43 per cent rather than 15 per cent. This clearly illustrates the major role which the export earnings factor, and the terms of trade factor implicit in it, has played in Latin America specifically, much more so than in the rest of the Third World. The significant exception is Africa where the loss of export earnings in fact accounted for 3.1 percentage points, even more than in Latin America, although in relative terms at just under 40 per cent slightly less than in Latin America. In Asia, on the other hand, export earnings improved (largely because of a larger share of manufactures in exports and also because of heavier increases in export volume) and the increases in the debt service ratio, which were in fact quite heavy compared with Latin America, were entirely due to the increase in debt volume.

In those Latin American countries where the debt service ratio fell during 1980–85 (Brazil, Peru, Nicaragua, Paraguay, Venezuela, Dominican Republic) export earnings were better maintained during 1980–85 than in the Latin American countries for which the debt service ratio increased (Colombia, Argentina, Uruguay, Jamaica, El Salvador, Guatemala, Bolivia, Mexico, Costa Rica, Chile, Barbados, Honduras, Equador, Trinidad and Panama). In the countries with falling debt service ratios, loss of export earnings added 0.15 percentage points to the ratio, whereas in Latin American countries with rising debt service ratios changes in export earnings added 2.6 percentage points. This is still another indication of the crucial role played by the change in export earnings in determining debt service ratios. Within the change in export earnings, movements in terms of trade played a crucial role in the primary sector.

For the 13 largest debtor countries as a whole, loss of export earnings accounted for 0.6 percentage points out of a total rise in the debt service ratio by 7.9 percentage points during 1980–85, that is rather less than 10 per cent, less than for developing countries as a whole. For the Latin American countries among these three largest debtor countries, in Argentina loss of export earnings accounted for a 3.3 percentage points rise in the debt service ratio, although this was compensated by other factors so that the debt ratio in fact declined. Chile had the largest loss of export earnings as a contributory factor to the increase in debt service (12.1 percentage points), accounting for more than the whole of the total increase in the ration. In Peru, as in Venezuela, a big loss in export earnings (6.1 percentage points on the debt service ratio) was over-compensated by other factors. In Mexico and Brazil due to heavy increases in volume of exports and diversification into manufactures, export earnings helped to reduce the debt service ratio by 10.3 and 8.3 percentage points respectively. In the case of Brazil this improvement accounted for about 50 per cent of the total fall in the debt service ratio, while in the case of Mexico it was over-compensated by the heavy increase in the volume of debt, raising the debt service ratio sharply.

The authors of the above calculations[2] also find a negative correlation between the impact of export earnings on the debt service ratio and the contribution of changes in rates of interest of amortization, indicating that countries worst hit by falls in export earnings have received relief in the form of rescheduling and softer borrowing. Expectedly, there is significant positive correlation between the share of primary exports in total exports and the contribution of falls in export earnings to the debt service ratio indicating that the terms of trade problem is centred on primary commodities rather than on manufactures.[3]

Impact of debt pressure on terms of trade

So far, we have dealt with the direct role of deteriorating terms of trade and the associated fall in export earnings as a contributory factor to the accumulation and escalation of debts during the last 15 years or so. Perhaps less well-known is the opposite connection, that is, the way in which debt pressures have been a causative factor in the decline in commodity prices and deterioration of terms of trade. All the same, this opposite connection should also be fairly clear. Under the pressure of debt payment obligations, developing countries have to try to achieve export surpluses. Theoretically, such surpluses could be achieved by way of import reduction combined with effective and efficient import substitution. In fact, there have been heavy import reductions in the 1980s in Latin America – a fact too well-known to need much documentation. The volume of imports for Latin America as a whole fell between 1980 and 1988 by 24 per cent; over the whole period 1980–88 the average reduction during these eight years was 25 per cent per annum amounting to a cumulative reduction over the eight years of 203 per cent equivalent to a loss of two years of imports. Unfortunately, this did not represent effective import substitution, but was at the expense of growth and development. This is shown by the fact that over the decade of the 1980s the cumulative loss of per capita GDP amounted to 10 per cent, literally a 'lost decade'. Thus, the reduction in imports represented import strangulation, and not constructive import substitution.

This leaves export expansion as an alternative route. In fact, the debt pressures created a need for earning foreign exchange at any price, even at heavy cost – 'desperation exports' in the graphic words of Senator Bradley. This pressure was further added to by the neo-classical, anti-Keynesian and anti-Prebischian ideology of 'outward orientation' as representing the only recipe for healthy, 'sustainable' growth and development, governing the stabilization and adjustment procedures of the IMF and World Bank. Under the double pressure of the 'facts of life', that is, the need to make debt payments in a hostile international environment, and of the neo-classical adjustment ideology, Latin American countries were pressed to undergo processes of stabilization and structural adjustment, prominently including exchange depreciation and other incentives for intensified exports. Latin American countries generally underwent depreciation of their real exchange rates, that is even after taking into account domestic inflation in excess of that of their main trade partners. Real exchange rates now are typically 30–40 per cent lower than at the opening of the decade. The 1985 real effective

Table 6.1 Volume and unit value indices of exports of different parts of the market economy world, 1980–87

Regions & Indices	Years							
	1980	*1981*	*1982*	*1983*	*1984*	*1985*	*1986*	*1987*
I. First World (developed market economies)								
Volume	100	102	101	104	114	118	121	122
Unit value	100	96	92	88	86	85	97	108
II. Third World								
Volume	100	94	88	91	96	93	114	119
Unit value	100	105	97	88	87	85	64	71
Terms of trade[*]	100	109	105	100	101	100	66	66
A. Major Petroleum Exporters								
Volume	100	84	72	68	67	61	78	72
Unit value	100	112	106	93	91	89	52	61
Terms of trade[*]	100	117	115	106	106	105	54	56
B. Other Third World Countries								
Volume	100	113	119	128	141	144	156	174
Unit value	100	93	84	82	83	80	78	83
Terms of trade[*]	100	97	91	93	96	94	80	77

[*]Relative unit values: unit values of exports of the different regions of the Third World inflated by the unit values of exports of the First World.

Source: UNCTAD, *Handbook of International Trade and Development Statistics*, 1987.

exchange rates showed the following rates of depreciation compared with 1980: Argentina 45 per cent, Brazil 29 per cent, Mexico 31 per cent, Venezuela 33 per cent.

The currency depreciations increased export supplies but also made exports cheaper to the customer countries, thus increasing export volumes at the expense of deteriorating terms of trade. This amounted to a 'reverse' transfer of capital, similar and additional to the better-known reverse transfer of capital represented by the debt payments themselves.[4] To the extent that the growth in export volume was bought at the expense of deteriorating terms of trade, it represented a case of 'immiserizing growth'.

The data for this decade confirm the existence of a transfer burden in the form of worsened terms of trade, in addition to the budgetary and investment burden of the debt payments and reverse capital transfer which has taken place (see Table 6.1).

On the basis of 1980 = 100, the terms of trade of Third World countries had worsened in 1987, by 34 per cent; if major oil exporters are excluded the drop was 23 per cent. This was associated with a terrific export drive by the non-oil Third World countries, with volume increasing year by year in the decade to a 74 per cent expansion in 1987. Thus, the terms of trade deterioration cut the capacity

Table 6.2   Growth of exports between different regions of the world, 1981–83/1984–86 (annual average percentage rate)

Origin	*Destination*				
	World	*First World*	*Third World*		
			Total	*OPEC*	*Others*
First World (developed market economies)	3.7	6.1	−3.7	−12.8	0.8
Third World					
Total	−2.6	−3.1	−4.2	−4.5	−4.2
OPEC	−14.0	−16.0	−10.6	−5.5	−11.1
Others	5.5	7.0	0.5	−4.2	2.1

Source: UNCTAD, *Handbook of International Trade and Development Statistics*, 1987, pp. 62–3.

to import from rising export volume from 74 per cent to 34 per cent (174/0.77 = 134), or by over half (confirming earlier results as to the serious magnitude of the contribution of terms of trade deterioration to debt burdens). For the Third World as a whole (including major oil exporters), this contribution is actually over 100 per cent since the terms of trade deterioration (34 per cent) is greater than expansion of export volume (19 per cent) so that capacity to import was actually reduced. For the oil exporters taken alone, the deterioration in terms of trade (44 per cent) was the major factor in the decline of capacity to import exceeding the drop in export volume (28 per cent). By contrast, the OECD (First World) countries were in the happier position of combining increased export volumes with improved terms of trade with the Third World.

Most of the growth of exports of the OECD countries was due to trade among themselves where the question of overall terms of trade does not arise (improvements by some countries automatically cancelling out deterioration in others), whereas most of the export volume expansion of the Third World countries was to the OECD countries, with exports among themselves hardly expanding at all (0.5 per cent per annum). This is further analysed in Table 6.2. (It should be noted that Table 6.2 relates to a different time period and base period from Table 6.1, and no direct comparisons should be made.)

Even the non-OPEC developing countries increased trade among each other only at a rate of 30 per cent of that of trade expansion with the First World (2.1 per cent per annum against 7 per cent per annum). Including OPEC countries, the Third World reduced trade volumes both with the First World and among themselves, but more so among themselves. South–South trade remains the poor relation of the world trading system, still the hope of tomorrow rather than today. At the same time, it remains a 'black box' of the world economy whose lowly status remains inexplicable – inexplicable, that is, on purely economic grounds. Classical theory would lead us to believe that today Third World intra-trade should be more intensive than the intra-trade of industrial countries since they differ more in comparative advantage and resource structure – but then classical theory also told us that the terms of trade of primary exporting countries would improve *vis-à-vis* industrial countries. Hence the World Bank and IMF frantically produced commodity price projections consistently diverging from reality.[5] For the Bank and Fund, P–S was 'the truth that dare not speak its name' – the Great Satan!

The overall data of Table 6.1 may be supplemented for the Latin American major countries (Table 6.3).

The aggregate pattern of expansion of export volume partially wiped out by deterioration of terms of trade can be seen to apply clearly only to Costa Rica and to Uruguay. In a number of countries the deterioration in terms of trade either comes on top of a reduction in export volume (Bolivia, Jamaica, Nicaragua, Peru and Venezuela) or else wipes out the whole rather than only part of the increase in export volume (Argentina, Chile, Ecuador, Mexico). The best-looking cases are those of Brazil and Colombia where improved terms of trade went hand in hand with increased export volume. (However, it will be noted that in both countries the improvement in terms of trade applied only to the terminal year 1986; in previous years and over the average of the decade there was terms of trade deterioration com-pared with 1980). These two countries are the only ones out of 13 Latin American debtor countries where terms of trade actually improved. The situation for Latin America is more diffuse than for other Third World countries, practically all of which reflect the over-all pattern of an expansion of export volume greatly weakened in its impact on capacity to import by deterioration in terms of trade.

Between 1980 and 1985, the quantity of copper exports of the Third World rose by 12 per cent and its price fell by 35 per cent so that the value of exports fell by 28 per cent. For 10 'core' commodities mainly exported by Third World countries, volume of exports rose by 8 per cent while export unit value fell by 26 per cent so that the value of exports fell by 21 per cent (see UNCTAD *Handbook of International Trade and Development Statistics*, 1987, pp. 242–3). The implied elasti-city of demand (around 0.3 in each case) agrees with other empirical findings. It creates an assumption that simultaneous supply expan-sion by producers leads to aggregate immiseration.

From the viewpoint of this essay, the important question is whether this pattern of export volume expansion combined with terms of trade deterioration is in fact related to debt pressure. For the Latin American countries this seems to be the case: cross-country calculations show that higher debt pressure (as measured by the debt service export ratio) was positively correlated with expansion of export volumes but negatively correlated with unit values and

Table 6.3   Value, unit value and volume of exports and terms of trade of some major Latin American debtor nations, 1980–86

	1980	*1981*	*1982*	*1983*	*1984*	*1985*	*1986*
Argentina							
Value	100	114	95	98	101	105	85
Unit value	100	98	83	76	83	78	71
Volume	100	117	115	128	122	134	120
Terms of trade	100	102	88	84	92	87	75
Bolivia[x]							
Value	100	95	87	79	75	65	52
Unit value	100	80	71	74	67	66	56
Volume	100	118	121	107	111	98	93
Terms of trade	100	85	77	82	77	75	59
Brazil							
Value	100	118	100	109	134	127	111
Unit value	100	89	84	83	85	81	88
Volume	100	132	120	130	158	157	127
Terms of trade	100	88	86	91	94	90	111
Chile							
Value	100	84	79	82	78	82	90
Unit value	100	82	73	75	67	67	66
Volume	100	102	109	110	117	122	136
Terms of trade	100	85	78	82	75	75	75
Colombia							
Value	100	75	78	78	88	90	129
Unit value	100	83	87	82	83	84	109
Volume	100	90	90	96	106	107	119
Terms of trade	100	86	93	89	93	94	119
Costa Rica							
Value	100	101	87	86	98	99	102
Unit Value	100	81	77	75	82	80	85
Volume	100	124	113	115	120	123	120
Terms of trade	100	84	82	83	92	90	95
Ecuador[x]							
Value	100	102	94	89	104	112	88
Unit value	100	100	94	88	87	88	67
Volume	100	102	100	101	119	128	131
Terms of Trade	100	105	100	96	98	97	69
Jamaica							
Value	100	101	80	76	78	59	62
Unit Value	100	91	84	82	77	64	66
Volume	100	111	94	92	101	91	94
Terms of trade	100	92	89	91	87	73	83

Mexico[x]							
Value	100	131	117	135	154	143	103
Unit value	100	106	101	92	89	88	62
Volume	100	123	116	147	173	161	165
Terms of trade	100	112	109	101	101	99	66
Nicaragua							
Value	100	111	90	95	86	67	62
Unit Value	1001	72	63	61	63	65	69
Volume	100	154	143	155	136	103	90
Terms of trade	100	74	68	69	72	74	80
Peru							
Value	100	83	82	77	80	69	63
Unit value	100	93	81	78	75	74	65
Volume	100	90	102	99	106	93	97
Terms of trade	100	99	89	88	87	85	70
Uruguay							
Value	100	115	97	99	87	81	103
Unit value	100	97	81	75	85	76	73
Volume	100	118	119	131	103	105	141
Terms of trade	100	98	84	81	93	84	85
Venezuela[x]							
Value	100	101	83	75	72	62	50
Unit Value	100	113	105	92	89	87	51
Volume	100	89	78	82	80	70	98
Terms of trade	100	120	114	103	102	99	54

[x] Export structure dominated by 'fuels' (Standard International Trade Classification code 3).

Source: UNCTAD *Handbook of International Trade and Development Statistics*, 1987, pp. 529–47.

terms of trade. Export volume is also negatively correlated with terms of trade. Thus the signs are in line with the 'desperation sale' hypothesis. The correlation though significant is not very close and the coefficient of determination is low – this again is expected since obviously many factors other than debt pressures influence export volumes and terms of trade, in particular the composition of exports, both between different commodities and between commodities and manufactures.

During the 1981–86 period as a whole, the terms of trade of developing countries as a whole deteriorated by 13.9 per cent but for the group of 'highly indebted countries' by 17.3 per cent – yet another indication of the link between debt pressures and terms of trade deterioration. If the figures are recalculated for the non-highly indebted countries separately, the gap becomes one of 11.5 per cent for this group as against the 17.3 per cent deterioration for the highly indebted countries. On this (admittedly conjectural) reckoning, an additional 6.8 per cent deterioration could be considered as the transfer burden of debt payment.

Senator Bradley's characterization of 'desperation exports' could also serve as a reminder that the export pressure and associated terms of trade pressure, representing the transfer cost of debt payment, has a political as well as a purely market dimension. The industrial countries tend to resent the additional exports of developing countries as a threat to employment and market control and take protectionist action in the name of 'anti-dumping'. The threat may be more perceived than real, but the protectionist reaction is real enough. There also lurks here one of the vicious circles (Gunnar Myrdal's 'cumulative causation') so frequent in development economics: as there is protectionist reaction to the increased exports of debtor countries at reduced prices, prices have to be even further reduced to get in underneath the protectionist barriers, in turn feeding more protectionist action, and so *ad infinitum*. An even more important vicious circle stems from the fact that a deterioration of terms of trade makes the country less 'creditworthy' and reduces its chances of paying debts with the help of new resources rather than exports; this in turn leads to more cut-price 'desperation exports', and so on, recalling Irving Fisher's dictum that 'liquidation defeats itself'. The road to debt repayment, no less than the road to development, is truly paved with vicious circles!

The harmful case of 'immiserizing growth' is increasingly recognized as a weakness resulting from the present approach to stabilization and structural adjustment – by the IMF and World Bank (IMF WB). The present IMF WB approach is designed as a country-by-country approach: that is to say the task of IMF WB conditionality is to ensure that each individual country separately, within a negotiated standby or structural adjustment agreement, is expected to increase its own exports, by real exchange rate depreciation, added incentives to exporters, and so forth. No account is taken of the impact of such an export expansion by Country A on the export of

Countries B, C, D, etc., which produce competing exports. Yet, at the same time, countries B, C, D, etc., are also separately advised to push *their* exports, through broadly identical measures of exchange rate depreciation, outward orientation, and so on: this will be partly at the expense of Country A and take away the intended benefit to Country A. At the end of the process all the countries involved, A, B, C, D, etc., would be no better and may be worse off than before. The real beneficiaries are the importing countries (although on a broader view they may also be ultimate losers in such a no-win anti-development approach).

This is no rational way of running international affairs. We are getting the worst of both possible worlds. The IMF WB approach is too country-specific in the sense that the country missions are not given any mandate to study the impact on other developing countries; yet at the same time the approach is not country-specific enough in the sense that the recommendations addressed to various countries show a surprising similarity to each other. It is evident – and has been shown – that the measures recommended to various countries show a 70–80 per cent overlap of identity. It is frankly unbelievable that the great variety of circumstances among different developing countries should justify such identical policy packages, unless the measures are more inspired by ideology and preconceived theory than derived from concrete analysis of specific country situations. But this is exactly what one would expect when major policy shifts are based on three-week visiting missions of IMF and WB staff members with qualifications in financial analysis closeted with debtor country officials of central banks and ministries of finance with similar concentration on financial analysis (many perhaps themselves former IMF WB staff members).

This 'fallacy of composition' of expecting that what may be good for individual debtor countries must also be good for debtor countries as a whole, is particularly serious in the case of competing exporters of primary commodities, facing inelastic demand so that large price cuts are necessary to achieve given increases in export volume and where there is often an oligopolistic supply situation, where three, four or five producing countries may each have a market share sufficient to have a marked influence on other countries. For example, if Chile devalues and expands its share of the copper market, this is bound to affect the shares of Zambia and Zaire and vice versa; and if all three try to do this simultaneously the results would be general 'immiserization'. The same situation exists in coffee, tea, cocoa, rubber and other markets for primary commodities of great importance to developing countries. The current adjustment approach lags behind other areas of economic policy where the existence of 'externalities' has long been recognized. Professionally there would be agreement that such circumstances call for export taxes in the context of devaluations – but that is not part of the ideology of 'outward orientation'.

Evidence of such a link between expansion of export volume in the service of adjustment programmes and deteriorating terms of trade is not lacking. The most recent and most striking piece of evidence comes from an impeccable source – the World Bank itself – although it applies to Africa rather than Latin America. In its report (with the UNDP), on *Africa's Adjustment and Growth in the 1980s*, the World Bank presents data designed to show that countries with 'strong reform programmes' are doing better than the countries without such programmes. Yet in fact we find that, on the Bank's own figures, the much better export volume performance of the 'good boys' has been purchased at the expense of a marked deterioration in their terms of trade, both absolutely and in comparison with the 'bad boys' who failed to expand their export volumes. This in fact is only to be expected and confirms the view that the outward orientation and export drives associated with debt pressures and IMF World Bank type of adjustment programmes put downward pressure on export prices, making the debt burden to that extent heavier rather than lighter. The accelerated growth of export *volume* from −0.7 per cent per annum to +4.9 per cent per annum of the 'good' countries (always comparing the recent period 1985–87 with the earlier period 1980–84) was bought at the expense of a sharp acceleration in the deterioration in their terms of trade, to 4.7 per cent per annum in 1985–87, as against 0.5 per cent per annum in the earlier period. Thus, in that more recent period, the increase in export volume was practically fully wiped out by the deterioration in terms of trade, so that the growth in import volume of 6.1 per cent must have been entirely attributable to non-trade factors, that is additional external support. By contrast, the 'bad boys', although they also achieved a certain improvement in their export volume performance (from −5.7 per cent per annum to −3.3 per cent per annum) were compensated for this smaller improvement by seeing their terms of trade improved by 1.4 per cent per annum so it must follow that the fall by 4.0 per cent per annum in their import volume was mainly due to their being cut off from external support.[6]

Elsewhere I have examined more general claims that 'outward orientation works'.[7] The general finding is that statistical claims to this effect must be taken with a grain of salt. The connection breaks down for the unfavourable climate of the 1980s; it also breaks down when we apply it to low-income countries as distinct from middle-income countries. Altogether, as in the case of the African report, a good deal of suspect manipulation of data is needed to make a case. We shall see that even in the case of manufactured exports and of the Latin American middle-income countries, export expansion under debt pressure has exacted a price in the area of terms of trade.

III

While the early terms of trade debate was conducted in the context of exchange of primary commodities against manufacture, there has since been a tremendous expansion in the exports of manufactures by developing countries. While the manufactured exports of the First World countries (the 'developed market-economy region') rose in value at an annual average rate of 17 per cent during 1965–80 (and 13 per cent during 1970–84), the manufactured exports of the Third World (the 'developing market economy region') increased at annual average rates of 24 per cent and 22 per cent respectively during the same periods.[8] These manufactures of the Third World found their destination also in the First World: during 1965–80 and 1970–84, manufactured exports of the Third World to the First World rose at annual average rates of 25 per cent and 22 per cent respectively. Even the tremendous rise in oil prices during the 1970s and early 1980s cannot overshadow the fact that the share of manufactures in the exports of the Third to the First World rose above 23 per cent (if we include fuel exports) or 58 per cent (if we consider only non-fuel exports) during 1980–84. See Table 6.4.

For this reason it is important to look at the relationship of trends in terms of trade in manufactures and debt pressures. In particular it is important to answer the question as to what extent, if any, the shift towards manufactured exports has offered an avenue of escape for

Table 6.4   Shares of manufactures[*] in total exports of the Third World countries during 1965–85 (selected countries, average percentages)[*1]

Country or region	Periods						
	1965–67	*1968–70*	*1971–73*	*1974–76*	*1977–79*	*1980–82*	*1983–85*
Argentina	10.0	15.7	21.5	27.1	27.9	28.6	19.5
	(11.7)	(15.7)	(24.3)	(30.7)	(27.4)	(27.8)	(19.0)
Bolivia	65.4	59.6	54.2	42.4	41.3	33.1	26.9
	(60.6)	(55.7)	(45.5)	(41.7)	(33.8)	(34.4)	(32.1)
Brazil	11.6	13.7	21.4	28.0	35.0	42.1	44.9
	(9.8)	(10.5)	(14.7)	(22.8)	(34.1)	(40.4)	(44.6)
Caribbean Group	18.6	19.84	21.6	18.8	23.0	25.6	13.4
	(8.4)	(8.9)	(10.30)	(15.9)	(19.5)	(26.62)	(14.7)
Chile	75.7	79.8	72.9	68.7	63.5	54.4	49.0
	(65.1)	(62.8)	(58.8)	(63.5)	(61.0)	(59.0)	(54.9)
China	46.1	48.3	52.2	49.6	51.6	54.2	50.5
	(48.9)	(48.7)	(51.2)	(45.0)	(46.1)	(57.4)	(56.6)
Ecuador	7.5	9.7	6.4	6.2	7.8	18.5	1.8
	(5.9)	(7.1)	(2.7)	(3.7)	(5.8)	(16.3)	(1.4)
Egypt	24.2	29.9	30.5	31.9	33.6	36.1	13.8
	(26.3)	(35.0)	(33.5)	(31.8)	(28.5)	(39.4)	(14.4)
Ghana	8.2	15.6	15.3	13.3	19.7	42.5	16.3
	(3.9)	(10.5)	(10.1)	(11.3)	(21.4)	(34.8)	(11.6)
Hong Kong	89.9	93.1	93.8	93.5	93.6	93.2	96.5
	(86.9)	(90.5)	(90.3)	(91.3)	(93.1)	(92.5)	(95.8)
India	50.5	55.1	53.9	54.9	60.9	57.5	52.3
	(58.5)	(61.2)	(57.4)	(57.6)	(66.3)	(57.7)	(49.6)
Indonesia	13.0	9.1	8.5	5.4	7.3	7.6	10.7
	(6.4)	(4.0)	(3.7)	(4.4)	(5.5)	(9.2)	(14.5)
Kenya	24.1	18.1	19.6	21.2	18.6	24.9	12.0
	(18.2)	(12.6)	(10.2)	(17.7)	(18.5)	(25.8)	(14.4)
Korea	63.9	76.5	83.8	85.1	87.8	91.0	91.6
	(54.9)	(66.5)	(76.7)	(81.7)	(86.8)	(90.6)	(98.8)
Malaysia	29.3	29.0	29.7	30.8	29.7	30.9	29.1
	(26.8)	(26.0)	(26.5)	(32.2)	(26.7)	(31.8)	(31.5)
Mexico	29.7	37.1	46.5	48.3	36.8	30.6	29.2
	(22.0)	(25.2)	(35.0)	(37.5)	(31.0)	(31.7)	(28.6)
Morocco	10.1	12.5	17.1	16.6	26.7	34.0	41.5
	(4.8)	(5.7)	(9.0)	(16.8)	(21.9)	(35.2)	(41.2)
Nigeria	11.1	11.2	7.9	4.2	5.1	4.8	1.5
	(4.9)	(4.8)	(2.8)	(2.5)	(2.9)	(5.7)	(1.8)
Pakistan	44.1	55.9	59.7	57.3	59.0	55.6	66.4
	(57.0)	(52.2)	(54.7)	(63.4)	(56.2)	(56.0)	(61.3)

Paraguay	12.3	12.8	16.9	19.7	21.0	16.5	11.1
	(9.5)	(9.1)	(13.3)	(15.5)	(20.7)	(14.1)	(8.5)
Peru	34.8	35.6	31.8	38.9	44.1	41.5	37.4
	(19.2)	(16.9)	(19.9)	(32.0)	(41.6)	(43.1)	(38.2)
Philippines	7.8	9.4	12.4	21.8	34.3	45.7	48.2
	(5.6)	(5.2)	(8.2)	(16.1)	(30.8)	(45.0)	(48.5)
Singapore	33.7	30.1	43.8	44.7	49.0	57.7	55.5
	(16.3)	(12.6)	(21.5)	(33.5)	(41.6)	(59.0)	(51.1)
Taiwan	41.3	65.6	78.1	80.2	84.3	88.1	91.7
	(33.0)	(58.8)	(73.7)	(79.7)	(83.0)	(87.8)	(91.9)
Thailand	14.2	21.1	26.6	25.2	32.3	36.9	38.7
	(16.5)	(25.6)	(30.6)	(33.0)	(33.1)	(34.6)	(37.0)
Tunisia	42.6	26.2	22.6	26.5	37.9	41.6	47.6
	(21.0)	(7.2)	(6.5)	(17.3)	(26.1)	(45.4)	(52.0)
Uruguay	25.6	28.7	15.0	31.9	45.0	37.7	34.3
	(33.1)	(32.7)	(19.0)	(32.8)	(45.7)	(36.9)	(32.2)
Venezuela	3.8	4.9	7.3	3.6	6.4	7.9	5.5
	(0.7)	(0.9)	(1.7)	(2.2)	(4.5)	(9.2)	(6.8)
Yugoslavia	65.4	70.6	74.1	78.7	77.1	82.5	82.2
	(62.1)	(66.1)	(72.9)	(76.8)	(74.7)	(83.3)	(82.6)

*In the broad category, 'Manufactures', we have included all commodities classified in the SITC (Standard International Trade Classification) section 5 to 9. That means, unclassified items (SITC section 9) are also included.

*1Shares in total values of exports. Figures in parentheses are shares in total volume of exports.

Source: Calculated on the basis of unpublished data stored by United Nations and made available by Mr Fred Campano, Chief, Perspective Studies Section, DIESA/DRPA, United Nations.

developing countries from the vicious circle between debt pressures and deteriorating terms of trade.

Relevant data are not easily available for examination of the behaviour of terms of trade for manufactures. The United Nations used to publish some data on unit values of commodities flowing between the two regions of the market economy world but after 1980 these data were discontinued. On the basis of the published data, one study has already been carried out to examine the behaviour of terms of trade of different categories of primary products exported by the Third World to the First World *vis-à-vis* different SITC (Standard International Trade Classification) sections of products exported by the First World to the Third World over the period 1950–80 (see Sarkar, 1986a). It concluded that the terms of trade of the Third World deteriorated mainly due to exchange of primary products for manufactures, machinery (SITC section 7) and other manufactures (SITC Section 6 and 8) of the First World. But the study could not cover the field of trade in manufactures between the two regions due to lack of data. The Statistical Office of the United Nations published unit value indices of manufactured exports of the two regions of the market economy world starting from 1970 (with a discontinuity over 1971–74). But these series are not strictly appropriate for a study of terms of trade between the two regions, just as the unit value of export and the terms of trade series for the two regions available in different UN publications are not relevant for a study of the behaviour of aggregate terms of trade between the two regions. This is so because these data are not generated after netting out intra-regional (South–South and North–North) trade. This intra-regional trade accounted for 75 per cent of total exports of the First World and 24 per cent of total exports of the Third World during 1950–80 (Sarkar, 1988; and Table 6.5).

However, in the absence of better data, it may still be useful to study the behaviour of relative movements of unit values of manufactures of the two regions. The present study is concerned with this. We have calculated the ratio of unit values of manufactured exports of the two regions over the period 1975–87 and have conducted a time series trend study. Furthermore, we obtained some unpublished data for total exports of manufactures by individual countries over the period 1965–85.[9] These data enabled us to calculate the values of exports and imports of manufactures of some Third World countries. On the basis of these data, we have undertaken a time series study of the behaviour of manufacture–manufacture terms of trade (the ratio values of manufactured exports of some major industrial countries. of the unit value index of manufactured exports to the unit value index of manufactured imports) of some Third World countries. Moreover, we have examined the movements in the unit values of manufacture exports of these Third World countries in relation to the unit Our findings are presented in the next section. These cast some doubts on the 'unequal exchange' extension of the Prebisch–Singer thesis as far as the long-term trends in barter terms of trade are concerned.

IV

From the various issues of the *Monthly Bulletin of Statistics* (United Nations), we get unit value indices of manufactured exports for both

Table 6.5   Trends in the unit values of manufactured exports of the Third World countries relative to those of major industrial countries, 1965–85

| | *Estimates*[*] | | | | |
	b	t-ratio	$\bar{R}^2$	F-ratio	$D - W$
Argentina *vs*					
France	0.0166	3.93	0.57	13.72	1.79
Germany	0.0149	3.34	0.41	7.52	1.80
Italy	0.0175	3.46	0.55	12.51	1.80
Japan	0.0227	2.97	0.63	16.99	1.55
UK	0.0013	0.10	0.52	11.35	1.90
USA	−0.0094	−0.33	0.60	15.54	1.55
Bolivia *vs*					
France	0.0281	4.22	0.70	23.36	1.82
Germany	0.0267	5.42	0.78	35.35	2.00
Italy	0.0294	2.96	0.76	30.36	1.72
Japan	0.0350	2.78	0.79	37.77	1.64
UK	0.0145	0.99	0.61	15.79	1.64
USA	0.0064	0.19	0.63	17.50	1.28
Brazil *vs*					
France	−0.0063	−0.43	0.41	7.56	2.06
Germany	−0.0033	−0.36	0.30	5.05	1.94
Italy	−0.0053	−0.37	0.39	7.16	2.28
Japan	−0.0064	−0.29	0.59	14.66	1.92
UK	−0.0354	−0.13	0.70	22.78	2.08
USA	−0.0956	−0.66	0.82	44.78	1.71
Caribbean group *vs*					
France	0.0125	4.40	0.77	32.87	1.65
Germany	0.0125	2.52	0.66	19.80	1.60
Italy	0.0131	2.85	0.74	27.73	2.02
Japan	0.0184	2.32	0.72	25.37	1.80
UK	−0.0056	−0.48	0.60	15.04	1.66
USA	−0.0388	−0.43	0.71	24.73	1.51
Chile *vs*					
France	−0.0470	−5.03	0.72	25.71	1.92
Germany	−0.0493	−4.56	0.76	31.44	1.77
Italy	−0.0453	−5.76	0.73	26.47	1.98
Japan	−0.0404	−4.81	0.69	21.89	1.84
UK	−0.0583	−5.15	0.78	35.66	2.00
USA	−0.0591	−5.44	0.79	36.89	1.84
China *vs*					
France	−0.0127	−0.89	0.39	6.95	2.27
Germany	0.0101	1.02	0.33	5.63	2.13

Table 6.5   (*Cont.*)

	Estimates[*]				
	b	t-ratio	$\bar{R}^2$	F-ratio	$D - W$
Italy	−0.0119	−0.75	0.37	6.63	2.24
Japan	−0.0121	−0.59	0.51	10.90	2.07
UK	−0.0433	−1.34	0.74	27.77	1.82
USA	−0.0671	−1.00	0.76	30.90	1.53
Ecuador *vs*					
France	−0.0071	−0.89	0.26	4.37	1.84
Germany	−0.0067	−0.57	0.38	6.88	1.71
Italy	−0.0064	−1.24	0.07	1.71	1.89
Japan	−0.0009	−0.19	−0.06	0.48	1.91
UK	−0.0967	−2.00	0.58	13.87	1.84
USA	−0.0211	−2.70	0.65	18.97	2.18
Egypt *vs*					
France	0.0260	1.31	0.60	15.16	1.48
Germany	0.0266	1.46	0.59	14.85	1.36
Italy	0.0262	1.18	0.59	14.82	1.57
Japan	0.0300	1.18	0.69	21.72	1.25
UK	0.0085	0.29	0.56	12.89	1.36
USA	−0.0008	−0.20	0.61	15.66	1.39
Ghana *vs*					
France	0.0077	0.78	0.43	8.20	1.70
Germany	0.0101	0.69	0.53	11.63	1.50
Italy	0.0083	0.80	0.50	10.50	1.64
Japan	0.0136	0.90	0.58	14.34	1.56
UK	−0.0045	−0.72	0.23	3.82	1.36
USA	−0.0163	−0.68	0.49	10.16	1.64
Hongkong *vs*					
France	0.0072	0.61	0.39	7.16	1.95
Germany	0.0073	0.67	0.36	6.46	1.92
Italy	0.0087	0.86	0.32	5.53	2.07
Japan	0.0132	1.45	0.59	14.82	1.89
UK	−0.0123	−0.53	0.56	12.94	1.86
USA	−0.0253	−0.67	0.64	18.19	1.44
India *vs*					
France	0.0209	2.85	0.56	12.96	1.85
Germany	0.0209	2.09	0.46	9.17	1.87
Italy	0.0204	4.44	0.58	13.89	1.95
Japan	0.0262	6.30	0.78	34.49	1.78
UK	0.0098	1.00	0.41	7.66	1.94
USA	0.0084	1.00	0.29	4.97	1.78

Indonesia *vs*				
France	0.0119	1.87	0.31	5.31	1.73
Germany	0.0209	2.09	0.46	9.17	1.87
Italy	0.0103	1.06	0.40	7.37	1.78
Japan	0.0064	0.29	0.68	21.01	1.73
UK	−0.0090	−0.52	0.38	6.81	2.02
USA	−0.0363	−0.56	0.55	12.51	1.31
Kenya *vs*				
France	−0.0255	−0.68	0.49	9.99	2.16
Germany	−0.0095	−1.26	0.37	6.54	2.04
Italy	0.0046	1.50	0.55	6.92	2.03
Japan	−0.0276	−0.54	0.62	16.74	1.92
UK	−0.0547	−1.40	0.84	52.40	1.75
USA	−0.1213	−0.62	0.82	44.75	1.09
Korea *vs*				
France	−0.0007	−0.17	−0.02	0.82	2.04
Germany	−0.0024	−0.34	0.19	3.28	1.84
Italy	0.0012	0.49	−0.08	0.32	2.13
Japan	0.0050	1.27	0.34	5.83	1.59
UK	−0.0123	−2.01	0.41	7.70	2.44
USA	−0.0176	−2.21	0.60	15.37	2.10
Malaysia *vs*				
France	0.0056	4.99	0.69	22.30	1.83
Germany	0.0271	4.79	0.73	27.10	1.94
Italy	0.0292	4.28	0.68	21.16	1.80
Japan	0.0356	4.06	0.78	35.45	1.74
UK	0.0182	2.96	0.52	9.19	1.64
USA	0.0160	1.06	0.47	9.27	1.38
Mexico *vs*				
France	−2.99	−0.0044	0.13	2.46	1.77
Germany	−0.0007	−0.0994	0.11	2.14	1.57
Italy	0.0008	0.13	0.03	1.31	1.90
Japan					
UK	−0.0164	−0.99	0.61	16.01	1.64
USA	−0.0227	−1.04	0.66	19.50	1.58
Morocco *vs*				
France	−0.0487	−9.14	0.97	271.69	1.74
Germany	−0.0470	−4.25	0.95	167.38	1.42
Italy	−0.0479	−16.64	0.96	219.84	1.90
Japan	−0.0426	−8.52	0.92	103.39	1.71
UK	−0.0641	−6.34	0.96	235.71	1.44
USA	−0.0710	−4.59	0.97	288.99	1.45
Nigeria *vs*				
France	0.0059	1.11	0.02	1.20	1.88
Germany	0.0035	1.01	−0.05	0.05	1.82

Table 6.5   (*Cont.*)

	Estimates[*]				
	b	t-ratio	$\bar{R}^2$	F-ratio	$D - W$
Italy	0.0071	1.01	0.08	1.82	1.92
Japan	0.0133	1.41	0.36	6.33	1.72
UK	−0.0048	−0.37	0.31	5.32	1.84
USA	−0.0087	−0.39	0.47	9.41	1.47
Pakistan *vs*					
France	0.0337	3.04	0.53	11.59	1.67
Germany	0.0324	3.00	0.52	11.20	1.70
Italy	0.0348	3.50	0.54	12.00	1.75
Japan	0.0401	4.00	0.63	17.25	1.63
UK	0.0215	1.20	0.39	7.17	1.78
USA	0.0191	1.05	0.42	7.82	1.68
Paraguay *vs*					
France	0.0026	0.25	0.11	2.16	1.94
Germany	0.0025	0.21	0.13	2.47	2.01
Italy	0.0027	0.33	0.02	1.25	1.94
Japan	0.0074	1.29	0.05	1.55	1.89
UK	−0.0087	−0.53	0.45	7.06	1.93
USA	−0.0104	−0.83	0.32	5.42	2.03
Peru *vs*					
France	−0.0478	−6.89	0.79	36.98	2.07
Germany	−0.0500	−6.97	0.82	45.53	1.95
Italy	−0.0462	−7.62	0.79	37.34	2.15
Japan	−0.0415	−7.20	0.81	41.38	2.02
UK	−0.0611	−5.41	0.82	43.07	2.11
USA	−0.0633	−5.22	0.82	44.77	1.87
Philippines *vs*					
France	−0.0176	−1.38	0.37	6.56	1.86
Germany	−0.0173	−1.51	0.38	6.85	1.75
Italy	−0.0158	−1.28	0.30	5.01	1.97
Japan	−0.0120	−0.83	0.29	4.87	1.59
UK	−0.0361	−1.61	0.57	13.48	1.86
USA	−0.0499	−1.45	0.66	19.19	1.83
Singapore *vs*					
France	0.0142	2.35	0.33	5.76	2.05
Germany	0.0176	1.40	0.37	6.51	2.12
Italy	0.0138	3.51	0.34	5.98	1.76
Japan	0.0198	4.81	0.61	16.02	1.85
UK	0.0045	0.40	0.31	5.18	1.99
USA	0.0028	0.33	0.21	3.49	1.97

Taiwan *vs*				
France	−0.0060	−1.30	0.03	1.30	1.99
Germany	−0.0079	−1.53	0.14	2.55	2.01
Italy	−0.0043	−1.22	−0.03	0.76	2.02
Japan	0.0000	0.01	−0.06	0.48	1.89
UK	−0.0232	−1.89	0.56	13.03	2.23
USA	−0.0387	−1.21	0.63	17.49	1.76
Thailand *vs*				
France	0.0145	3.76	0.44	8.63	2.26
Germany	0.0141	2.96	0.44	8.72	2.25
Italy	0.0164	3.28	0.51	10.82	2.20
Japan	0.0235	3.01	0.67	20.09	1.81
UK	0.0057	1.09	0.11	2.14	1.75
USA	0.0037	0.27	0.38	6.83	1.46
Tunisia *vs*				
France	−0.0429	−5.55	0.95	176.07	1.76
Germany	−0.0414	−5.10	0.93	122.73	1.28
Italy	−0.0396	−6.69	0.92	109.51	2.24
Japan	−0.0348	−4.63	0.86	61.47	1.75
UK	−0.0642	−3.96	0.95	172.26	1.25
USA	−0.0826	−2.59	0.96	240.96	1.15
Uruguay *vs*				
France	0.0168	6.07	0.75	29.36	1.65
Germany	0.0156	4.09	0.62	16.62	1.81
Italy	0.0173	8.74	0.74	28.08	2.16
Japan	0.0230	7.75	0.79	36.91	1.77
UK	0.0050	0.56	0.42	7.80	1.89
USA	−0.0066	0.23	0.60	15.50	1.25
Venezuela *vs*				
France	−0.0161	−2.96	0.35	6.19	1.98
Germany	−0.0180	−2.80	0.36	6.36	1.97
Italy	−0.0143	−3.78	0.38	6.82	1.99
Japan	−0.0092	−2.28	0.17	2.93	1.93
UK	−0.0289	−3.28	0.63	17.03	2.42
USA	−0.0322	−2.68	0.60	15.02	2.06

the regions of market economies (the First and Third Worlds), measured in both US dollars and SDRs, over the period 1975–87. Accordingly, we can construct two series on the unit values of manufactured exports of the Third World relative to those of the First World (one in terms of dollars and the other in terms of SDRs). Ignoring intraregional trade, let us call these relative unit values the (net) barter terms of trade in manufactures between the Third World and the First

World. Multiplying these relative unit value figures by the quantum indices of manufactured exports of the Third World, we obtain their income terms of trade (again ignoring intra-regional trade).[10] Multiplying the reciprocal of barter terms of trade of the Third World by the quantum index of exports of manufactures of the First World, we obtain the income terms of trade of the First World (with the same qualification) for their manufactures trade.

To examine the nature of trends present in these series, we have fitted an exponential trend equation through Cochrane–Orcutt Iteration to remove autocorrelated errors from the estimates. Results are reported in Table 6.6. It is evident from the table that in both US dollars and SDRs, unit values of manufactured exports of the Third World declined by 1–2 per cent per annum in relation to those of the First World. The values of $\bar{R}^2$ indicate that these trends are not smooth. Moreover, the trend coefficients estimated here have very high standard errors and do not survive the *t*-test (indicating a lack of statistical significance). But while the trend figures for individual years is uncertain, over the period of 20 years covered (1965–85), an annual trend of $-1\ 1/2$ per cent per annum would result in a decline of over 35 per cent. This can hardly be treated as 'insignificant', even if the annual trend figure is so in the statistical sense.

However, due to the tremendous growth in manufactured exports of the Third World, their 'income terms of trade' rose unambiguously at an annual average rate of about 10 per cent. This rate of growth of income terms surpassed the rate of growth of income terms of trade of the First World which grew at an annual average rate of 5 to 6 per cent (not reported in Table 6.5). So if we take the ratio of income terms of trade of the two regions, the index exhibits an upward movement at an annual average rate of 3 to 4 per cent in favour of the Third World (see Table 6.6).

From this aggregative study, let us now turn to country cases. As indicated earlier, we obtained some unpublished trade data for some individual countries. For our case study, we have chosen a sample of 28 individual countries and one group of countries. Our sample covers all the countries considered as 'Major Exporters of Manufactures' in the 'developing' region of the market economy world (see UNCTAD *Handbook of International Trade and Development Statistics*, 1986 Supplement, p.v.). These constitute the 'Gang of Four' (South Korea, Singapore, Taiwan and Hong Kong) and three

Table 6.6   Trends in net barter – and income terms of trade in manufactures of the third world *vis-à-vis* the First World, 1975–87

Index	*Estimates*[*1]		
	Annual average rate of change (%)	R^{-2}	*Durbin–Watson statistic*
I. Net Barter Terms of Trade (NBTT)			
– relative unit values in US dollars	-1.88^{x}	0.34	1.80
– relative unit values in SDR	-1.36^{x}	0.22	1.72
II. Absolute Income Terms of Trade (ITT)			
– quantum index of exports × relative unit values (NBTT) in dollars	9.34^{*}	0.97	1.86
– quantum index of exports × relative unit values (NBTT) in SDR	9.52^{*}	0.97	1.86
III. Relative Income Terms of Trade			
– Third World ITT (in dollars)/First World ITT (in dollars)	4.47^{*}	0.73	1.28
– Third World ITT (in SDR)/First World ITT (in SDR)	4.60^{*}	0.75	1.48

Note: [x] Not significant at 10% level.
[*]   Significant at less than 5% level.
[*1]   Estimates are obtained by fitting an exponential trend equation. First-order autocorrelated errors are sought to be removed by Cochrane–Orcutt iterative procedure.
Source: Calculated on the basis of data available in *Monthly Bulletin of Statistics* (United Nations), various issues.

other countries – Argentina, Brazil and Yugoslavia. Besides these seven countries, we have considered another 20 individual Third World countries and a group (the Caribbean group of countries). We have also included China in our sample. Table 6.7 shows the importance of manufactured products[11] in the value and volume of total exports of each of the countries covered over the period of our study, 1965–85. It may be noted that the share of manufactures in total value and volume of exports rose rapidly for countries like Brazil, Korea, Morocco, Philippines, Singapore, Taiwan, Thailand and Yugoslavia, over the whole 1965–86 period. For countries like Argentina, India and Pakistan, the share of manufactures rose steadily up to a point near the end of the 1970s and then it showed a tendency to fall. On the contrary, for countries like Bolivia and Chile, the importance of manufactured products in total exports declined steadily.

For some countries we find abrupt rises or falls in the share of manufactures (for example Ghana, Ecuador and Egypt); countries like Ecuador, Nigeria and Venezuela had very low shares of manufactures (they are basically oil exporters). Thus we have a sample covering different groups of countries having different experiences regarding the relative growth of value and volume of manufactured exports over the 1965–85 period.

For each country or region we show the ratio of unit value of manufactured exports to that of manufactured imports. This gives the manufacture-manufacture (net Barter) terms of trade of a country *vis-à-vis* the rest of the world. Multiplying the unit value ratio by the quantum index of manufactured exports we arrive at figure of income terms of trade in manufactures. To examine the nature of trends present in the series, an exponential trend equation has been fitted in each case. Through the Cochrane–Orcutt iteration technique, autocorrelated errors are removed from the estimates as done in the case of our aggregative study. The estimates are reported in Table 6.7.

The results for the 29 cases (28 countries and 1 region) may be summarized as follows: 14 negative trends, of which 6 significant and 8 not clearly significant; 15 positive trends, of which 8 significant and 7 not clearly significant. Thus the results are evenly divided – about half not clearly significant and the others divided between positive and negative trends in terms of trade. Thus changes in terms of trade in manufactures seem to have been natural, neither compensating for nor exacerbating adverse change in overall terms of trade or exchange of primary products for manufactures.

There is, however, a clear tendency for the negative trends for the 14 'negative' countries to be stronger (−2.8 per cent per annum), than the positive trends for the 15 'positive' countries (+1.3 per cent

Table 6.7 Trends in manufacture–manufacture terms of trade[1] of a selected number of Third World countries, 1965–85

	Estimates[2]		
	Annual average rate of change (%)	*$\bar{R}^2$*	*Durbin–Watson statistic*
I Negative trends			
Brazil	−2.65	0.67	2.06
Chile	−5.18[*]	0.79	1.91
China	−0.32	0.33	1.23
Ecuador	−1.14[*]	0.38	1.91
Kenya	−4.85	0.86	1.30
Mexico	−1.15	0.59	1.58
Morocco	−5.04[*]	0.97	1.23
Paraguay	−0.24	0.08	1.98
Peru	−5.19[*]	0.84	2.02
Philippines	−2.41	0.48	1.70
Taiwan	−0.60	0.04	1.98
Tunisia	−4.38[*]	0.95	1.35
Venezuela	−1.90[*]	0.55	1.98
Yugoslavia	−0.31	−0.10	2.00
II Positive trends			
Argentina	1.56[*]	0.56	1.66
Bolivia	2.76[*]	0.75	1.40
Caribbean Group	1.02[*]	0.72	1.84
Egypt	3.37[*]	0.51	1.47
Ghana	0.37	0.46	1.28
Hong Kong	0.78	0.56	1.69
India	1.78[*]	0.58	1.89
Indonesia	0.06	0.41	1.47
Korea	0.07	0.04	1.89
Malaysia	0.94	0.56	1.62
Nigeria	0.31	0.06	1.76
Pakistan	3.61[*]	0.49	1.81
Singapore	0.78	0.13	1.88
Thailand	1.54[*]	0.53	1.90
Uruguay	1.13[*]	0.67	2.05

per annum). Thus the overall unweighted average for the 29 countries is −0.65 per cent per annum broadly confirming the results of the aggregate analysis. All these figures are unweighted (simple) averages, treating each country case as a separate, equally important, test of the hypothesis. If we concentrate on countries with marked trends (over 2 per cent per annum) we find seven countries with negative trends and only three with positive trends. Of the Latin American countries, seven had negative trends and only three positive (average −1.2 per cent); by contrast among the Asian countries only two were negative but eight positive (average +0.9 per cent). Here we clearly have a contributory factor to the differential balance of payments and debt pressure experience of the two continents.

Of the 14 highly-indebted countries in Table 6.7, no less than nine are in the negative group and only five in the positive group. This would support the view that debt pressures and associated export pressures have a negative influence on terms of trade. The average trend (simple average) for the 14 highly indebted countries is −1.3 per cent per annum.

It is interesting to compare the behaviour of unit values of manufactured exports of Third World countries with those of some major industrial countries. Accordingly we have derived the ratios of unit value of manufactured exports of each of the 29 countries and region covered in our sample to those of six industrial countries, France, Germany, Italy, Japan, UK and the USA. As before we have fitted an exponential trend equation to each series on relative unit values of manufactured exports. The results are reported in Table 6.5.

It can be observed that five (out of six) countries that faced a significant deterioration in their manufacture–manufacture terms of trade during 1965 (Chile, Morocco, Peru, Tunisia and Venezuela) experienced declines in their unit values of manufactured exports relative to those of all the six industrial countries considered here. The other country, Ecuador, faced a statistically significant declining trend in its unit value of manufactured exports only *vis-à-vis* the USA. In fact all the six countries faced the highest rates of declines in their manufactured export unit values *vis-à-vis* those of the USA. Not only that, no country experienced an improvement in its unit value of manufactured exports *vis-à-vis* the USA.

If these unit value ratios can be taken as rough proxies of the manufacture–manufacture terms of trade between the two countries, one belonging to the Third World and the other belonging to the First World, we must conclude that there is no clear evidence in support of the 'unequal exchange' extension of the Prebisch–Singer 'deterioration hypothesis', although there is some evidence for this

(a) for Latin America and (b) for trade with the USA. This finding in a way supports the prophecy of Prebisch. As the first Secretary General of UNCTAD, 'with an effort of imagination', he visualized a situation in the distant future when adverse terms of trade would disappear 'as a result of the worldwide process of industrialization' (Prebisch, 1964, p. 15).

However, more relevant concepts in the context of the Theory of Unequal Exchange are the double factoral terms of trade. Although our study is not directly concerned with this concept of terms of trade in the field of manufactured exports and imports, available data presented in Table 6.4 indicate that there exists a wide gap in the growth of labour productivity between the First World and the Third World.

During 1960–70 the annual average rate of growth of labour productivity in manufacturing production of the First World was 4.1 per cent while for the Third World, it was 2.3 per cent. This gap widened further in the next decade, 1970–80: while labour productivity grew at an annual average rate of 2.8 per cent in the field of manufacturing production of the First World, it rose at a meagre rate of 0.4 per cent in the Third World. Hence, given the absence of major overall trends in the manufacture–manufacture terms of trade of the Third World *vis-à-vis* the First World, the double factoral terms of trade turned against the Third World. Thus while our study casts some doubts on the 'unequal exchange' extension of the Prebisch–Singer thesis so far as it is concerned with the behaviour of manufacture–manufacture (net) barter terms of trade, the barter terms of trade by their very absence of a clear improvement failed to reflect the respective productivity trends, and in that sense trade in manufactures contributed to increased inequality in the distribution of gains from trade. But the major factor remains the long-term deterioration in the (net barter) terms of trade of primary products *vis-à-vis* manufactures (see also Sarkar, 1986 and other). It is only when we move to factoral terms of trade that trade in manufactures emerges as important overall although in Latin America it also contributes to a deterioration of barter terms of trade.

It also suggests that the real core of the Prebisch (or Prebisch–Singer) thesis is the loss of productivity gains which applies both to primary products/manufactures and manufactures/manufactures trade, rather than the movement of barter terms of trade which has led to a spate of statistical debate. This final conclusion fits in well with those reached by Spraos (1983) in *Inequalizing Trade*.

Notes

1   This is based on data in H. D. Gibson and A. P. Thirlwall, 'An International Comparison of the Causes of Changes in the Debt Service Ratio 1980–1985' (mimeo).
2   *Ibid.*, p. 11.
3   *Ibid.*, p. 11.
4   This, in fact, is part of the 'double taxation' or 'multiple taxation' of export earnings mentioned in an earlier part of this essay.
5   See Peter G. Warr, *Predictive Performance of the World Bank's Commodity Price Projections*. The Australian National University Research School of Pacific Studies, Department of Economics and National Centre for Development Studies, Working Papers in Trade and Development no. 88/2, February 1988.
6   These figures are based on table 20 (Summary of economic performance indicators) of the World Bank/UNDP Report on 'Africa's Adjustment and Growth in the 1980s' (p. 30) and represent the simple averages (not the weighted averages also given in the same table in parenthesis).
7   'The World Development Report 1987 on the Blessings of "Outward Orientation": A Necessary Correction', *The Journal of Development Studies*, vol 24, 2 January 1988 pp. 232–6 and 'Trade Policy and Growth of Developing Countries: Some New Data', with Patricia Gray, *World Development*, vol 16, no 3, 1988, pp. 368–74.
8   See UNCTAD *Handbook of International Trade and Development Statistics*, 1983 (pp. 94–9) and 1986 (pp. 72–9).
9   These data were compiled for use in the World Trade Matrix which is at the centre of the Link modelling system at the University of Pennsylvania. All trade data (exports and imports) are on an f.o.b. basis.
10   As argued before, intra-regional trade is dominant for the First World and not insignificant for the Third World. But, due to lack of better data, we are using the terms, income terms of trade and net barter terms of trade although the indices calculated and studied here will be good proxies only if unit values do not differ much between intra-regional and inter-regional flows of products due to identical market conditions.
11   Generally, in UN presentation of data, the broad category 'Manufactures' includes only those products which are classified in the SITC (Standard International Trade Classification) sections 5 to 8 (chemicals, machinery and other manufactures). But for our country case study, 'unclassified items' (SITC section 9) are also included in the broad category 'Manufactures'. This definition is used for all the date presented and analysed in Tables 6.4, 6.5 and 6.6.

References

Cline, W. R. (1985) 'International Debt: From Crisis to Recovery?', *American Economic Review*, May 1985, pp. 185–90.

Emmanuel, A. (1979) *Unequal Exchange* (Eng. trans.) (New York: Monthly Review Press).

Grilli, E. R. and M. C. Yang (1988) 'Primary Commodity Prices, Manufactured Goods Prices, and the Terms of Trade', *Economic Review*, vol. 2, no. 1.

Kindleberger, O. (1956) *The Terms of Trade: A European Case Study* (London: Chapman & Hall; New York: Wiley).

——(1958) 'The Terms of Trade and Economic Development', *Review of Economics and Statistics*', vol. 40, pp. 72–85.

Prebisch, R. (1950) *The Economic Development of Latin America and Its Principal Problems* (New York: United Nations Economic Commission for Latin America).

——(1959) 'Commercial Policy in the Underdeveloped Countries', *American Economic Review*, vol. 49, no. 2.

——(1964) *Towards a New Trade Policy for Development* (New York: United Nations for UNCTAD).

Sapsford, D. (1985) 'The Statistical Debate on the Net Barter Terms of Trade between Primary Commodities and Manufactures: A Comment and Some Additional Evidence', *Economic Journal*, vol. 95, no. 397.

Sarkar, P. (1986a) 'The Terms of Trade Experience of Britain Since the Nineteenth Century', *Journal of Development Studies*, vol. 23, no. 1.

——(1986b) 'The Singer–Prebisch Hypothesis: A Statistical Evaluation', *Cambridge Journal of Economics*, December.

——(1986c) 'Patterns of Trade and Movements of Interregional Terms of Trade between the Developing and the Developed Market Economies, 1950–80', *Economic Bulletin for Asia and the Pacific*, vol. 37, no. 2.

——(1988) 'The South–South Economic Cooperation in the World of North–South Unequal Exchange', mimeo: CICD, Ljubljana, Yugoslavia.

Singer, H. W. (1950) 'The Distribution of Gains between Investing and Borrowing Countries', *American Economic Review*, vol. 40, May.

——(1984) 'Terms of Trade Controversy and the Evolution of Soft Financing: Early Years in the UN: 1947–1951', in M. Meier and D. Seers (eds), *Pioneers in Development*: A World Bank Publication (New York and Oxford: Published for the World Bank by Oxford University Press, pp. 273–303).

Spraos, J. (1980) 'The Statistical Debate on the Net Barter Terms of Trade between Primary Commodities and Manufactures', *Economic Journal*, vol. 90, no. 357, January, pp. 107–28.

——(1983) *Inequalizing Trade?* (Oxford: Clarendon Press).

Thirlwall, A. P. and J. Bergevin (1985) 'Trends, Cycles and Asymmetries in the Terms of Trade of Primary Commodities from Developed and Less Developed Countries', *World Development*, vol. 13, no. 7.

7
Beyond the Debt Crisis[*]

The effects of the 'lost decade' of the 1980s on the Third World have been devastating – more than is usually realized. It will be an almost impossible task for Third World countries to make up for the losses in the coming decades. In this sense, the 'lost decade' will be with us for a long time to come. This essay speculates about the long-term trends, both favourable and unfavourable, for Third World countries, and expresses some doubts whether the currently predominant neo-liberal counter-revolution will really serve to lay the foundation of future solid and sustainable growth. A more eclectic and country-specific approach is advocated.

I will begin in the time-honoured fashion of economists: 'Let us assume that by general agreement all debts are wiped out tomorrow – 100 per cent. What difference will this make to the world in general and the developing countries in particular?' If I hear ironic laughter at this assumption as being so out of line with what is possible in the real world, perhaps this is as much a comment on the real world as on my assumption. In the real world, of course, the fact is that with all the hectic efforts of devising new instruments of debt relief, with Baker and Brady plans coming and going, and with all the preemption of negotiating time and limited administrative capacities involved, we are back today more or less where we were in 1982 with the volume of debt undiminished. The chief beneficiaries seem to be the

---

* Originally prepared as a panel paper for the 20th World Conference of the Society for International Development in Amsterdam, The Netherlands, in May 1991. Published in *Journal für Entwicklungspolitik*, vol. 3, 1991, pp. 3–7.

commercial banks and that mysterious entity the 'world financial system' which has been protected and safeguarded, rather than the developing countries.

The first thing to realize is the tremendous devastation which the nine years of the debt crisis (dating it from the Mexican moratorium in 1982) have wrought upon the developing countries. Compared with the GDP growth rate of 1965–80, the developing countries have lost during the past decade cumulatively income as follows: low-income countries other than China and India 35 per cent of GDP; lower middle-income countries 39 per cent; upper middle-income countries 23 per cent; sub-Saharan Africa 40 per cent; Latin American and Caribbean 45 per cent; the severely indebted countries also 45 per cent. These would be the jumps in income required to bring the Third World back to the 1965–80 line. In manufacturing – which I still consider the flagship of economic development – the cumulative setbacks have been even more severe: 32 per cent for the low-income countries other than India and China; 53 per cent for the lower middle-income countries; no less than 85 per cent for sub-Saharan Africa; 57 per cent for Latin America and the Caribbean. Only the upper middle-income countries managed to keep this cumulative loss to a relatively modest level of 10 per cent.

Not all of this economic devastation (compared with 1965–80) is due to the debt crisis. The industrialized OECD countries have also had their setbacks but with a cumulative setback of 7 per cent for GDP and only 4 per cent for manufacturing these setbacks seem minimal compared with those of the Third World and could easily be made up in the next ten years by better economic management on behalf of the G7 and by restoring the growth objective to a more equal place relative to control of inflation – more of Keynes and less of Milton Friedman!

By contrast, to return the Third World countries during the next decade back to the 1965–80 line, so as to make up for the cumulative loss during the 1980s, would require nothing less than a miracle. GDP of low-income countries would have to grow by 8.5 per cent per annum; lower middle-income countries by 9.4 per cent per annum; upper middle-income countries by 7.9 per cent per annum; sub-Saharan Africa by 8.8 per cent per annum; Latin America and the Caribbean by 10.5 per cent per annum. In other words, the task is impossible (except perhaps for the upper middle-income countries) and if ever at any point in the future we are to get back to the interrupted 1965–80 line, it will take very much longer than a decade. The job may have to be spread out over 30–40 years at least. So we will be walking in the shadow of the debt crisis for a generation or more, even if the debts are wiped out tomorrow. It will be a long run and 'in the long run we are all dead'. In spite of the much-vaunted 'outward orientation' achieved during the 1980s, it is true, even in the case of trade, that arrears have to be made up. The rate of growth of exports of low-income countries other than China and India fell from 5.9 per cent per annum in 1965–80 to 0.5 per cent in 1980–88; their exports would have to increase by no less than 11.3 per cent per annum to come back again to the 1965–80 growth line. For sub-Saharan Africa the figures are even worse. In the case of the lower middle-income countries, the impact of outward orientation on export volume has been minimal, from growth at 5.8 per cent in 1965–80 to 6.0 per cent in 1980–88. It is only in the case of upper middle-income countries and of Latin America that there has been a visible shift to outward orientation reflected in the volume of exports. And these figures relate to the *volume* of exports and do not therefore reflect the deterioration of terms of trade which has occurred not only for the primary commodity exports but also for the manufactured exports of developing countries.[1] Nor does it show the import strangulation – directly related to the cuts in investment already noted. Imports of low-income countries other than China and India have fallen at the rate of 3.2 per cent in the recent decade after rising by 4.5 per cent per annum 1965–80. They would have to rise by no less than 12.2 per cent per annum in the next decade to make up for this shortfall. For the severely indebted countries as a whole, as well as for Latin America and the Caribbean and for sub-Saharan Africa, this downward shift and shortfall is even greater. It is noteworthy that, while the OECD members also showed a drop in their growth of exports (some of it explained by the import strangulation in developing countries), they were able to increase the growth rate in the volume of their imports (from 4.2% to 5.1%), largely due to their improved terms of trade – the counterpart of the deteriorated terms of trade of Third World countries.

As against this, the neo-liberal counter-revolutionaries, who today control some of the strategic positions in the development institutions, will argue that this is a false calculation based on excessively static assumptions. Many of the developing countries have improved the quality of their policies through structural adjustment pro-grammes and thus 'laid the foundations for subsequent sustainable growth', in the favourite phrase of this school. In this picture of the world, the past decade was a period of necessary consolidation, of *reculer pour mieux sauter*. Perhaps so – only the future can tell. If this view is correct, and if the Third World countries are really in better shape now for subsequent growth, then perhaps catching up with the 1965–80 line is not impossible, at least gradually in the course of time.

But there is also the opposite view, that is, that what has happened in the past decade, far from 'laying the foundations of subsequent growth' has done exactly the opposite, that is it has *destroyed* the foundations for subsequent growth. This view can find support from the particularly heavy decline of investment in the indebted coun-tries and Third World countries generally. Investment has declined even more than GNP, that is, it has declined as a proportion of GNP. Physical capital investment is not the only – perhaps not the major – source of growth, but it is an important determinant of future growth. Gross domestic investment in the severely indebted coun-tries, after growing by 8.4 per cent per annum in 1965–80, has over the past decade *declined* by 3.1 per cent per annum. This is a swing, in the direction of decline, of 11.5 per cent or no less than 115 per cent cumulatively over the decade. This means that the volume of invest-ment in these countries over the next decade would have to be more than double that of the last decade in order to bring them back to the 1965–80 line. The corresponding figures for sub-Saharan Africa and for Latin America are equally bad or worse. Thus I think there is another scenario, at least as plausible as that of 'laying the founda-tions of subsequent growth'. That is the scenario, first introduced into development economics by Gunnar Myrdal, of cumulative pro-cesses and vicious circles leading countries into a poverty trap.

In any case, scepticism about our having 'laid the foundations of subsequent growth' does not depend on belief in physical capital investment, Harrod–Domar, ICOR and all that. The picture is no different if we talk about human capital. Central government expend-iture on education has fallen from 20.5 per cent to 9.0 per cent in low-income countries; from 17.5 per cent to 13.3 per cent in lower middle-income countries; from 15.4 per cent to 11.0 per cent in Latin America and the Caribbean; and from 15.6 per cent to 10.8 per cent in the severely indebted countries. There are similar declines in health expenditures as a proportion of government expenditure from 5.5 per cent to 2.8 per cent in low-income countries; 5.7 per cent to 4.0 per cent in lower middle-income countries and from 5.9 per cent to 4.4 per cent in the severely indebted countries. Again it will take many years before such a cumulative shortfall can be made up. All this does not look like laying the foundations for growth in terms of the human resource basis.

So there is some reason to be sceptical about the view that the Third World economies are now 'leaner and fitter' to face the world ahead beyond the debt crisis. They are certainly leaner but whether they are fitter remains to be seen. Probably true in the case of much of Asia, probably untrue in the case of Africa, Latin America, and the Middle East.

But it seems not very useful to dream in terms of a return to paradise lost. Nor is it very productive to sit down wearing sackcloth and sprinkling ashes on our heads, wailing in doom and gloom. Far better to accept the setbacks of the 'lost decade' as water under the bridge and ask ourselves: Where do we go from here? How can we do better in the future?

Economic projections are notoriously tricky and our record as forecasters is very patchy to say the least. The World Bank projections, whether on commodity prices, growth rates or results of structural adjustment programmes, have proved chronically over-optimistic and had to be repeatedly revised downward. As a result, the World Bank, and all of us, have become more humble about our projections and hedge them with careful assumptions. There is practically no area, from the 'peace dividend', financial flows, the Uruguay round, oil prices, future technologies, and so on, where you could not make plausible optimistic assumptions about the impact on developing countries or equally plausible pessimistic assumptions; so I am taking my courage in both hands in making the following propositions:

1   The international context for the growth of developing countries will continue to be unfavourable. The growth rate of industrial countries is expected to continue to be sluggish even if recessions can be avoided. The surplus countries in particular seem determined to put the objective of inflation control above that of more rapid growth and fuller employment. The job of global economic

co-ordination, now largely in the hands of the G7, is clearly not properly done – see their meeting of April 1991 when it was clear that each country acted by its own domestic lights, without much thought for the impact on other countries, least of all the Third World. Professional economists can talk themselves hoarse to explain that all could benefit if externalities, in the form of impact on the rest of the world with feedback effects on the acting country itself, were properly taken into account. The point seems to get lost in the G7 and its bland communiqués. It would be rash to expect the 'locomotive of growth' which the industrial countries are to provide for the rest of the world to move very fast in the next decade.

2   We are gradually learning to be more humble, not only about projections in general, but also about the right kind of development policies, about what works or does not work. At one time we believed in planning and the government as the guardian of the public good. More recently, we believed in privatization, free markets and the invisible hand. We are now swinging back to a more moderate position between these two ideological extremes, in the form of a belief in 'good governance' which each of us is then free to interpret as we think best. As a result, domestic development policies could become more pragmatic with mixtures of planning, free markets and experiments with 'social market' systems. This may make development policies much more diverse and trendless, certainly more so than the broadly uniform and identical policies imposed under debt pressure by the Bretton Woods institutions on developing countries today. (Remember that we have assumed elimination of debts and hence reduced leverage and reduced outside pressure on developing countries.) This is already foreshadowed in current World Bank projections where the main line of hedging now runs as follows: prospects for developing countries are much less determined by the international context than by their domestic policies, but developing countries differ sharply in the quality of their domestic policies (in 'good governance'); hence their future growth rates will differ sharply, and average growth rates are difficult to predict as well as not particularly meaningful. We may note that this type of projection tends to be self-fulfilling, that is, if average projected growth rates turn out to be too high it follows that the governance of developing countries

has been less than good. This hedge also depends on the assumption that the international context is less important than domestic policies – a proposition on which one can differ and which would be difficult to quantify.

3   On financial flows it is difficult to be optimistic. If there is full debt relief one can hardly see private investment and commercial bank lending resuming with any vigour. Official development assistance will have to provide the bulk of resources, yet this assistance has stubbornly refused to rise above even half the theoretically accepted level of 0.7 per cent of GNP. Eastern Europe and Russia will be big competitors for financial assistance. The Gulf, from being a major source of outward capital flows to developing countries, may well absorb resources rather than provide them. The air is presently thick with assurances that aid to Eastern Europe, the Gulf, to domestic social sectors, and so on will not be at the expense of developing countries, but I would not be willing to bet too confidently on this. Furthermore, if the above assumption about sluggish growth in industrial countries for the sake of inflation control is correct, this may mean rising unemployment; and this in turn may mean that financial resources are domestically absorbed to cope with social problems and unemployment since 'charity begins at home'.

4   Technology may work as much against developing countries as in their favour. True that biotechnology, improved health technology, globalization of production due to improved communications technology and so forth may work in their favour, but with increased replacement of natural raw materials, and increased importance of high skills rather than cheap labour, closer integration of research and development (R&D) with production will operate against them. Nobody can be sure today where the balance will lie. In this area it may be true to say that countries with good technology policies could gain by maximizing the advantages and minimizing the disadvantages, and vice versa.

I hope that we will all meet in good health in ten years' time, at the 25th SID World Conference, and will then be able to say that in the 1990s we have put the 'lost decade' of the 1980s behind us.

Note

1 See P. Sarkar and H. W. Singer, 'Manufactured Exports of Developing Countries and their Terms of Trade since 1965, *World Development*, vol. 19, no.4, April 1991.

Part IV

Structural Adjustment and Stabilization

8
Are Structural Adjustment Programmes Successful?[*]

The answer to the question 'Are the Structural Adjustment Programmes Successful?' raises a number of difficult statistical and analytical problems. How would a country subject to a structural adjustment programme have done without the programme? This is a question of counterfactual evidence, not subject to rigorous proof or disproof. The method preferred by the Bretton Woods Institutions is to compare countries with a programme to countries without a programme, or 'strong adjusters' which have stuck with their programmes to 'weak adjusters' which have abandoned or failed to implement their programmes. But the two groups may differ in other relevant respects. There is also the well-known difficulty of establishing causation: are countries successful because they implemented programmes or were they able to implement programmes because they were successful? Finally, there must be a doubt whether the successful countries were successful because of the programmes or because of the supporting finance which accompanied the programmes: would the countries have been successful if they had just got the finance and would the countries without a programme have been successful if they had got the finance?

Before this question can be answered we must obviously make a number of distinctions. A structural adjustment programme (SAP) may be called successful if it achieves the objectives of the programme itself, but may not be successful from the point of view of optimum

---

* Originally published in *Pakistan Journal of Applied Economics*, vol. XI, nos 1 and 2, 1995, pp. 1–15.

development of the country. This would be the case if the objectives of the programme differ from what is in the best interest of the development of the country. To give a few examples: the objective of the structural adjustment programme may be the integration of the economies of the adjusting countries into the world economy, through outward orientation and alignment of domestic prices with international prices; but the best possible development strategy for a country may call for greater emphasis on the domestic market and for a degree of protection or even a period of relative insulation from external influences. Or the objective of structural adjustment programmes may be to stabilize the balance of payments position and thus enable a country to service its foreign debts; but this would not necessarily be the development priority of the country itself. The 'Washington Consensus' under which the Bretton Woods Institutions (BWI) operate holds that there can be no such conflicts. Integration into the world economy, 'getting prices right', by aligning domestic prices with international prices, maintaining a good international credit rating by servicing foreign debts and attracting foreign investments by maintaining a sound balance of payments position, etc., – all these are 'fundamentals' which are held by the Washington Consensus to be in the best interests of development at any time and under any circumstances. Thus the question whether an adjustment programme is successful in terms of its own objectives as defined by the Washington Consensus is different from the question whether the Washington Consensus contains the right recipe for development of all countries at all times.

A key objective of the structural adjustment programmes inspired by the Washington Consensus is to extend the role of the market and reduce the role of government intervention by way of planning and regulation as well as direct production. This emphasis on 'market friendliness' has both international and domestic aspects. It is based on the assumption that the market is right: there are no market failures or if there are, they are less serious or can be more easily rectified than government failures. This is perceived to be in contrast to the bad old ways of the 1950s when the reverse assumption was made, that is, that government failures could be disregarded in comparison with market failures. The international aspect of market friendliness consists in the acceptance of international prices as the benchmark of comparative advantages and measures of competitiveness; this places emphasis on the selection of the correct exchange rate so that the assumedly correct market incentives of international prices can feed through into the national economy, resulting in proper emphasis on the production of tradeables as against non-tradeables. Tradeables of course include not only exports and potential exports but also import substitutes and potential import substitutes. This is recognized in theory although in practice the emphasis tends to be on exports rather than on import substitution. Similarly, allocation of resources, non-tradeables as well as tradeables, must be governed by market prices. 'Getting prices right', in the sense of having prices as close as possible to what a free market would produce, are held to be the key to sustainable growth.

Critics might question this model on various grounds. First of all, international prices are not always free market prices and as such suitable benchmarks for countries undergoing structural adjustment. For example, international cereal prices can hardly be said to be the result of free market forces; rather they are artificially low as a result of agricultural subsidies to farmers in Europe and the USA resulting in large surpluses overhanging the market and putting downward pressure on prices. Thus countries deciding their domestic priorities for domestic food production *versus* imports on the basis of international prices would allocate less to domestic production and rely more on food imports than true free market principles would suggest. This is sometimes acknowledged by accepting food security as a desirable objective in itself, apart from market friendliness, but this is really an acknowledgement that there are important market failures in this area.

Secondly, critics would point out that in developing countries, and especially in the poorer developing countries, the institutions and qualifications necessary for the operation of domestic markets are simply not there. This lack refers to essential infrastructure such as roads, telecommunications, and so on, and also to the lack of an entrepreneurial and business class with the necessary information, access to credit, and so forth to organize production in response to price incentives. The structural adjustment programmes, and even more the IMF stabilization programmes, are based on the assumption that the first and most essential step is to get the macroeconomic fundamentals right and supply will respond to the right environment and proper price incentives and thus lead to sustainable growth. This seems to neglect some of the structural obstacles to supply response. The emphasis on the macroeconomic and demand side is further reinforced by the cross-conditionality between the IMF and World Bank under which the World Bank structural adjustment programmes will not apply unless and until the IMF stabilization targets have been fulfilled. The World Bank had acknowledged this difficulty by putting increasing emphasis on 'capacity building' and 'institution building'.

Thirdly, many critics are not ready to accept the blanket proposition that government failures are more important than market failures. This seems to disregard the above-mentioned weaknesses of market structures in developing countries. It also seems to disregard the great variety of circumstances in different developing countries. A more realistic picture would be to say that we would find a great variety of circumstances in different countries: reasonably good governance combined with promising market structures; good governance but poor market structures; poor governance but promising markets; and poor governance as well as poor markets. In the latter situation, which may be widespread among the poorest countries, it seems not particularly useful to approach structural adjustment from the point of view of 'getting government out of business'. Altogether the doctrine of market superiority may have been developed more on the basis of conditions in advanced industrial countries rather than developing countries. Moreover, it is not easy to square with the experience of such successful East Asian economies as Korea and Taiwan, or for that matter with the earlier experience of successful industrial countries such as Japan (although the World Bank in its recent study of the East Asian Miracle has done its best to squeeze their experience into the paradigm of the Washington Consensus).

Fourthly, critics are also doubtful about the priority given to internal causes of underdevelopment or balance of payments difficulties over and above external or international sources. Such an emphasis is inherent when poor governance and harmful government intervention is treated as the main culprit. The World Bank and IMF tend to reply that, while international factors such as deteriorating terms of trade, protectionism in industrial countries (e.g., in textiles and agriculture), debt burdens and so forth may be important, they must be accepted as facts of life beyond the control of developing countries. However, there are two related replies to this: (a) that the Bretton

Woods institutions were not created to force countries to adjust themselves to an unfavourable international environment, but rather to change the international environment for the better; and (b) the Bretton Woods institutions are criticized for not putting corresponding pressure on rich countries and balance of payments surplus countries to undergo the same degree of structural adjustment expected from developing countries which are in a much weaker position to undergo the rigours of structural adjustment. This also is contrary to the original intentions: for example, in the original documentation for Bretton Woods, Keynes had proposed an international tax on balance of payments surpluses and the IMF is supposed, in theory, to exert the same degree of 'surveillance' over all member countries, rich as well as poor, surplus as well as deficit. The World Bank in its turn was set up on a purely project basis without having any business in the area of conditionality or structural adjustment. A further point of the critics in this area is that such external obstacles as deteriorating terms of trade for countries exporting primary products are by no means entirely external or exogenous. Rather, as discussed later in this essay, the country-by-country approach adopted in structural adjustment negotiation results in a fallacy of composition leading to downward pressure on commodity prices, to the benefit of importing countries where low commodity prices help to control inflation.

So far, we have looked at the objectives of structural adjustment. We now turn to consider the question raised in the title of this essay, that is whether these programmes were successful, while accepting their objectives. In other words: were these programmes successful in terms of their own objectives?[1]

Perhaps the most authoritative statement by the World Bank, both on the methodology of measuring the success of SAPs and the actual results of such measurements, is in the proceedings of a World Bank Symposium on *Adjustment Lending Revisited*, held in September 1990.[2] In the key contribution to this symposium, 'World Bank Supported Adjustment Programs: Country Performance and Effectiveness' by Vittorio Corbo and Patricio Rojas, the following four criteria are singled out as indicators of country performance: rate of real GDP growth; ratio of domestic saving to GDP; ratio of investment to GDP; and ratio of exports to GDP. Countries under SAPs, or 'early-intensive adjustment lending (EIAL) countries' are compared with other (less intensive) adjustment lending (OAL) countries and also with countries which have received no adjustment loans (NAL countries).[3] The records of the three categories of countries (EIAL, OAL and NAL) for the periods 1981–84 and 1985–88, as compared with a pre-SAP base period of 1970–80, are then contrasted and taken as tests of the success of SAPs. This is the essence of the procedure, although the technique is more sophisticated than indicated here, since selected indicators of policy stance as well as external shocks (such as deterioration in terms of trade and rising real interest rates) are also taken into account.

What can we say about this methodology? The countries without SAPs – the NAL countries – are used as a control group for the countries with SAPs, among which again the countries with less intensive SAPs – the OAL countries – serve as a control group for the countries with more intensive SAPs – the EIAL countries. This method of cross-country comparison is clearly superior to the alternative method of inter-temporal comparisons of countries with SAPs. This inter-temporal method would compare a given country before and after SAPs, and attribute any change to the impact of the SAP. This is clearly unsatisfactory and subject to all the hazards of counterfactual evidence. A change in the performance of a country in the post-SAP period compared with the pre-SAP period may be due to any number of factors, and it is naive to assume that in the absence of a SAP there would have been no change in the relevant performance criteria. The control group method actually adopted makes a less stringent assumption, that is, that without the SAPs the performance criteria of countries undergoing SAPs would have been the same as for countries without SAPs. Even this is a risky assumption – one would have to be sure that the SAP countries are in all relevant respects fully comparable to the non-SAP countries. Such relevant respects would include in particular size of countries, regional distribution of countries, degree of urbanization or industrialization, trade-intensity, technological capacity, to name only a few. But while the method is still risky it seems the best we can do, and in any case the assumption of other things being equal between SAP and non-SAP countries can be tested and to some extent corrected for (as indeed the World Bank now does in its new more sophisticated approach to measurement of SAP success evidenced in the symposium).

If we first look at the results obtained for the four selected performance criteria, we would expect to establish a clear demonstration of
success of SAPs is a smooth transition up the ladder of adjustment as
it were, that is the OAL countries with mild adjustment doing better
than the NAL countries without adjustment and the EIAL countries
with intensive adjustment doing better still than the OAL countries.
In fact, we find that this is true only for one of the four main
indicators, namely the ratio of exports to GDP. If we look at the
median values (which in view of the limited number of countries in
each group seem more appropriate than average values) we find that
the NAL countries suffered a fall in the export ratio in 1985–88
compared with 1970–80 of 6.3 percentage points, the OAL countries
had a smaller fall of 2.5 percentage points, whereas the EIAL countries showed an actual increase in the ratio by 2.3 percentage points.
So far so good – leaving aside for the moment the question whether
the ratio of exports to GDP is in fact a good indicator of 'success'. But
none of the other three indicators gives such an unequivocal picture
of success.

One other indicator – presumably the most important single indicator of success – namely the rate of GDP growth, shows at least a
partial picture of success. Compared with the non-adjusting NAL
countries which showed a decline of 2.4 percentage points in the
rate of growth, both categories of adjusting countries did better.
However, as between the mildly adjusting OAL countries and the
intensely adjusting EIAL countries the former did distinctly better
than the latter, losing only 0.5 percentage points of growth as against
1.9 per cent for the intensely adjusting countries. So the picture of
success is somewhat blurred, but perhaps broadly one can count this
as another indicator of success.

However, the two other indicators show unequivocally an opposite
picture of failure, in the sense that the adjusting countries did worse
than the non-adjusting countries. Admittedly for the ratio of domestic saving to GDP the differences are slight: a loss of 1.5 percentage
points for the NAL countries, 2.1 per cent for the OAL countries and
3.4 per cent for the EIAL countries. For the ratio of investment to
GDP, on the other hand, the differences are not only in the opposite
direction to those indicating 'success' but the differences are also very
sharp: again of 0.2 per cent for NAL countries, a loss of 3.7 per cent for
OAL countries and a loss of no less than 7.3 percentage points for the

EIAL countries. All this is on the assumption that high ratios of saving and investment are a good thing and can properly be treated as performance indicators.

So the overall picture given by the four indicators is at best mixed, with two pointing in one direction and two in the other. The result most clearly pointing in the other direction concerns the ratio of investment to GDP; the negative finding in this respect has also been confirmed by other researchers and is accepted by the World Bank researchers. However, they then immediately raise the question whether the ratio of investment is in fact a proper performance indicator and argue that this finding 'should be interpreted carefully'.[4] It is argued that such a careful interpretation might show that the reduction in investment was in the area of 'low-efficiency public (and private) investment programmes' and that the efficiency or quality of investment must have improved since the lower rate of investment goes together with better growth of GDP.[5]

All this is fair enough, but should not the same argument that the findings 'should be interpreted carefully' also be applied to the indicators where the picture is favourable to the success hypothesis? For example, is a high ratio of exports to GDP really an indicator of success? The figure does not tell us anything about the terms on which the higher export ratio has been achieved. Has the increase in exports been part of a general export drive which has led to weak prices and adverse terms of trade? Have the increased exports been in the nature of cash crops at the expense of local food supplies and local food security? Have the exports required a high percentage of imported inputs so that their contribution to overall import capacity has been negligible? Have the export proceeds been absorbed in increased debt service so that they are not available to finance developmental imports? Careful interpretation must be general, not selective.

The finding of a negative impact of World Bank policy-based lending on the rate of investment is also confirmed by the even more recent analysis by Mosley, Harrigan and Toye.[6] However, since they – contrary to the World Bank symposium – do not find any clear evidence for a positive effect on GDP growth, they cannot share the World Bank's explanation that the decline in the rate of investment has been overcompensated by an increase in the efficiency of investment. This is an imputation by the present author – matter of efficiency of investment is not dealt with explicitly by Mosley, Harrigan and Toye.

We are now coming to a particularly serious question concerning the success of SAPs. The data show reasonable GDP growth for 1985–88 for the intensely adjusting countries (3.7 per cent median growth, compared with only 3.1 per cent for the OAL countries and 2.2 per cent for the NAL countries). But in welfare terms what matters is GDY (gross domestic income) rather than GDP that is GDP adjusted for changes in terms of trade. Now another table shows that the terms of trade of the intensely adjusting countries resulted in a loss of income in 1985–88 relative to 1970–80 of no less than 6.0 per cent of GDP. Hence the GDY figure would show a very different result from the GDP figure. Admittedly, we are now shifting the debate from the relative performance of adjusting countries to their absolute success or failure, but as Frances Stewart rightly pointed out at the World Bank Symposium, absolute performance may be more significant than relative performance.

The terms of trade losses are in fact shown among the data in the Corbo – Rojas study discussed at the World Bank Symposium. However, they are introduced and treated as 'external shocks'. This begs the question whether terms of trade changes are in fact external or whether they are not to some extent endogenous to the adjustment process. The SAPs, especially when taken in combination with IMF stabilization programmes, typically include a number of measures such as exchange rate devaluation, designed to increase 'outward orientation' which in the IMF/World Bank picture is a good thing in itself. Yet the data for recent years clearly show that the increased outward orientation has been at the expense of deteriorating terms of trade. Certainly exchange rate devaluation (if it succeeds in raising the volume of exports) would normally be expected to have that effect. It should be added, however, that in the context of the World Bank study, that is, in comparative terms of adjusting relative to non-adjusting countries than for the adjusting countries. This fact does not really dispose of the possibility of endogenous terms of trade effects: the outward orientation and pressure to export inherent in stabilization/adjustment programmes would also affect the non-adjusting countries which export products competitive with those of adjusting countries. All this will be difficult to disentangle and any attempt to do this may lead us into a statistical quagmire but this is no reason to disregard such spill-over effects and interdependencies.

Beyond this looms still another question: in looking at statistical associations between SAPs and performance indicators we have to ask ourselves which is cause and which is effect. It may seem natural in the type of comparative analysis presented by the World Bank authors to take it for granted that adjustment is the cause, and GDP growth, savings ratios, investment ratios and export ratios are the effects. But this is not necessarily true. It is conceivable that a good performance in respect of growth rates and savings/investment/ export ratios makes countries 'creditworthy' in the sense of qualifying for support through additional programme lending which in turn is subject to SAP conditionalities. This would mean that a good past performance is causal for the attraction of SAP lending and other external capital flows, and good past performance, in turn, may plausibly be assumed to have some association with subsequent performance. Such considerations would considerably blur the cause/ effect relationship. In any case, it is a well-established principle that correlation or association does not tell us which is cause and which is effect. All such complications are presumably well-known to the World Bank analysts, but one would think that they should work in the direction of considerable caution in treating the performance indicators as success indicators for structural adjustment.

SAPs are a form of programme lending and thus provide additional finance as well as exacting policy changes. This additional flow of finance to adjusting countries is then further amplified through bilateral donors and non-official sources taking the World Bank loans as a 'seal of approval' and increasing their own lending or investment to adjusting countries. This does not, of course, mean that non-adjusting countries do not also attract World Bank loans, both programme and project, as well as other external finance, especially if the reason for their non-adjustment is good domestic policies and absence of external troubles. But there seems a need to extend the scope of statistical analysis to cover such problems. It will be easy to disentangle statistically what part of any improved performance is due to the loans *per se* and what part to the conditionality attached to these loans. Presumably the World Bank would argue that there is no need to make such a distinction because the loans and the conditionality form an integral whole. Yet, when we are concerned to isolate the effects of the required structural reforms the distinction does seem relevant and important.

It has previously been pointed out that the control group of non-adjusting countries may not be an ideal statistical control group since they are also affected by the adjustment of adjusting countries. This observation can now be extended: the adjustment of adjusting Country A also affects the performance indicators in adjusting Country B and vice versa. All the countries in the statistical sample are inter-dependent. Underlying this statistical point is a major analytical doubt concerning the SAPs: the SAP approach is on a country-by-country basis and what is more makes the 'small country assumption', that is, that the country is without market power and faced with perfectly elastic demand for its exports. In other words, it is assumed that the structural changes in, say, trade policy or foreign exchange policy leading to outward orientation and improved export perfor-mance do not affect the overall situation of developing countries, for example, their terms of trade, trade access, commodity prices, and so on. While this is clearly doubtful when dealing with individual countries with a significant market share in specific commodity mar-kets or – less likely – in the market for manufactures, it becomes patently unacceptable when dealing with many countries simulta-neously, although with each of them on a country-by-country basis. The IMF and World Bank themselves now show signs of recognition of the 'fallacy of composition' involved in the small-country assump-tion for the case of many simultaneous country SAPs. This recogni-tion is emerging in the case of major primary commodities, such as cocoa, where the supply side of the market is shared by a limited number of countries, each of which has a significant market share. However, the doubts expressed in the professional literature are much wider than this.[7]

To take account of these wider doubts, it would be necessary to change the whole country-by-country framework of SAPs. It would be necessary either to negotiate SAPs simultaneously on the basis of a global macroeconomic model for estimating overall impacts, or else in the negotiation of country SAPs to take much more account of the impact on other developing countries before recommending specific adjustment measures. The present procedure may be said to be at the same time both too country-specific and not country-specific enough. It is too country-specific in the sense that the negotiation is country-by-country with insufficient attention to the impact on other countries; and not country-specific enough in the sense that the individual country programmes tend to recommend more or less the same type of measures and the same ingredients for the individual country SAPs. Although it is not easy to be statistically precise, it appears that the bulk of the country SAPs are identical to each other in the type of measures recommended. This can be taken as *prima facie* evidence that the programmes are too much inspired by a common theory or ideology and as a result take insufficient account of country specificities and differences. Thus, the question mark over the use of non-adjusting countries as a control group for measuring the success of SAPs is only a part of a much broader question-mark hanging over the whole SAP process as presently operated.

A spirited criticism of over-generalized SAPs has come from Gerald Helleiner, one of the participants in the World Bank Symposium:

> Unhappiness with 'global' prescriptions has rarely been as vociferous as it has become in recent years in the context of the 'conditionality' attached to IMF, World Bank and other official lending. The IMF and the World Bank usually deny that they employ a single 'model' for all their member countries. Whether these institutions, qua institutions, do or do not, there can be little doubt that within them, generalised prescriptions abound.[8]

A further question arises from the relationship between the World Bank and the IMF. Given the present rules and practice of cross-conditionality, it must be assumed that practically all the adjusting countries in the World Bank analysis have been subject to IMF stabilization programmes. This may also be true of some of the non-adjusting countries, but clearly to a much lesser degree. The question then arises: to what extent are the observed results of SAPs attributable to the SAP or to what extent are they attributable to IMF stabilization? If one assumes that the non-adjusting countries were free of IMF stabilization programmes, then one could say that the observed results measure the combined impact of World Bank and IMF programmes. In that case perhaps the distinction would not matter too much, since both organizations follow similar policies. However, the World Bank Symposium does not draw any distinction, either among the adjusting or the non-adjusting countries, between those also subject to IMF programmes and those not subject to such programmes.

Meanwhile, the Fund has undertaken its own series of empirical studies to examine the effects of Fund-supported programmes. The macroeconomic performance criteria used by the Fund are partly overlapping with those used by the Bank, although with more emphasis on the balance of payments and rate of inflation. The IMF empirical results, like those of the Bank, include the impact on GDP growth rates but with a different result. The Fund analysis admits that the Fund programmes 'involve some cost in terms of a decline in the growth rate',[9] but also that 'the negative effects on growth were reduced when the evaluation period was lengthened'.[10] The Bank analysis, on the other hand, claims a positive effect on GDP growth (although as pointed out this result is somewhat blurred). If both these analyses are correct they would form a coherent picture: the impact on GDP growth of IMF stabilization programmes, which usually precede World Bank SAPs, is at first negative, then this negative effect is gradually reduced and, by the time the World Bank SAP takes over, is converted into a positive effect. While consistent, this result cannot be said to be firmly established by the empirical data.

This last consideration raises the question of sequencing of Fund and Bank programmes respectively. The normal sequencing is of a Fund stabilization programme first, mainly directed towards reducing inflation and improving the balance of payments, later followed by a Bank SAP. This sequence is based on the theory that you first need demand-reducing stabilization as the only sound basis for subsequent sustainable growth, and when that is achieved you turn to the supply side for the institutional and trade policies designed to encourage efficiency and growth. In other words, the underlying theory is one of *reculer pour mieux sauter* – retrench or step back first in order to move or jump forward.

However, this theory is subject to some doubt. The initial retrenchment carries a danger of becoming cumulative or irreversible. It may also conflict with the idea of improving long-term supply-side efficiency. For example, if the initial retrenchment leads to an increase in poverty and malnutrition, this certainly would not be helpful in improving the efficiency of the future labour force, especially when it is accompanied by cuts in education and health services. There is now increasing criticism of the present sequencing, and the World

Bank is urged to come in with its supply-side measures and financial support earlier and more strongly, and perhaps even reverse the traditional sequencing. As Gerald Helleiner stated at the World Bank Symposium: 'there does not seem to be agreement as to the universal productivity of the new general advice on the sequencing of reform'.[11]

In a detailed study of sequencing in the agricultural sector, with special reference to sub-Saharan Africa, Lawrence Smith and Neil Spooner criticize the poor sequencing of adjustment policies at the sectoral, market and micro-levels. They also comment on the priority sequencing given to stabilization and attribute this to 'The influence of the IMF and its insistence on the pursuit of an orthodox stabilization policy'.[12] Their general judgement on the performance of SAPs in sub-Saharan Africa is that it has been at the best patchy and in many cases disappointing.[13]

The priority in sequencing given to IMF stabilization and the improvement of the external balance is connected with the fact that almost invariably in the 1980s the need for structural adjustment and SAP lending has arisen from the debt crisis – the inability of developing countries to service their debts in full. To some extent, the whole purpose of SAPs is to enable countries to resume debt servicing, although possibly on the basis of reduced debt, with agreed debt reductions and debt rescheduling going hand-in-hand with the SAP. In so far as resumed debt servicing is the effect and purpose of structural adjustment, it could be said that the beneficiaries are the creditors rather than the developing countries. No doubt there would also be beneficial effects for the adjusting country in that it becomes more creditworthy for future lending and investment as a result of debt service resumption, and the developing countries share a general interest in protecting that mysterious entity 'the world financial system' from disruption and collapse. It is also true that the resumption of debt service under SAPs hopefully comes from resumed and sustainable growth rather than further squeezing of consumption, domestic investment or imports. However, the fact remains that to the extent that the increase in GDP or in exports goes to finance debt service, there is no immediate or direct impact on the welfare of the adjusting country. The essential purpose of exports must be to provide finance for development-essential or welfare-essential imports. It is noteworthy that the World Bank analysts use the ratio of exports to GDP as a performance indicator and not the ratio of imports to GDP. In the latter case they would probably have found a negative impact of SAPs, but they could then have explained away this negative finding by assuming that this represents efficient import substitution – import substitution made efficient by the adjustment of the exchange rate, removal of price distortions, reduction of inflation, and so on. Such an explanation would be as plausible as the one used in respect of the negative finding concerning the rate of investment. In fact, however, it will almost certainly be found in country analysis that the import squeeze generally did not represent efficient import substitution, or any other kind of import substitution, but went together with a decline in domestic production of the relevant tradeables.

Dealing with African and other low-income countries, Helleiner finds 'no statistically significant link between the change in export share of GDP and growth. Indeed, the sign on this relationship is consistently negative'. On the other hand, when the change in export shares was replaced by the change in import shares, the finding is modified at least to the limited extent that 'although in some estimated equations the sign was now positive, the relationship with growth was still statistically insignificant'.[14]

The link with the debt crisis and the potential benefits of adjustment for creditors and the 'world financial system' should serve to direct our minds to a basic problem of the SAPs, that is they are unilaterally and asymmetrically applied to indebted developing countries in balance of payments deficit, while they are not applied to richer creditor countries, especially those with a balance of payments surplus. This is of course inevitable, given the linkage between SAPs and policy-based World Bank lending, but all the same it is wrong and incompatible with effective global macroeconomic management. In his original proposals for Bretton Woods, Keynes was emphatic in prescribing symmetrical adjustment for surplus as well as deficit countries. In fact, in conditions of recession and unemployment he wanted the adjustment pressure to be put more on surplus than on deficit countries. For this purpose, he advocated a tax of one per cent a month on balance of payments surpluses, the proceeds to be recycled to the deficit countries.[15]

In so far as the need for adjustment arises from the debt crisis, the responsibility for letting the debts accumulate so merrily during the

1970s must surely be shared between the improvident lenders, the industrial countries mal-adjusting to the OPEC shocks, and the improvident borrowers in the mal-adjusting developing countries. The IMF, in spite of the mandate for 'surveillance' in its Terms of Agreement, and the World Bank have of course no means, either political or financial, to put symmetrical or more than symmetrical pressure on creditor and surplus countries. They might argue that it is useless to rake over the history of the debt crisis and allocate responsibility: the debt crisis and the world recession are facts of life to which the developing countries will have to 'adjust'. But the Keynesian counter-argument to this would be that the Bretton Woods institutions were set up, not to enforce the facts of life on developing countries, but to change the facts of life.[16]

The four performance criteria of GDP growth and the ratios of saving, investment, and export are limited to some major macroeconomic aggregates. They lack a 'human face' as pointed out as early as 1987 in the well-known UNICEF study.[17] GDP growth tells us nothing about income distribution and the numbers living in poverty. In any case, the World Bank itself has now come to be more and more insistent that the pattern of income growth may be more important than the rate of growth. The 'positive' effect of adjustment on the savings ratio could in fact be the result of increasing inequality of income distribution, given the association between propensity to save and income levels. One could also be sufficiently Keynesian to be doubtful about the usefulness of higher savings in periods of recession and unemployment (although this doubt would not be shared by the IMF and World Bank with their priority on reducing inflation). As for the export ratio, some doubts have already been expressed about possible negative welfare implications.

In line with the UNICEF study and also with recent thinking in the UNDP *Human Development Reports*, the macroeconomic aggregate indicators might well be replaced or supplemented by indicators with a more human face. Admittedly the World Bank itself, following the UNICEF criticism, has become more and more concerned with the social dimensions of adjustment, and the World Bank Symposium itself included discussion of the social impact. But the thinking still seems to be largely in terms of dealing with social impacts in terms of compensatory measures and secondary action to provide 'safety nets'. The essential measure of success or failure of SAPs is still seen in terms of the four macroeconomic aggregates. Underlying this approach must be some version, however more sophisticated and more qualified, of the old 'trickle-down' approach, or at least the idea that you must first bake the cake before you can distribute it. The trouble is that the way you bake the cake determines the possibility of distributing it.

The Managing Director of the IMF, Michel Camdessus, singled out neglect of the 'social pillar' as the major weakness of adjustment approaches. In a recent address to the UN Economic and Social Council in July 1992 he stated:

> We still have to make a major effort to see to it that the social aspects of our strategies are dealt with on a co-ordinated basis, with suitable structures and means of financing. For the moment, we are a long way from that: the attention given to these problems has been disjointed or sporadic, the social component of our interventions – and I mean all of us, bilateral and multilateral donors – is financially inadequate, comes too late, and sometimes is disorganised.[18]

The upshot of all this must be to emphasize the great uncertainty and lack of unambiguous knowledge about the impact of the instruments in the orthodox repertoire of SAP measures. In these circumstances, there is a case for being less self-confident in prescriptions. Instead there is a good case for considering alternative approaches, and evaluating their results without ideological prejudice.

Notes

1   The rest of this essay, which answers this question, was previously published under the title 'Structural Adjustment Programmes: Evaluating Success', in J. W. Gunning, H. Kox, W. Tims and Y. Wit (eds), *Trade, Aid and Development* (London: Macmillan – now Palgrave, 1994).
2   See, V. Corbo, S. Fischer and S.B. Webb, *Adjustment Lending Revisited: Policies to Restore Growth*, (Washington, DC: World Bank, 1992).
3   *Ibid.*, pp. 23–39.
4   *Ibid.*, p. 33.
5   The reference to 'low-efficiency public (and private) investment programmes' is revealing – why not private (and public) investment programmes? Or at least 'public and private programmes' without the brackets? I think we do not have to look very far for an answer to these questions.

6 P. Mosley, J. Harrigan and J. Toye, *Aid and Power. The World Bank and Policy-Based Lending* (London and New York: Routledge, 1991). The reference is to Volume 1, *Analysis and Policy Proposals*: 'if adjustment lending has hidden benefits, it also has a hidden cost. This is the downward pressure which it has exerted, in conjunction with IMF stabilisation programmes, on the level of investment in developing countries' (p. 303).

7 See, D. Evans *et al.*, 'Trade Reform and the Small Country Assumption', in I. Goldin and L. A. Winters (eds), *Open Economies: Structural Adjustment and Agriculture*, OECD Centre for Economic Policy Research (Cambridge: Cambridge University Press, 1992).

8 G. K. Helleiner, 'Outward Orientation, Import Instability and African Economic Growth: An Empirical Investigation', in S. Lall and F. Stewart (eds), *Theory and Reality in Development* (London: Macmillan – now Palgrave, 1986), p. 139.

9 M.S. Khan, 'Macro Effects of Fund-Supported Programmes', *IMF Staff Papers* no.37 (June 1990), p. 222.

10 *Ibid.*

11 Helleiner, 'Outward Orientation', *op. cit.*, p. 181.

12 L.D. Smith and N.J. Spooner, 'The Sequencing of Structural Adjustment Policy Instruments in the Agricultural Sector', in C. Milner and A.J. Rayner (eds) *Policy Adjustment in Africa: Case-Studies in Economic Development*, Vol. I (London: Macmillan – now Palgrave, 1992), pp. 61–80.

13 *Ibid.*, p. 61.

14 Helleiner, 'Outward Orientation', *op. cit.*, p. 146.

15 See, H.W. Singer, 'The Vision of Keynes: The Bretton Woods Institutions', in E. Jensen and T. Fisher (eds), *The United Kingdom, The United Nations* (London: Macmillan – now Palgrave, 1990), pp. 235–45.

16 See, H.W. Singer, *Lessons of Post-War Development Experience: 1945–1988*, IDS Discussion Paper no. 260 (1989).

17 G.A. Cornia, R. Jolly and F. Stewart (eds), *Adjustment with a Human Face: Protecting the Vulnerable and Promoting Growth* (Oxford: Clarendon Press, 1987).

18 Quoted from *IMF Survey*, 3 August 1992, pp. 255–6.

9

Alternative Approaches to Adjustment and Stabilization*

Much thought has been given to modifying the strict character of orthodox IMF approaches to stabilization and orthodox Bank approaches to adjustment. In view of the considerable uncertainity and lack of knowledge about acceptable sustainable stabilization/adjustment policies, there is a good case for considering alternative approaches. These are briefly mentioned and listed here:

1 There should be more dialogue and persuasion rather than imposed conditionality. This is basically non-controversial and thinking in the IMF and World Bank itself is moving in the same direction.
2 There must be recognition that at least part of the present difficulties of many developing countries necessitating stabilization and adjustment are due to external reasons over which the developing countries have no control, for example, weak commodity prices, deteriorating terms of trade, high rates of interest, slower growth in the industrial countries, protectionism, absorption of available funds through the US balance of payments and budget deficits, failure to co-ordinate the use of Japanese and German surpluses, and so on. The IMF/Bank argue that while this may be true yet the need for adjustment is not affected, and the present

* This essay was part of a series of lectures given by the author at a seminar organized by the Food and Agriculture Organization of the United Nations (FAO). Originally published in *Third World Economics*, no. 72, September 1993, pp. 12–16.

unfavourable international circumstances must be accepted as a fact of life. But those asking for alternative approaches argue that this does justify special consideration for the debtor countries. It also calls for more symmetrical adjustment on the part of the industrial countries (especially the surplus countries). The Bretton Woods institutions were created not just only to help developing countries to adjust to the international facts of life but rather to change them.

3 Some of the critics have also argued that the IMF and World Bank themselves carry some of the responsibility for the magnitude of the debt crisis, in the sense of inadequate warnings and preventive action during the period 1974–82, that is, from the first big rise in oil prices to the full eruption of the debt crisis with Mexico's suspension of payments.

   During that period OPEC was happy to put its surpluses into the commercial banks of the USA, the UK, Switzerland, and so on, for recycling (instead of supplying cheap oil to developing countries). The commercial banks were only too eager to press loans without conditionality and often without much concern for creditworthiness upon developing countries at favourable rates of interest, many developing countries equally eagerly accepted these funds as an easy remedy for their balance of payments problems without sufficient concern for productive investment and ultimate repayment, and the major industrial countries were happy to continue this system because it removed any threat to the international financial system and gave them time to adjust to the rise in oil prices and counteract OPEC pressures, and so on. In this sense, everyone carried some responsibility for the debt crisis, including the IMF and World Bank themselves for standing too much on the sidelines during that period. In the view of the critics of the orthodox approach to adjustment this widely shared responsibility established a case for also sharing the burden of adjustment today.

4 In the matter of acceptable and sustainable stabilization/adjustment policies and the impact of given policy instruments, there is still considerable uncertainty and lack of knowledge. These are matters of great complexity and the impact of the instruments in the orthodox repertoire is by no means clear. The empirical evidence is mixed. In these circumstances, there is a case for being less self-confident in prescribing measures such as devaluations,

abolition of food subsidies, the move towards market prices, fiscal policy, and so on. Instead, there is a good case for considering alternative approaches, and evaluating their results without ideological prejudice.

5 Adjustment is a difficult process with serious political and social implications. Hence sufficient time must be given to make the process more gradual and soften the political and social impact. This means that more time should be given to debtor countries and other countries in difficulties than is often allowed for. By contrast, stabilization measures can be enacted almost instantly, but for that very reason they tend to have an immediate shock effect which also carries its own political and social dangers. Any alternative approach should make greater allowance for such shock effects and difficulties.

6 The last point is closely related to the advocacy of more external finance being made available, as a *quid pro quo* for accepting the great sacrifices and risks often involved. There is a danger of a vicious circle in that external finance is conditional upon strict adherence to the adjustment programme, while the adjustment programme depends on the maintenance of external finance. There is a risk – which experience has shown to be all too real – that even temporary and perhaps unavoidable lapses from the original adjustment targets may result in a cessation of external support and the collapse of the whole programme.

7 This last point also leads to the suggestion that in alternative approaches the number of conditions and targets should be a matter of discussion rather than automatic suspension of external support – in other words, fewer and more flexible targets. In particular, the suggestion has been made that the conditionality of stabilization/adjustment programmes should be restricted to actual outcome targets (such as balance of payments deficits, growth rates, food production, and so on) rather than instruments (such as devaluation, budget deficits, credit restrictions, pricing policies, and so on).

8 New unfavourable changes in external circumstances subsequent to the conclusion of agreements should be taken into account and more readily admitted as reasons for modification of original conditions. Alternatively, there should be compensation facilities. While this has in principle been accepted, for example in the

IMF Compensatory Financing Facility (CFF) or the EEC's STABEX, there is a present danger that these compensatory facilities are being eroded and themselves becoming subject to stricter conditionality.

9   There should be more concern with income distribution and the social impact of stabilization and adjustment programmes. Many programmes have resulted in severe cuts in real wages. The UNiCEF study on *Adjustment With a Human Face* has documented widespread harmful impacts on child nutrition, educational and health facilities and infant mortality. Reductions in food subsidies, increases in food prices, and cuts in social expenditure often have had a harsh impact on poorer and vulnerable groups. There is a danger that destruction of human capital may defeat the longer term objective of adjustment, that is, to lay the foundations for subsequent sustainable growth.

Many adjustment programmes involve a reduction of 'urban bias'. While the shift from urban to rural incomes is *per se* a move towards greater equality of income distribution (since rural incomes tend to be lower than urban incomes), there is a risk that this may be offset by an unfavourable redistribution of incomes within the rural sector towards the larger and more prosperous farmers who are better able to take advantage of the new price incentives offered, at the expense of small farmers or landless people. In any case, we do not want to solve the rural poverty problem at the expense of creating urban poverty – it should be possible for programmes to protect poor and vulnerable groups, both rural and urban.

10 There is also concern about the present timing and sequencing of IMF and World Bank action, and their mutual relation. The IMF stabilization measures, usually working in a contractionist and deflationary direction, tend to come first and have immediate effect. The structural adjustment measures and the longer-term structural adjustment finance which at least in principle are more growth-oriented, take a much longer time to be effective. This relationship is embodied in cross-conditionality with the IMF providing a 'seal of approval'. The basic idea is that stabilization, often involving devaluation, greater reliance on market prices, reduction of government deficits, trade liberalization, and so on, is needed in order to lay the foundations of subsequent economic

growth. But there is a danger that the contractionist pressures become cumulative and stand in the way of resumption of economic growth, rather than 'laying the foundations'. Another danger is that the sacrifices and pressures of the transitional stabilization period become politically and socially unsupportable and prevent countries from reaping the benefits expected from the subsequent adjustment period.

The present paradigm is that of *reculer pour mieux sauter*, of a temporary retreat providing the room for manoeuvre needed for a new forward jump. But the danger is that the paradigm becomes one of stepping back down a slippery slope from which it is difficult to recover or gain ground for a forward jump. The critics want to reverse the sequence between support for longer-term growth-oriented adjustment support and the more immediate need for stabilization to improve the balance of payments. They want a policy of 'growing out of debt'. In particular, the critics point to the import compression or 'import strangulation' presently imposed by the balance of payments crisis upon Latin American and African countries as making it possible to import the goods needed for new export promotion, or even for efficient import substitution. For example, in the case of agriculture, import strangulation may prevent debtor countries from importing the goods, such as fertilizer, agricultural machinery, transport equipment, and so on, needed to enable such stabilization measures as increased prices for agricultural producers to have the intended effect of stimulating production.

11 Related to this criticism is the suggestion that there should be more emphasis on the 'real economy' rather than macroeconomic aggregates – more concern with supply, specifically with supply bottlenecks. It is felt that the negotiations concerning stabilization and adjustment are presently too much confined to the financial sphere, taking place between financial experts of the IMF or World Bank on the one hand, and of ministries of finance and central banks of debtor countries on the other hand. It is felt that the conditions of the various sectors of the 'real economy' such as agriculture, industry, transport, institutions, and so on are insufficiently built into the negotiations and programmes. This may lead to excessive belief in the efficacy of financial incentives, such as higher prices, a belief which may

then be frustrated by such factors as lack of transport to collect crops, lack of storage, difficulties of supplying fertilizers or seeds to farmers, and so on. Similarly, changes in exchange rates are supposed to lead to greater exports or efficient import substitution, but this may be frustrated by a scarcity of inputs needed for expansion of exports and/or efficient import substitutes. In this context, greater emphasis on sectoral rather than overall adjustment lending may be indicated.

12   To reduce the harshness of the impact of adjustment programmes on poor and vulnerable groups, a number of suggestions have been made to build in compensatory measures into the adjustment process itself, as distinct from providing *ex post* safety nets such as the IMF Compensatory Financing Facility or STABEX. One current proposal under examination is for the use of food aid as part of adjustment programmes. This could be in the form of programme food aid since food is naturally targetted on poorer and vulnerable groups for whom food is a more important part of expenditure. But it is more effective to use food aid selectively targetted on poor groups lacking effective purchasing power for food so as to make sure the additional food aid does not interfere with the objective of increasing domestic food production. Alternatively, the food aid can take the form of specific projects directed at vulnerable groups endangered by adjustment difficulties, for example by way of food-for-work projects, feeding programmes for poorer children, and so on. The use of counterpart funds from the sale of programme food could provide the local finances for projects included in adjustment programmes. Counterpart funds could also serve to reduce the budget deficit which is usually also one of the objectives of adjustment programmes.

13   Some modifications are also suggested in the present country-by-country approach. It is true that adjustment problems and optimal adjustment policies are country specific, and there is a need for careful country specific analysis. On the other hand, the impact of what is recommended to Country. A on other countries, also subject to advice on adjustment policies, cannot be disregarded. For instance, if devaluation is recommended to say, Kenya, in order to increase the export of tea, the impact of this on the tea exports of say, Sri Lanka cannot be disregarded. If Sri

Lanka at the same time is induced to devalue its currency to bolster its tea exports, the backlash on Kenya will undo at least some of the intended advantages of Kenya's own devaluation; in the end both countries may be worse off, with the tea importing countries as the main beneficiaries.

More generally, concern exists about the effect of outward orientation, that is promotion of exports, which underlies many adjustment programmes, on export prices and terms of trade. It is also not always clear that devaluation with higher prices for export crops, in terms of local currency, always gets through to the producers and if it does whether the resulting increase in exports is not at the expense of food promotion for domestic use. The orthodox approach emphasizes that import substitution must be efficient (and that it is efficient if viable at 'proper' adjusted exchange rates). But the critics would extend this qualification also to export promotion and stipulate that export promotion must also be 'efficient' and can be inefficient, especially for developing countries as a whole. The concern is often expressed in the form that the country-by-country approach is open to a 'fallacy of composition'.

14 The monitoring of performance in stabilization and adjustment programmes has also become a matter of debate. It is suggested, for example, that more social indicators should be used, such as reduction of infant mortality, school enrolment rates, literacy, provision of employment, reduction poverty, and so on, so that countries doing well in these respects are given credit for their performance.

Similarly, suggestions have been made that performance might be monitored by an impartial source such as the UN or UNDP. Also that monitoring should pay attention to the overall performance in all targets taken as a whole so that under-performance in one individual target should not automatically trigger off suspension of promised assistance.

15 As a general trend, there is increasing recognition of the need for adjustment programmes to be more 'growth-oriented'. The point emphasized is that sectoral shifts and industrial restructuring are all easier in the context of growth. The same is true of shifts in income distribution, as was recognized in the development strategy of 'Redistribution With Growth' advocated by the

World Bank in the 'McNamara era' of the early and mid-1970s. The principle that adjustment should be more 'growth-oriented' is not controversial; the Bretton Woods institutions themselves are increasingly accepting this point. But there still remains an area of doubt as to what extent stabilization, often involving 'austerity', is a precondition for growth and hence must come first; as against the view that growth orientation should dominate both stabilization as well as adjustment. In a growth-oriented stabilization approach, the avoidance of import strangulation and maintenance of rates of investment would be more important objectives than they are now compared with a better balance of payments equilibrium or control of inflation.

16 A particularly important criticism of the orthodox approach is that it is not country-specific enough, in the sense that the programmes reflect too much a 'standard' approach, dominated by monetarist or neo-liberal doctrines and ideology. This criticism refers to a general presumption of these programmes that market failures are less important than government failures; that rational allocation of existing resources, broadly identified with allocation on market principles, is a more immediate objective than promotion of growth by increasing resources, or at least the precondition for it; that 'getting prices right' is of primary importance and that price incentives are vital and effective; that developing countries will benefit from trade liberalization, and so on. These criticisms of a 'standard' approach are denied by the IMF and World Bank but various analyses have shown that the country programmes in fact bear considerable resemblance to each other in the above and other respects. The critics ask for greater or more balanced emphasis on market failures as well as government failures; on need for supportive infrastructure as well as price incentives; dangers and risks of competitive devaluation of debtor countries; need for more symmetrical adjustment by creditor countries, and so on. The case of the critics is that the programmes are both not country-specific enough (in the above sense), and too country-specific (in the sense of following a country-by-country approach without sufficient consideration given to the 'fallacy of composition').

Part V
Food Aid

10
The Opportunity and the Challenge: H. W. Singer's Contribution to the International Debate on Food Aid*

by D. J. Shaw

> One of the most prominent early members of the epistemic community, notable for his many contributions toward making food aid a tool of economic development, was Hans Singer.
>
> (Hopkins, 1992, p. 236)

Introduction

Of all the many issues and concerns that Hans Singer has addressed in his long and illustrious career, one of his greatest international contributions has been in the field of food aid. There are few aspects of the subject that he has not touched on at one time or another. The epistemic community has long recognized that no other person has made such a dominant impact in the international debate on the subject (Clay and Shaw, 1987; Sapsford and Chen, 1998). He also played a strategic role in the creation of the World Food Programme (WFP), the food aid organization of the United Nations system (Shaw, 1998a; Shaw, 2001). And he has been a consultant to bilateral and non-governmental food aid programmes. His views on food aid as providing an opportunity as well as a challenge to achieving food security for the neediest people in the poorest countries have provided a balanced assessment and reasoned account when much of the criticism has

---

* An abridged version of this essay appear in the *Canadian Journal of Development Studies*, vol.XXII, No.1, March 2001, pp. 7–31.

been based on prejudice, polemical argument and anecdotal evidence. Many, but by no means all, of his contributions to engendering a rational debate are referenced here. What motivated him to take an interest in food aid, and what have been some of his many outstanding contributions to this controversial form of international assistance?

In many ways, food aid acted as a resource that has bound Singer's deep and abiding interest in issues such as unemployment, human capital formation, social welfare, trade, redistribution with growth, soft lending and strong international institutions for the benefit of developing countries, stimulated by the early influence of Schumpeter, Keynes, Beveridge and Archbishop Temple, and his early work on unemployment in the depressed areas of the United Kingdom and on social security and the welfare state (Oakeshott, Owen and Singer, 1937; Singer, 1940, 1943,1984a, 1992). After his work in the United Nations (1947–69), he stimulated the creation of an informal 'food aid cluster' in the Institute of Development Studies (IDS) at the University of Sussex in England, where he became professorial fellow, and initiated a series of food aid seminars for which IDS became famous as well as served as a consultant to a number of bilateral and NGO food aid programmes and WFP. Much of his work on food aid and related subjects after 1969 was conducted with members of the cluster and others at IDS and elsewhere.[1] He played a major role in sorting through the debris of the international debate on food aid that generated more heat than light to identify the issues, review the evidence, and suggest areas where new fronts might be established or old ones re-opened. Although areas of controversy and disagreement remain, he helped to demarcate the boundaries of consensus and to uncover the inconsistencies and prejudices.

Emerging interest in food aid

Singer played an active part in attempts to establish a soft financing aid facility at the United Nations, known as the UN Special Fund for Economic Development (SUNFED), throughout the 1950s. It was while undertaking this work that his emerging interest in food aid occurred:

> It was also in casting around for possible financing for SUNFED that I became very interested in 1954 in the establishment, under

Public Law 480, of the U.S. food aid program and the possibility of an international food aid program which had begun to emerge in Rome. (There was also a direct link with the local counterpart funds arising from P.L. 480 and the financing of IDA). This interest led me to my involvement in laying the ground for the U.N./FAO World Food Programme, and it has remained an active interest. (Singer, 1984a, p. 301)

SUNFED was not approved, mainly due to opposition in the United States. Instead a new soft financing window was adopted by the International Bank for Reconstruction and Development (IBRD) in 1959 inthe form of the International Development Association (IDA).[2] Subsequently, in 1960, when acting as an adviser to UN Secretary-General Dag Hammarskjöld, Singer drafted a proposal for a multilateral food aid agency that would be responsible for targeting food aid towards development projects. This would have avoided much of the criticism that had been generated against the United States bulk-supply food aid programme of creating disincentives to agricultural production in developing countries and disrupting international agricultural trade (Schultz, 1960). In a letter to Eugene Black, then president of the IBRD, Hammarskjöld proposed that the bank establish a separate management division to undertake multilateral food aid targeted on the reconstruction and development projects that the bank was financing. The proposal was declined (Hopkins, 1992, p. 242).[3]

The schism between multilateral soft financing and food aid, with the former going to the World Bank and the latter to WFP, was to have lasting negative repercussions. It was to result in a lower level of co-ordination of financial and food aid than might have otherwise occurred, to the mutual detriment of both types of assistance. It was also to result in different methods of appraisal, operational procedures and evaluation, even mind-sets, and to odious comparisons in which food aid came to be regarded as a 'second-class' resource. This also reflected the state of affairs in bilateral aid programmes where food aid was handled differently from other forms of assistance, by separate administrative units, and with special legislative, financial and operating procedures, inhibiting the fusion of the different forms of aid. On the other hand, the birth of WFP might be seen as part of a wider compromise in which food aid and pre-investment financing were given to the United Nations as 'consolation prizes' for the loss of a soft-financing facility to the IBRD.[4]

Dissenting view

Singer's early interest in food aid might also be attributed to what might be called a 'dissenting view', which characterized his work in other fields (Arestis and Sawyer, 1992, pp. 526–32).[5] Many economists and development practitioners were contemptuous of food aid as very inferior to financial aid. Moreover, food aid seemed to be entirely a North American matter and linked with US interests in getting rid of burdensome surpluses, subsidizing US farmers, and developing US export markets. In addition, food aid was met with much scepticisms and resistance because of its alleged disincentive effects, by lowering domestic food prices in recipient countries and thus discouraging local food production.

Singer dissented from this view for a number of reasons. First, there seemed to be no empirical evidence that the enormous volume of food aid that had gone into Western Europe under the Marshall Plan (see below), and into many other countries, had prevented them from increasing their own domestic food production. The clinching case was India, which received large amounts of US food aid in the late 1950s and early 1960s and used the revenue obtained from the sale of food aid commodities to finance investments in transport and irrigation infrastructure, which created the foundation of the Green Revolution (see below). Secondly, Singer foresaw that the availability of food surpluses would not remain limited to Canada and the USA but would become widespread among other developed countries, thus making possible a co-ordinated and fully multilateral food aid system. Thirdly, the debate about whether food aid was 'inferior' to financial aid was to him largely beside the point. Food aid was available whereas financial aid was limited. The question was therefore whether food aid could achieve positive results in terms of economic growth, employment creation and relief from hunger and poverty. Fourthly, even though food aid had evil origins in the agricultural policies of developed countries, which led to the accumulation of surpluses and were harmful to developing countries, Singer felt that this need not prevent 'plucking the flower of development from the nettle of surpluses'. Finally, to him the disincentive effects attributed to food aid were not inherent but were the result of bad planning and administration. Properly designed and managed, food aid could be used to promote local agricultural production.

An expanded programme of surplus food utilization

Singer and other members of the epistemic community thus turned their attention to the establishment of an independent multilateral food aid agency that the FAO and the UN were advocating and, for different reasons, both US presidential candidates in the election campaign of 1960, Vice-President Richard Nixon and Senator John F. Kennedy, were supporting (Wallerstein, 1980, pp. 38–42). The chance came when, following a proposal made by President Eisenhower at the United Nations on 22 September 1960 (UN, 1960a), the UN General Assembly passed a resolution on the 'Provision of food surpluses to food-deficit peoples through the United Nation system' and invited the FAO director-general, in consultation with the UN secretary-general, to undertake a study on how this might be done (UN, 1960b). The director-general of FAO, B. R. Sen, appointed a group of five 'high-level, independent experts' to assist him in preparing the study. Hans Singer, who enjoyed the confidence of the executive heads of both the UN and FAO, was appointed chairperson of the group.

The group met at the height of the Keynesian consensus with its emphasis on full employment, active government demand management, and the welfare state. Of the five members of the group, three were direct student of Keynes, the fourth was an economic development thinker in his own right, but fully in the Keynesian vein, and the fifth was an agricultural expert in the American 'New Deal' tradition of President Roosevelt.[6] It was no surprise, therefore, that the group's report had a strong Keynesian flavour (FAO, 1961). The emphasis was to deal with the surplus problem not by curtailing production but by expanding demand. Food surpluses were seen as an important part of the resources needed for economic development in developing countries. Far from being a waste, they could be a blessing, if matched by other resources, and used as an essential part of a coherent aid programme (as in the Marshall Plan[7]) and, to borrow from the Keynesian concept, would 'turn the stone of surpluses into bread for development'.[8]

Singer held a special position in the group. Not only was he chairperson but he represented the interests of the United Nations in general and the UN secretary-general in particular, and enjoyed the respect of the FAO director-general. He brought to the group the unique and profound experience he had gained in working on the proposals for SUNFED and an UN Expanded Programme of Technical Assistance (EPTA), and an interest in a multilateral form of the US food aid programme (PL480). Given such a like-minded group, the wealth of documentation and experience available, and the support of the FAO secretariat that had been working on the concept of a multilateral food security facility since the abortive proposal was made for a 'world food board' in 1946 (FAO, 1946), it is hardly surprising that its report was handed to the FAO director-general only 19 days after the commencement of its work at FAO in Rome.

Certain basic considerations influenced the group's report. Information available at the time indicated that over half the world's population was either undernourished or malnourished. In light of this fact, and the existence of large unused food stocks, the group viewed the world food problem as one of deficiencies, not surpluses. Underdevelopment was recognized as the basic cause. Developing countries within the world economy were akin to underprivileged, low-income people within the national economies of developed countries. The expert group observed that with the growth of wealth within the developed countries, inequalities of income had diminished. Equality of opportunity, full employment and a minimum of subsistence were accepted parts of the social philosophy of the welfare state in the developed countries. Nothing similar obtained within the international community as a whole. The basic aim should be to apply the principles of social progress accepted within the rich countries to the world as a whole. 'Only if this is done can we talk of an international community'.

The group was inspired by the earlier pioneering work of FAO and the example of the Marshall Plan, and ensured that its recommendations were in accordance with the FAO *Principles of Surplus Disposal*, which had established three general principles (FAO, 1954). The solution to problems of agricultural surpluses should be sought through efforts to increase consumption rather than through measures to restrict supplies. Disposal of excess stocks should be done in an orderly manner to avoid sharp falls in prices on world markets.

And there should be an undertaking from both importing and exporting countries that disposal of surpluses would be done without harmful interference to normal patterns of agricultural production and international trade.

In a spirit of optimism that matched the time, the group considered that the resources to implement a far-reaching aid programme were already available. In its opinion, a transfer of two-thirds to three-quarters of 1 per cent of the gross national product (GNP) of the developed countries over a period of five years, and probably less for another decade, would provide sufficient means for helping people in developing countries help themselves. This represented a much smaller international redistribution of income than the national redistribution of income achieved through progressive taxation within many developed countries, and much less than achieved under the Marshall Plan. The group pointedly added that to think that the developed world could not spare that amount for an international programme of economic aid was to show 'failure of imagination and failure of will'.

A central part of the expert group's case was that surplus food could form an important part of capital in its original sense of a 'subsistence fund'. If sufficient food could not be supplied to meet increased demand from the additionally employed construction workers, either more resources (circulating capital) would have to be spent on food imports or the amount of additional investment would have to be reduced. Additionally, employed workers would have to be fed during the construction period, before the fruits of the labour could supply their needs or enable them to buy their subsistence. Without such a fund, additional investment would not be possible and inflation would become rampant. Food surpluses used for economic development would enable hungry people to produce either their own food or other products to buy food. Freedom from hunger could ultimately be achieved only through freedom from poverty.

The group estimated that about $12 500 million of agricultural commodities would become available as 'surpluses' over a five-year period for use outside normal commercial market channels. It recommended that two-thirds of the aid resources should be used for economic development programmes, including national food reserves and an international emergency food reserve. The aim would be to provide developing countries with a positive incentive for maximum national effort to increase the rate of growth. The remaining aid resources would be used to promote social development including: land reform programmes; school feeding; support to poor students in secondary and higher levels of education and in training programmes; and relief and welfare programmes for the old, handicapped and destitute. A country programming, not project, approach was advocated for determining the criteria for the productive use of aid capital, including food aid, which would also take fungibility into account (Singer, 1965).

While recognizing that the major part of international aid would continue to be provided bilaterally, the group recommended that it should be supplied within a multilateral framework. This would ensure that bilateral and international aid activities would be provided within coherent and consistent country assistance programmes. The chief constraint was the capacity of developing countries to absorb surplus food supplies into their economies at a high level of effectiveness. Planning and programming machinery in the developing countries, the international organizations, and among donor countries required to be developed to take better, and more immediate, advantage of the availability of surpluses to further economic and social development.

The views of the expert group were taken fully into account in the report of the FAO director-general. Although a number of its recommendations were well in advance of their time, their value was subsequently recognized. Critically, they were well received by officials in key positions in the United States. In a memorandum to President Kennedy, the US ambassador to the UN, Adlai Stevenson, described it as 'One of the most remarkable documents on the subject'.[9] Willard Cochrane, director of the US Department of Agriculture's Agricultural Economic Services, found it 'an excellent report. The analysis of the role of food aid in economic development is, in my opinion, highly competent and informative. I know of no better analysis in the literature on economic development'.[10] Within less than a year after the expert group had submitted its report to the FAO director-general in February 1961, WFP was established.

Writing over 20 years later, Singer recognized that the expert group's report had 'errors' and 'omissions' (Singer, 1983, pp. 36–7). The report drew a distinction between economic development and social welfare, which is now regarded as unnecessary and unacceptable. The expert group was predominantly concerned with the link between increased food aid and increased investment and support for higher marginal increased investment, along with the multiplier effects of increased investment and higher incomes on consumption, some of which would be additional food consumption. This essentially Keynesian analysis neglected the chain of causation leading from higher consumption and better nutrition to increased productivity and increased investment. (This may be as, or more, important than the opposite sequence emphasized in the Keynesian model of higher investment leading to higher consumption). Singer suggested that a development model stressing income distribution and basic needs might have been more appropriate. One consequence would probably have been that the proportion of food aid allocated to consumption would have been larger than one-third. The report might also have had more to say about the special role which food aid might have played in creating human capital through better nutrition of children, thus helping in the development of both physical and mental capacities and increasing the productivity of subsequent physical investment.

Singer also felt that the report underestimated the extent to which food aid programmes would become diversified. Although some burden-sharing was envisaged, the bulk of food surpluses was seen as occurring in the United States. One important exception to this was the discussion in the report about food surpluses in developing countries. The report made the point that if there were arrangements to utilize the cereal surpluses of developed countries, arrangement should also be made to take the surpluses from developing countries out of the market, whose producers would have to be compensated since they could not afford to provide their commodities as aid. The emergence of the European Community (now Union) as a major donor was a development not foreseen in the report and one which had an important impact on the range of commodities available and on the channels for food aid. Singer admitted that the report was 'seriously in error' when it came to discussing the size and composition of surpluses and the relationship of food aid to other forms of aid. But there were good reasons for making optimistic assumptions at the beginning of the 1960s about the total volume of cereal aid, which were not realized.

There were also a number of important areas that the report did not address. These included: man-made emergencies, which were less prevalent at the beginning of the 1960s; the problems of malnutrition and the nutritional requirements of pre-school children and expectant and nursing mothers; and the benefits of triangular transactions for providing food aid. Singer recalled that when presenting the expert group's report to the FAO director-general (B. R. Sen) and the UN secretary-general (U Thant), he was doubtful of its title 'Expanded Program of Surplus Food Utilization' and raised the question as to whether it should be something more 'developmental and humanitarian' (Singer, 1991a). He was largely responsible for maintaining the United Nations' interest in launching WFP as a joint UN/ FAO undertaking. He recorded that the expert group was very much aware of the vision of the first FAO director-general, Sir John (later Lord) Boyd Orr, in proposing the creation of a 'world food board' and added 'Although, like much of Keynes's vision at Bretton Woods, this proved to be Utopian, I can say we felt that in a modest way we were following in the footsteps of both Boyd Orr and of Keynes'. Singer also recognized the debt the expert group had to the earlier work of FAO on the use of food surpluses, particularly the pilot study conducted on the use of food aid for development in India (FAO, 1955).

First UN development decade

The expert group's ideas were carried forward in the context of the first United Nations Development Decade of the 1960s that President Kennedy had proposed in an address to the UN General Assembly on 25 September 1961 (US, 1962, p. 623). Singer drafted the 'Proposals for Action' to be implemented during the development decade, which showed a strong Keynesian flavour (Singer, 1986, p. 35; UN, 1962). Reference was made to the roles that WFP could play in meeting emergencies and in supporting development projects. A number of 'new approaches' were identified including: the concept of national planning for social as well as economic development; the importance of the human factor in development and the urgent need to mobilize human resources; and the need to tackle the problems of unemployment and underemployment throughout the developing world.

At the same time, WFP was seen as representing an experimental extension of the idea of multilateral aid in terms of physical commodities. Developed countries were urged to think more about the possibilities of bringing their surplus resources and capacities to bear on the promotion of development in developing countries. The report suggested that the whole area of supplementary aid in the form of surplus commodities and the utilization of surplus capacity deserved further exploration within the United Nations, where equal weight would be given to the legitimate protection of commercial trade and the interests of producers in developing countries as well as the inherent potential of such aid for speeding up development.

Multilateral food aid

Singer has remained a strong supporter of food aid supplied through multilateral channels and, despite its difficulties, considers that WFP deserves a high place in the list of UN achievements (Singer, 2001; Shaw and Singer, 1998). Singer singled out five major achievements of WFP. First, by giving it a multilateral dimension, WFP has helped to depoliticize food aid and use it as an instrument for achieving universally recognized objectives as both development aid and as relief assistance in conflict and emergency situations. In addition, multilateral procurement and delivery of food aid can be more cost-effective and result in better resource management than unco-ordinated, and often conflictive, bilateral aid. Singer recognized that WFP has acquired considerable expertise and experience in the administration of food aid and has become a major transport and logistical arm of the UN system. Over the years, a supply system has been developed that is appreciated by both recipient countries and donors alike. This expertise is at the service of bilateral donors and increasingly used by them, especially in large-scale and complex emergencies. And WFP has developed an indispensable food aid information system which is at the disposal of decision-makers throughout the world.

Secondly, WFP has helped to establish a policy framework for food aid for both development and in times of emergency. Guidelines and criteria for food aid were developed which, although not always followed by bilateral food aid programmes, still provide the best available policy framework for food aid globally (WFP, 1979). As part of its functions, WFP also administers the International Emergency

Food Reserve (IEFR), the only international facility available to respond quickly to emergencies whenever and wherever they occur (WFP, 1978b). Although the IEFR has not lived up to its original expectations, it now includes an Immediate Response Account (IRA), a cash reserve to purchase food to respond to emergency food needs quickly. Both the IEFR and the IRA are still too small and unpredictable, and their use not fully multilaterally controlled, to ensure that all emergency needs are satisfied speedily, but the framework for effective action is in place once the political will to expand and use these facilities is fully generated.

Thirdly, Singer observed that WFP successfully pioneered the project approach to food aid through labour-intensive food-for-work programmes and the development of human resources through providing support for nutrition, health, education and training project for vulnerable groups and abjectly poor people in the most needy countries before the mobilization and development of human resources were fully recognized as key factors in development.

Fourthly, Singer noted that WFP has emerged as the principal international channel for emergency food aid and a natural co-ordinator in large-scale and complex emergency food relief operations following both natural and man-made disasters. Finally, with its dual functions of providing both development and relief assistance, Singer sees WFP as well placed to play a major role in what has come to be called the 'continuum' between relief and development (see below). Singer considers that there is still much to be done to create a link between relief and development. Food aid could be visualized as a means for preventing conflicts and resolving tensions before they developed into full-scale emergencies. A future task of the WFP will be to stimulate the international community to remove the artificial dichotomy between emergency and development assistance in the process from crisis to recovery and development, and to broaden the humanitarian consensus from acute emergency relief to the full circle of disaster prevention and preparedness linked to rehabilitation, reconstruction after emergencies and development.

Food aid for development

The 'most complete guide and assessment of the literature' on food aid for development is still that carried out by Singer, which was commissioned by the WFP in the 1970s and 1980s (Ruttan, 1996, p. 188, ff 91; WFP, 1978a; Maxwell and Singer, 1979; Clay and Singer, 1985). Singer identified four main potential advantages of food aid. It could lift a constraint on growth and self-reliance by providing the real resources necessary to expand investment or dampen inflationary repercussions of the implementation of development plans. It could particularly benefit disadvantaged groups, notably through nutrition improvement or food-for-work projects or by food subsidy programmes. It could help governments set up food reserve and price stabilization schemes. And it was at least partly additional in the sense that in its absence financial aid and commercial food imports would not be forthcoming.

Against these four advantages, Singer identified four potential disadvantages. Food aid could have a disincentive effect on local agriculture, through the price mechanism, by its effect on government policy or by attracting agricultural labourers to food-for-work sites. The allocation of food aid between recipient countries reflected the economic, political and military interests of donor countries rather than criteria of need. Food aid could result in greater dependence than self-reliance. And food aid could be second-best, expensive, double-tied, dependent on surpluses, irregular, bureaucratic, and often inappropriate. Singer argued that a closer examination of these eight aspects of the food aid debate showed that these effects could take place, but were not inevitable.

Singer concluded that an important task was to specify the conditions under which food aid could promote development in the developing countries, for which he established 'guiding principles' that are of continuing validity. Food aid could be useful in those cases where shortage of food was a constraint on growth or on the more equal distribution of income, without causing disincentive. In the case of least-developed and net food-importing developing countries, Singer advocated greater use of the waiver of usual marketing requirements (UMRs), for which there was provision in the FAO *Principles of Surplus Disposal*, which required that countries should import commercially at least a specified level of commercial imports in addition to any imports of the same commodities received as food aid (FAO, 1992, pp. 9–10). This would release scarce foreign exchange, which could be used for developmental purposes, with a particular focus on helping poor, food-insecure people. Food aid was best deployed in general support of a broadly-based, poverty-oriented development plan. It should be planned in advance and its availability should be guaranteed. Food aid should preferably consist of commodities which were indigenous to the recipient country or part of the normal diet. It should be complemented by other forms of aid. And resources generated from the sale of food aid should be used for developmental purposes with a poverty-reduction focus.

Singer called for greater awareness of the problem of income distribution in the allocation of food aid; the desirability of medium-term planning of global food aid resources (only partly met by commitments under the Food Aid Convention); greater procurement of food commodities in developing countries for food aid; revision of the FAO *Principles of Surplus Disposal* in recognition that poor food-importing developing countries needed help in meeting the mounting cost of filling structural food deficits; and easier terms and simpler administrative arrangements for the provision of food aid. He also advocated greater innovation in the uses of food aid including: addressing the seasonal dimensions of hunger and poverty when poor people might be too hungry to work well at certain seasons of the year; a closer amalgamation of input aid (fertilizer, feed and seeds) with output aid (food); the development of a better statistical base for food aid of all kinds (see below); and a better appreciation of the dynamic contribution of food aid to growth and equality (Singer 1993).

Writing 20 years after the expert group study that led to the establishment of WFP, Singer identified six 'guiding principles for the next 20 years' (Singer, 1983). These were: more food aid, particularly to remedy malnutrition and to offset the rapid rise in food imports in Sub-Saharan Africa; more food aid in the form of cereals; more programme food aid; more food aid through multilateral channels; greater efficiency in food aid administration and operations; and better international arrangements for food aid.

Programme food aid, pricing, and counterpart funds

Singer was commissioned by the US Agency for International Development to carry out an assessment of the developmental impact and effectiveness of United States PL480 Title 1 bulk-supply food aid in 1982 (Clay and Singer, 1982). The overall assessment was that recognition of what were called 'donor-end' problems in the programming and operation of food aid played an important part of a balanced perspective on food aid. They also helped explain the considerable diversity of findings and views on the impact and developmental potential of food aid. This diversity could be attributed to two effects of food aid pulling in opposite directions. First, food aid reduced the immediate pressures on the recipient country economy. Secondly, food aid increased the resources of a country for development in general and increased domestic food production (or improved storage and distribution) in particular, which could lead to reduced dependency and greater self-help. Which of the two effects prevailed depended, primarily, on the policies of the recipient government, and secondarily on the policies of food aid donors, including the extent to which the balance of resources and concessionality moved the overall impact of food aid from a negative to a positive outcome.

Greater obstacles and complexities in the effective use of food aid were also to be expected in the shift of food aid toward poorer countries and communities. Using food aid as an instrument in a basic needs strategy, linked to income distribution and poverty reduction, also created problems in the targeting of food aid and the use of counterpart funds. Targeting on the really poor was notoriously difficult in that they were handicapped in their access to food-aided projects and programmes. And meeting the nutritional needs of the poor was not identical with promoting overall poverty-oriented development. Assessment of the impact of food aid was made difficult by the fact that food aid was only one of many factors in a complex structure that determined rural–urban terms of trade and income distribution. Food aid was difficult to identify as a separate factor and its relationship to other factors was often indirect and disputable. No food aid agreement, however detailed, could cover all these complex factors and interrelations. At best, it could create a presumption that the direct and indirect impact of food aid was in reducing poverty and strengthening self-reliance and the forces making for sustained development.

Concerning pricing policies for food aid, the best 'general advice' (subject to the overriding importance of specific country objectives and conditions) was that 'where possible food aid should be sold at domestic prices which in turn should not be below international prices' (Singer and Clay, 1983). Any subsidies connected with food aid should preferably consist of large subsidies or free distribution for specific groups of target recipients rather than a small subsidy spread over a large indiscriminate group. In this way, any spill-over from the subsidized market to commercial channels could be minimized. Food subsidies for consumers should also be matched by incentives to domestic producers. Governments receiving food aid should also have an overall development and food policy that treated domestic food production as a priority throughout. This was ultimately more important than a sophisticated and complex pricing strategy which could not be made effective. Policy aspirations should also not out-run managerial capacity and understanding of the food system.

As early as 1961, Singer exposed the 'multiplier fallacy' of counter-part funds resulting from surplus-food sales and the 'illusions' of the project approach to external aid (Singer, 1961, 1965, 1970). He revealed the 'myth' that local currency funds represented real resources and that their subsequent use, and possibly repeated reuse, could multiply the effects of foreign aid. This had to do with the 'crucial importance' of the nature and effectiveness of the original aid transaction, which was determined by the quality of the planning and use of aid at the time and the surplus food injected into the economy of the receiving country. If the aid was effectively used *at that stage* (original emphasis), it helped to mobilize the domestic resources of the receiving country. The subsequent use of counterpart funds could not add to the effectiveness of the use of the aid or remedy any failures in such use at the time the aid was given. Similarly, insofar as the counterpart funds were used for specific projects rather than general budgetary support, the 'illusion' of the project approach may be added to illusions about the real nature of counterpart funds. Singer felt that the project approach was itself basically illusionary since whatever the project label may be, aid really financed the marginal project that would be cut out if the foreign aid was not provided.

The illusion of project aid could to some extent be reduced if aided projects were discussed and selected within the framework of a general review of the broad policies of the recipient country and use of the overall resources at their disposal. Singer realistically saw that in the 'tangled world of aid politics and economics', the concreteness of aided projects was necessary to approve aid, even if it was 'the fallacy of misplaced concreteness'. Perhaps the educational and political value of donors and recipients working together on the formulation, appraisal and execution of specific development projects was sufficient to justify the drawbacks. Abandonment of the project approach to aid giving did not exclude control of the uses, purposes and sectors to which the aid was applied. On the contrary, non-project aid in many ways provided more effective leverage to the aid giver since it was eagerly sought by many developing countries and the release from project tying would often be accepted as an aspect of 'softness' in aid.

Food aid and the well-being of children

An additional motivation for Singer's interest in food aid was that at the time he was pursuing the idea of SUNFED he attended a lecture by Neville Scrimshaw, a leading nutritionist at MIT in Cambridge, Massachusetts, on the devastating effects of undernourishment and malnutrition on the physical and mental development of young children, which led him to recognize an important role for food aid in terms of human resource development.[11] Subsequently, Singer's pursued this interest in his work with UNICEF on children in the strategy of development (Singer, 1972; 1986, p. 35) and as a member of a team that studied the impact of the recession of the 1980s on children in developing countries (UNICEF, 1984). It also related to his concern with the ethics of aid. He considered that the moral case for aid was strengthened by concentration on vulnerable groups, particularly children, but also people living in abject poverty in the poorest countries and refugees and displaced persons in man-made emergencies. He considered that improved targeting of aid on these poverty groups was 'the most important item' on the aid agenda for those advocating aid on moral grounds (Singer, 1984b).

Singer set out his view extensively in a major paper on the role of food aid in promoting the welfare of children in developing countries (Singer and Longhurst, 1986). He concluded that with effective design and management, food aid could bring real benefits to children. Children were, almost by definition, always poorer than the average adult in developing countries. But mainly because large family size was an important element in poverty, and family size was also a negative function of educational and income levels, there were added social difficulties to realizing the needs of children in intra-household food distribution. The special characteristics of food aid as a form of development assistance was of particular relevance to children. These included its fungibility as a resource, the speed with which it could be committed, and its political acceptability as aid by both donors and recipients. Food aid had greater flexibility than other forms of aid in circumventing the barriers of reaching children, particularly if provided to women who had greater control of the use of food than cash in the household and a high propensity for child welfare. But food aid alone could not be expected to have significant benefits unless combined with other inputs related to health, education and living environments.

A particularly dangerous result of the rapid and radical economic adjustment measures inflicted on developing countries by external and internal pressures in the face of economic recession was to force them to concentrate on very short-term actions. Provision for children was, in economic terms, a long-run investment to which a country struggling for survival found it difficult to assign proper priority. Keynes' dictum that 'in the long run we are all dead' acquired a pungent meaning for countries in an adjustment crisis. The pressures to sacrifice long-term investment in human capital were strengthened by the fact that the negative effects on child development remained invisible in the absence of appropriate data, monitoring and evaluation, and would only be fully felt at some time in the future. The most vulnerable groups were least able to make their interests and needs felt in domestic and international discussions on adjustment and economic strategies, which focused largely on obtaining a financial seal of approval. But they should also have a 'human seal of approval' so as to bring about what came to be called 'Adjustment with a Human Face' (Cornia *et al.*, 1987). Within such a macroeconomic framework, it was preferable that additional resources (including food aid) should be provided in conjunction with, and as an integral part of, the adjustment process rather than as a result of separate and unrelated discussions carried out during or after adjustment negotiations before the human damage was done.

Structural adjustment and economic reform

It was a natural progression that took Singer from his concerns for children, particularly in the context of economic recession, to a wider interest in the role of food aid in structural adjustment and economic reform and the effects on poor households and communities, particularly in sub-Saharan Africa (Shaw and Singer, 1988; Singer, 1990a, 1991b). Singer was especially critical of the structural adjustment programmes of the IMF and the World Bank and the social costs they brought to poor people in developing countries. To take an extreme example, Singer argued that if malnutrition among young children increased and led to irreversible loss of physical and mental capacity, this could in no sense be described as 'laying the foundations for viable future economic growth', the purported reason for adjustment programmes.

Singer saw that mutual benefits could be forthcoming from an association of food aid with adjustment programmes. The adjustment process could be strengthened while food aid provided within the adjustment framework could be more effective. But this did not imply that food aid could be used like some kind of 'magic dust' to work wonders and overcome the mistakes and errors of badly-designed adjustment programmes. However, food aid did have special characteristics which were particularly appropriate for addressing the macroeconomic difficulties of developing countries and the microeconomic concerns of the poor in those countries by counter-balancing the tendency for adjustment programmes to be unduly austere and contractionist, rather than expansionist. But emphasis on the protection of vulnerable groups against 'austerity' should not be taken as support for a purely 'corrective' function of food aid under which an adjustment agreement is first negotiated, and then food aid is rushed in as special hardships became apparent. Rather, food aid should be included as a resource, both generally and with specific functions, in adjustment agreements from the very beginning.

Singer identified a number of contributions that food aid could make to structural adjustment. These included: contributing to overall available resources, to cushion the austerity of the adjustment process; setting free foreign exchange, helping with the stabilization of balance of payments as a necessary preliminary to resumed economic growth; sustaining incomes and employment of the poor, especially during the difficult transition period from retrenchment to resumed growth; protecting the vulnerable from the harsh short-run impact of stabilization and adjustment policies by maintaining essential economic and social services for them during the transition period; reducing budget deficits and inflation, an important element in stabilization and adjustment; helping to provide domestic food stability and food security, an essential political precondition for making adjustment acceptable and viable; supporting essential reform measures and sectoral programmes often related to food production; and helping, through counterpart funds, to provide local finance for projects and programmes within a structural adjustment context. With such a multitude of possible objectives and effects, it was important to be clear about intentions, and to choose the forms of food and financial aid, and other methods of combination, in the light of the main objectives.

Linking relief and development

Singer was an early proponent of linking relief and development strategies and of removing the dichotomy between 'emergency' and 'development' aid (Singer, 1994a; Singer 1996a). This division of external aid into two isolated compartments, each with its own terms, agenda, and operating agencies (even separate units within the same aid agency) had dichotomized what in the real experience of developing countries was not separate, the interrelationship between disasters and development. Singer supported the need for a 'continuum' of action from early warning and prevention of, and preparedness for, disasters to the transition from relief assistance to reconstruction, rehabilitation and development. This linkage, he reasoned, was not a linear but a circular process in which relief assistance supported and protected development and development mitigated the effects of disasters. This applied not only to disasters caused by nature (earthquakes, floods, drought) but also to man-made disasters in which the provision of food and work could help to mitigate, or even prevent the outbreak of, conflict.

Much would be gained, therefore, if the definition of emergency aid was expanded from an immediate, short-term response to a disaster to encompass pre- and post-disaster action in the 'continuum' between relief and development. Conceptually, disasters would no longer be seen in isolation and their effects on development would be taken fully into account. Resources and assistance would be provided for disaster prevention, preparedness and mitigation measures and would not dry up when required for reconstruction and rehabilitation after disasters have occurred, thereby helping the development process. And planning, design and implementation of assistance for both relief and development would be executed by integrated government and aid administrations within common legislative and executive procedures and financial provisions.

Intellectual investment and the disincentive controversy

Intellectual investment in the subject has been less than might be expected given the magnitude of food aid that has been provided. With notable exceptions, development economists have tended to avoid the subject, or came to it with a preconceived dislike, largely because it was perceived as surplus disposal as opposed to development assistance. The issues were blurred by participants in the policy debate who produced populist literature on the world food problem that emphasized philosophical and moral arguments and the responsibility of developed countries to 'feed the hungry-poor' (Ruttan, 1996, p. 187).

In the latter part of the 1970s, Singer, in co-operation with others, clearly revealed the contradictions in the economics literature on food aid (Isenman and Singer, 1977). Singer observed that many economists appeared to view food aid and non-food aid from 'remarkably different perspectives'. Most economists seemed to believe that aid recipients should use non-food aid to increase investment, employment and output in accordance with a well-thought-out development plan and/or signals provided by market forces. They would be horrified if the aid were used instead for short-term consumption increases or for low-priority development projects with uncertain impact. Yet, paradoxically, because of concern about disincentives and a lack of sufficient emphasis on how food aid could in fact add to employment and investment (and, perhaps, because of the particular association of food with basic human needs), many of these same economists urged that food aid virtually be required to be used for short-term consumption or for *ad hoc* 'additional' projects not included as top priority in development plans. At the same time, food aid was criticized because it benefited consumption instead of investment. While it was inconsistent to insist, implicitly, that food aid not be used for investment and to criticize food aid for not contributing to investment, both these views, each apparently reasonably derived from valid policy concerns, were well-established in the 'conventional wisdom' of food aid. Singer pointed out that increased consumption, when it meant, for example, improving nutritional levels of pre-school children or alleviating near-starvation among adults, could have a bigger impact on future output than a good deal of what was included under the accounting category of 'investment'. But the justification for food aid need not lie solely or primarily in such humanitarian consumption uses. Food aid, balanced with non-food aid, could also contribute to increases in investment, employment and output.

Singer illustrated his arguments by reviewing some of the analytical issues and literature relevant to the concern about the potential disincentive effects and risks of food aid, which he shared, with particular reference to the case of India, which had been one of the largest recipient of food aid. The disincentive argument ran as follows: increases in food supplies brought about by food aid depressed prices received by farmers and caused or supported inadequate agricultural policies by recipient governments, which together led to decreases in food production. (Food aid also disrupted agricultural trade, particularly of exporting developing countries). The stress on employment and more equal income distribution, with its attendant emphasis on agricultural and rural development, served to sharpen criticism of food aid. Many studies and policy discussions either dismissed, or missed entirely, the other purposes of food aid, as if it were to be judged solely on the basis of its contribution to food production. Other, somewhat overlapping, purposes included: improving the nutritional status of the hungry poor by increasing food supplies and containing food prices; directly and indirectly financing specific labour-intensive, development projects; building up food stocks for emergency and price stabilization purposes; and easing a major constraint on growth in output and employment by augmenting food supplies at a time of increasing demand, thereby containing inflation.[12]

A sizable proportion of total development aid could therefore be in the form of food aid without a significant cost in the efficiency of aid or in incentives for domestic agriculture. The uses of food aid flowed from its role in adding to a recipient country's import capacity. Since food aid was doubly-tied (to a specific set of commodities and often to specific uses), it was less valuable to the recipient in carrying out its development plans than an equal amount of unrestricted financial aid, except where the commodities imported and specified domestic uses corresponded to what the recipient would have done with unrestricted aid. What made food aid a subject worthy of special consideration was that it was partly additional in the sense that financial aid would not be decreased were it to be increased. There were a number of factors which made food aid at least partly additional. These included: a feeling among the general public and legislatures in donor countries that feeding the destitute, avoiding starvation and improving nutritional standards in developing countries should have priority as a form of development co-operation; political support for maintaining domestic agricultural protectionist policies in donor countries; and the relatively high capital cost of food storage, which meant that food aid from major donors was expected to remain at least partly additional, although this might not be true for particular bilateral donors.[13]

Singer examined both the price and policy effects of food aid on Indian agricultural production.[14] The depressing effect on prices was found to be much less than some analysts had expected, partly because food aid was used to increase government food distribution which, being subsidized, added to net food-grain demand. The large-scale food aid supplied by the United States should have been phased in more gradually (by stockpiling more and distributing less), but the short-term price effect on food production was found to be very limited, the medium-term income and price effect on food production (taking account of the effect of food aid in growth) was probably positive, and the medium-term effect on overall output, employment and nutrition (as distinct from foodgrain production only) was strongly positive.

Regarding the policy effects of food aid, Singer distinguished between criticism of the policy effect of aid and criticism of policies supported by aid but caused by political and economic factors far more powerful than aid. In the Indian case, the political and economic factors which up to the middle of the 1960s caused the preference for heavy industry over agriculture were far more powerful than food aid which, at most, played a supportive role. When there was a reorientation of Indian priorities toward agriculture after the mid-1960s, food aid was used to help the process not only by saving foreign exchange that would have had to have been spent on commercial imports but by directing a significant part of the fund generated from the sale of food aid commodities for investment in the infrastucture needed for the Green Revolution that resulted in a spectacular growth in Indian food production by raising crop yields through irrigation, technological progress and the use of high-yielding varieties of seed. This, in turn, required a policy commitment on the part of the Indian government and considerable resources, which food aid helped to provide.

The Indian example served to illustrate several general points about food aid. Food aid could be used to support both 'good' and 'bad' agricultural policies. It would be quite unrealistic for either critics or proponents of food aid (or other forms of aid) to take it for granted that it was necessarily a major or determining cause of such policies. If a country had a strong commitment to agriculture, and the political will and sound policies to carry out that commitment, it was likely to use food aid (and other forms of aid) in ways that supported its agricultural development effort. If not, food aid (and other aid) would be used to further whatever alternative economic objectives the government wished to pursue. Singer observed there had also been a rather paradoxical difference in the conventional views of the disincentive effects in recipient policy of food aid and non-food aid. Non-food aid to India was far larger than food aid and went primarily to support industry and related infrastructure. It would therefore be inconsistent to criticize food aid to India (or any country) on grounds that it led to underemphasis on agriculture in relation to industry unless the same criticism was directed to non-food aid. Singer concluded that it would be quite reasonable for donors and recipients to discuss mutual concerns about possible disincentive effects of large food aid programmes and what might be done about them. There might be advantages in carrying out such discussions under the aegis of a multilateral agency or a multi-donor consultative group, rather than on a bilateral basis.

Aid conditionality

Subsequently, Singer took on the controversial subject of aid conditionality (Singer, 1994b, 1995; Raffer and Singer, 1996, pp. 153–80). He explained the reasons behind the increasing trend for donors to put conditions on the assistance they provided through programme as well as project aid. First, was the concept of fungibility. Donors and aid organizations realized that if assistance was provided for a high-priority project, this set free the recipient government's own resources which would otherwise have gone into that project. The resources thus freed would then finance some other project – which could be military expenditure, additional salaries for high-ranking civil servants, and so on. Thus, in effect, the aid provided would finance projects which had not been examined and of which the aid donor was not even aware.

Secondly, experience showed that the success or failure of projects depended not only, or even mainly, on the virtues of the project itself but rather on the general efficiency of the recipient government and its policies. As Singer put it:

> As the rising tide lifts all boats, so a dynamic and growing economy can absorb and turn to advantage even a doubtful project and vice versa: where the economy is stagnant and macroeconomic policies counterproductive, even the best designed project will fail to yield its expected benefits and will be engulfed in the general failure (Raffer and Singer, 1996).

Projects were not carried out in a policy vacuum, hence project lending became more policy conditional and has shifted over to programme lending.

Thirdly, was a general undermining of the concept of sovereignty of developing countries on which the United Nations charter is based, which originally governed bilateral and multilateral aid, including the operations of the IMF and the World Bank (UN, 1945).[15] Singer attributed the undermining of the concept of sovereignty partly to the collapse of the Organization of Petroleum Exporting Countries (OPEC) and the build up of the debt burden for most developing countries. The dependence and weak international position of developing countries that followed (and also the deteriorating terms of trade) was combined with increasing scepticism about the nature and role of governments in the South. This was part of the neoclassical paradigm that came to be known as the 'Washington consensus', which became dominant in the 1980s. Previously, governments were supposed to be the Platonic guardians and best judges of national interest and aid was supposed to help them in their tasks. Later, in a 'remarkable reversal', governments were depicted as centres of corruption, policy failures, rent seekers and so on, while donors and aid agencies acquired a self-confident status of being in possession of the secrets of 'good governance' and the ability to sort out the 'good boys' from the bad. Conditionality became the instrument to discipline 'bad boys' and convert them into 'good boys', based on the firm (and often misplaced) conviction that donors and aid organizations knew what was best for recipient countries and that they had got hold of the 'sacred truth', that is the market-ruled principles ('basics') of neoclassical economics.

Criticism of the 'Washington consensus' revolved around the question of 'ownership' and the assumption of donors and aid organizations that they 'knew the right answers' to developing countries' problems. But if conditionality was imposed on countries against their wishes and their own judgement of what was best for them, they were unlikely to persevere with the aid programmes and fulfill all the conditions. Criticism also stemmed from what became known as the 'fallacy of composition'. Conditionality based on a common ideology or theory failed to make sufficient allowance for different circumstances, political systems, objectives and cultures. Singer observed that there were signs that the pendulum was swinging back from the 'Washington consensus' to something like a compromise with the earlier 'Keynesian consensus' but also embodying new concerns, including good governance, democracy and accountability and the environment, poverty reduction, human development and human rights. But the 'rhetoric was running far ahead of reality, as a comparison of the per capital ODA [Official Development Aid] received by democratic and authoritarian regimes shows' (UNDP, 1994, p. 76). Applying these aid conditions has proved to be difficult, and often contradictory, as double standards have been applied. Cutting off aid because people live in a country whose government violates the principles of conditionality amounted to punishing the population for the action of their government, and would affect those groups already suffering repression further deteriorating their lot. Briefly put, 'it may matter less to which country aid was given than to whom within that country'.

Redefining food aid in a liberalizing global economy

Singer recognized that the conclusion of the GATT Uruguay round of multilateral trade negotiations in 1994, the signing and ratification of the Final Act, and the setting up of the World Trade Organization (WTO) provided a major opportunity for establishing a new food aid regime within a liberalizing global economy (Singer, 1996c; Shaw and Singer, 1995). At the outset, this raised some basic questions including what should constitute food aid. Should it encompass the large volume of transactions in the 'grey area' between food aid, as defined under the FAO *Principles of Surplus Disposal*, and statistically recorded, and commercial trade in food commodities?

Singer pointed to the conceptual and statistical 'quagmire' in food aid. Under the present statistical convention, food aid is distinguished from food trade or commercial transactions by an element of concessionality. The Development Assistance Committee (DAC) of the Organisation for Economic Co-operation and Development (OECD), which comprises the major donor countries, agreed on a benchmark of 25 per cent below the commercial price as an arbitrary definition of the grant element in ODA. But, some immediate problems have arisen for food aid. As Singer pointed out, the international price of food is not a textbook free-market price with a significant reference function. The policies of subsidizing domestic agriculture in the major industrial countries have resulted in surpluses and surplus capacities, which have enabled and induced them to tie their aid to food. They have also depressed the commercial price of food in international trade. Hence, the 25 per cent concessionality limit that might define food aid is not 25 per cent off a truly free-market price, but 25 per cent off a world price that is itself at a discount to what commercial prices would be in a free, fully-liberalized market. If it were, many more transactions would come to be defined as 'food aid'.

Singer observed that a large part of so-called food 'trade' did not take place as straight market transactions at international prices, but is conducted through a labyrinth of various forms of bilateral agreement that provide discounts from the 'commercial' international price (itself reduced by overhanging surpluses and domestic production subsidies) in many direct and indirect ways. This made it difficult to quantify globally such transactions as export credits, guarantee and market enhancement programmes, and linkages with other trade concessions or with financial aid.[16]

Under the Final Act, export subsidies and domestic agricultural support measures are to be reduced partially and gradually. However, it is doubtful whether these reductions will catch all the hidden and indirect subsidies involved. If all the benefits from lowered prices were passed on to food-importing developing countries, Singer estimated that food aid would be approximately doubled compared to the 'statistical' food aid figure. With more radical assumptions, moving from partial to full market liberalization, and defining any discount from the much higher fully liberalized commercial international free market price for food commodities as 'food aid', the true volume of food aid thus broadly defined would be further increased.

However, as Singer pointed out, food aid implicit in the artificial lowering of international food prices and trade discounts, which he referred to as the food aid that 'dares not speak its name', was not targeted on the food-needy but was 'broadly and blindly' given across the board to all commercial importers, regardless of need, mainly for donor short-run political and commercial, market protection and penetration, purposes. The really needy, almost by definition, were not commercial importers or purchasers.

Singer identified other transactions which, in economic effect, amounted to food aid 'with different shades of grey'. As he put it, 'Once we cross the Rubicon into the "grey area", there are no obvious landmarks to tell us where to stop'. He questioned what shade of grey was the programme and emergency aid provided to the new republics of the former Soviet Union and Yugoslavia. Some, at least, of financial aid, especially that provided for structural-adjustment lending programmes, covered balance of payments deficits, thus enabling countries to acquire additional imports. Insofar as these imports consisted of food, it could be considered to be 'food aid'. In addition, the special facilities of the International Monetary Fund (IMF) used to finance food imports should, in reality, be seen as aid for food, or 'food aid'.[17] The food aid 'with different shades of grey' were not included in the statistics on food aid and demonstrated that a broader definition of food aid was required.

However, Singer noted that there was a countervailing element where the current definition of food aid could be said to be excessively wide. Part of the programme food aid that replaced commercial imports represented, in effect, financial aid in that it set foreign exchange free. The same could be said to apply to countries receiving emergency food aid for many years continuously, although in their case it was less likely that commercial imports could have been afforded. Another dimension in which food aid statistics may be overstated related to its value. Donors tended to value their food aid contributions at their budget costs, but these costs were inflated by the subsidies and high domestic prices involved in their own agricultural policies. Yet another possible overvaluation of food aid related to triangular transactions and local purchase whereby food commodities were procured in developing countries to be used as food aid. It was by no means clear how these transactions should appear in aid statistics. If a donor country, for example, bought maize in a developing country to be used as food aid in another developing country, the receiving country was designated as the food aid recipi-ent country. But the case could alternatively be presented as donor-financed trade between the two developing countries, which could result in double-counting. What should it be? To count it only as food aid might understate the financial aid provided: to count it as financial aid ran the opposite risk.

Singer considered that this last example illustrated that the real 'quagmire' was conceptual rather than statistical. When dealing with subsidized and financially-promoted trade, what part was 'trade' and what part 'aid'? What is, or should be, the grant element that distin-guishes trade from aid? And where is the borderline between finan-cial and food aid? The more the definition of food aid was broadened, the more it became clear that food aid must be understood and handled not in isolation, as in the past, but as an element in world food security and trade, and co-ordinated with financial and techn-ical assistance. A shift towards a broader conception of food aid would be all the more necessary as one of the outcomes of the GATT Uruguay round and the implementation of the Final Act. It would also be necessary as the historical links of food aid with surplus disposal and the resulting popularity of food aid, especially among the farming communities in the major food-exporting devel-oped countries, were weakened as a result of the liberalization of agricultural policy.

While the demand for food aid was likely to increase as a result of the higher cost of commercial food imports brought about by the

GATT Uruguay round, the supply of food aid was threatened by a reduction of surpluses and higher food prices, which would mean less volume of food aid for given budgetary allocations. According to the food aid provisions of the Final Act, a balance has to be found between these two forces by maintaining food aid at an 'adequate' level, presumably in volume terms, to offset fluctuations in production and prices.

Singer saw cutting the historical links between surpluses and food aid as a 'blessing in disguise'. This link had always been a flawed motivation for food aid, leading to major tensions between donors' domestic agricultural interests and the developmental needs of developing countries, and to the controversy and criticisms surrounding food aid. Much had been made of the possible disincentive effects of food aid on policy makers and producers in food aid recipient countries. Less had been heard about the disincentives created by policy-makers in the developed countries and the continuation of harmful agricultural policies on the grounds that some of the resulting surpluses could be disposed of as food aid. If, as a result if the GATT Uruguay round, the hidden food aid that, as Singer put it, 'dares not speak its name', was forced out into the open and placed under the disciplines of food aid established under the Final Act, it could then be purposefully targeted on developmental and humanitarian concerns for needy countries and people, rather than short-run political and commercial objectives. This would not only help to clear up the conceptual and statistical quagmire in food aid but, more importantly, would be a major step in dealing with the problem of hunger and, by extension, with the reduction of poverty in the developing world.

Singer noted that restrictive business practices, included in the 1948 Havana Charter of the abortive International Trade Organization, which Keynes had proposed but which was not ratified by the United States and other governments, are not included in the mandate of the WTO. Thus, there is no bar on multilateral corporations exercising their power in international trade to increase international prices even more than a reduction in supply brought about by the GATT Uruguay round would cause. Restrictive business practices are to be dealt with separately in the United Nations system, mainly by the United Nations Conference on Trade and Development (UNCTAD), but given the lack of financial and political support, this may not be effective. Singer therefore suggested that there was a definite need for a safety-net for the least-developed and net food-importing developing countries. Such a safety-net could either require financial assistance, which would involve the Bretton Woods institutions; or food aid, when the WFP would be involved; or may be trade-related, when it would require discussion in the WTO; or be generally related to global governance, when the UN would be concerned. In many cases, a mixture of all these solutions would probably be called into play, which would require co-ordinated action.

Development tool or obstacle?: responding to the critics

Singer is well-aware of the shortcomings and limitations of food aid, which he helped to reveal. Equally, he is concerned with the mistaken and misguided criticisms to which food aid is subjected, and has played an active role in responding to the critics (Singer, 1987, 1988, 1990b; Clay and Singer, 1983; Raffer and Singer, 1996, pp. 80–7). Published in 1987, his book on food aid (with John Wood and Tony Jennings) remains the best balanced account of food aid (Singer *et al.*, 1987).

Food aid has been criticized as being 'second-class' aid and an inferior substitute for financial aid. Singer recognized that genuinely untied financial aid was preferable to food aid. But most financial aid was tied, explicitly or implicitly, and when tied to food imports (aid for food) was better than financial aid tied to dubiously required high-priced capital goods or to armaments. Singer questioned whether a distinction could be made between financial and food aid. Financial aid was in fact the first step in the aid process. The next step was to convert the money provided into development goods and services, which raised a host of issues and problems, such as the sources of origin of the aid goods, procurement and utilization. In that sense, all aid was commodity aid. Food aid, properly executed, could be commended for simplifying procedures by cutting out the first or financial stage of the transaction and coming directly to the substantive second stage of commodity transfer.

There were other reasons for doubting whether there was a real distinction between financial and food aid and to allege that food aid was inferior. It was best, therefore, to judge food aid on its own merits rather than compare it with the costs and benefits of financial aid.

Where food aid substituted for commercial food imports, it saved the recipient government the foreign exchange that would have been spent. Thus, the food aid was directly equivalent to financial aid and, moreover, financial aid unconditionally available to the recipient government. Where food aid was monetized (sold) in the recipient country, this further blurred the borderline between financial and food aid.

Where food aid was additional to financial aid, the comparison was superfluous. There were political and commercial as well as humanitarian and legal reasons (such as international commitments under the Food Aid Convention or to the European Union's common food aid programme) which made donors inclined to give food aid where they would not give an equivalent amount of financial aid. Food aid, if properly targeted, had the advantage of directly addressing the needs of poor, food-insecure people and of being more gender-friendly to women, and thus their children. A higher proportion of food aid went to the poorer developing countries and benefited poor people than financial aid.

The potential disincentive effect of food aid on agricultural production in developing countries through adverse policy and price effects have been at the 'storm-centre' of the food aid debate. Concerning the policy effect, Singer questioned whether developing countries would, in the absence of food aid, have shown less 'urban bias' and done more to increase their own food production. The forces making for 'urban bias' were deeper and went much beyond the existence of food aid. It could even be argued that without food aid governments would squeeze their local farmers even harder to extract surpluses for the growing urban population. Conversely, part of the food constraint relaxed by food aid could allow governments to relax the monopoly grip of parastatal marketing organizations and permit farmers to sell their surplus food at free-market prices.

Singer observed that criticism of developing countries for neglecting their own food production, and for urban bias, did not come well from countries which themselves had shown such distortions and extreme forms of 'rural bias' in their own agricultural policies. Structural adjustment should be a two-way business. In the overall picture, the 'disincentive' due to low international food prices (in turn due to overhanging surpluses resulting from the European Union's Common Agricultural Policy (CAP) and similar protectionist policies in other major food-exporting developed countries), which encouraged imports, was more important than any disincentives due to food aid. Nor did such criticism come well from neo-liberal critics who preach the virtues of 'outward orientation' for developing countries. Replacing food imports by domestic production was an act of import substitution. The use of land for export crops rather than food for domestic consumption was the result of 'outward orientation' and the pressure to earn foreign exchange to repay increasing debts.

Food aid provided plenty of opportunity for those governments keen to promote their own food production to do so. Where food aid replaced commercial imports, the foreign exchange released could be used to import the inputs required to increase agricultural production and to produce the consumption goods that farmers need as an inducement to sell surplus food. Governments could also use the revenue derived from food aid sales for the promotion of domestic agriculture. Relaxation of the food constraint provided by food aid also enabled the recipient government to be more expansionist in its general policies. This, depending on the pattern of expansion, would increase the demand for local food and hence raise prices.

Where a government could not be trusted to use the relaxation of the food constraint in a manner favourable to domestic food production, donors could provide food aid conditional upon a shift of policy in that direction. This could be done in a number of ways, for example, by providing food aid: directly for agricultural purposes; as part of a structural adjustment programme; linked with an agreed food strategy; or through the use of counterpart funds in the agricultural and rural sectors.

Singer found the idea that the governments of developing countries eagerly seize on food aid as an opportunity to neglect domestic agricultural production hardly plausible politically. Developing countries were keen to establish and safeguard their national sovereignty. Dependency on food imports, and specifically on food aid, was incompatible with this political priority objective. This related to another criticism of food aid as a source of fiscal disincentives. The critics argued that food aid supplied in bulk for local sale provided governments with 'easy revenue'. This could tempt governments into relaxing their efforts to mobilize domestic savings through taxation. There was an inconsistency in this criticism, if at all well-founded. To the extent that the critics were preaching liberalization, greater reliance on the market, and limitation of the public sector as recipes for development, it could be expected that they would welcome this effect of food aid, namely, that it reduced the burden of taxation and enlarged the resources at the disposal of the private sector. Moreover, insofar as a relaxation of the tax grip reduced the tax burden on farmers and the rural sector, it could only help the objective of promoting local agricultural production.

Singer showed that a fall in domestic food prices as a result of food aid and the resultant disincentive to increased food production was by no means 'pre-ordained'. A recipient government could distribute the additional food to targeted groups free or at low or subsidized prices while maintaining or even raising prices for local producers. The idea of an automatic disincentive effect of food aid because it causes low domestic prices was based on the assumption of a single and unified market price applying to consumers and producers. However, as with the EU and the USA, food prices in most developing countries were subject to active government intervention. It was quite possible for governments in food aid recipient countries to operate a dual price system with low prices for consumers, or selected groups, and higher prices for producers. The fiscal resources to cover a resulting deficit could be obtained from the revenue derived from food aid sales.

An important qualification was that any reduced demand for locally produced food caused by the arrival of food aid from abroad could and should be offset by additional demand resulting from the additional incomes created by food-aid-induced and accelerated development. Such additional development would benefit local food producers by creating extra demand for food and maintaining or strengthening food prices. Economic history and cross-country analysis had shown that the major past recipients of food aid managed to use large-scale food aid as a basis for vigorous development of their domestic agriculture and had subsequently graduated out of food aid.

Another qualification to the disincentive effect arose from what Singer called 'the structure of food production' in developing countries. Where food was produced from subsistence farming, it would not be affected by any possible impact of food aid on local prices (except through subsistence transactions). Where food was produced by small-scale producers who supplied a marketable surplus in order to cover production and consumption needs and non-food related expenses, a fall in prices could have the effect of increasing marketable surpluses rather than reducing them. If farmers reduced the production of a given crop affected by lower prices because of food aid, land would be free to produce other crops. Such crop-diversification could be to the advantage of local farmers and the local economy. To assume that a lower price meant less output and higher price more production was generally an oversimplified application of neo-classical textbook analysis of a perfect capitalist market and was not applicable to the more complex and segmented food markets of developing countries. Incentives for farmers were governed by a spectrum of factors going well-beyond prices alone. 'Getting prices right' was important but not enough: the more expert advice was 'getting elasticities right'. Other types of neglect or discrimination were often more important than poor domestic terms of trade (prices obtained versus prices paid) of local food producers, as distinct from export crops, in causing a decline in local food production. The response of farmers was determined not by prices as such but by what they could buy with the price obtained. If the additional resources represented by food aid were used for additional imports or domestic production of, say, fertilizer, and its subsidized distribution to farmers, the profit margin for local food producers could be maintained or improved even if local food prices fell. The same applied to the availability of consumption goods and their accessibility in rural areas. If the revenue from food aid was used for that purpose, it could have a more powerful incentive to farmers to increase production and marketed surpluses than a higher price.

Finally, Singer responded to other criticisms of food aid, namely, that: it distorted consumption patterns; and it fostered urbanization and population growth. Food aid could have positive or negative effects on diets in recipient countries. It could lead to a taste for expensive foods that cost more per unit of energy and that could not be produced locally. Conversely, it could lead to a more efficient diet. Food habits were not immutable and could be changed by many factors, such as government import and pricing policies, changes in the relative prices of food commodities, increasing income, transport and logistical improvements, migration to urban areas, changes in fuel costs and women's participation in income-earning activities outside the home. To the extent that food aid substituted for imports which would have occurred anyway, the cause of changes in consumption habits must lie elsewhere (Cassen, 1986, p. 160). Moreover, the criticism would not apply to food aid provided through triangular transactions, local purchase and exchange arrangements under which the staple foods of the developing countries were supplied as food aid.

Similarly, many factors are at work which have led to increasing urbanization and population growth. Family size is affected by a number of socio-cultural factors but has been by no means as irrational or biologically determined as many had thought in the past. In very poor countries and communities, children, who become net positive economic assets at a young age, have been the best insurance against a disastrous reduction in family earnings through disability or old age. Contrary to the Malthusian view, birth rates among the poor have gone down, not up, as their standard of living (which in the poorest countries meant initially their standard of eating) has risen (Singer, 1976). While development led to a transitional period of sharply lower death rates before birth rates fell, the sooner and faster the death rate declined so too would the birth rate. Where food aid made a positive contribution to employment, nutrition, and other aspects of the development process, it could be said to be making a positive contribution to reducing population growth irrespective of whether a country had an official and effective family-planning programme.

In conclusion, Singer recognized that as with all forms of aid, the disincentive effects of food aid were possible and should be carefully guarded against, but they were by no means unavoidable, and were certainly not automatic. As with all aid, it depended on the policy environment and the precise ways in which food aid was used. Food aid provided an opportunity to promote growth and reduce poverty in developing countries. This opportunity may be taken or it may be wasted. That depended on the way food aid was given and the way in which it was absorbed. It depended on the purposes of the donor countries and the policies and efficiency of the recipients. Only careful analysis of situations in specific countries at specific periods of time could tell whether disincentive effects had occurred and whether such effects had been compensated, or overcompensated, for by the developmental benefits of food aid.

The main answer to the 'disincentive critics' was that they conducted the food aid debate in an unduly narrow framework. The direct or static impact of the arrival of food aid on markets and prices was only the first step in a chain of events which food aid could set in motion. By removing either a food or foreign-exchange or government finance bottleneck, food aid could set in motion a cumulative process of economic expansion which could lead to increased demand for local food. Thus, the immediate price disincentive on which the critics concentrated was only what Singer referred to as 'the left hook of a J-curve'. However, this was only plausible where food aid was a sufficiently significant factor.

The critics of food aid often omitted to consider the potential benefits as an offset to the disincentive effects which they emphasized. Similarly, the advocates of food aid could not have it both ways: just as the disincentive effects of food aid were potential rather then inevitable or automatic, the same applied to its potential developmental benefits. This placed a good deal of emphasis on the quality of planning and policies for development in food aid recipient countries, whether in the sense of overall macroeconomic policy or of microeconomic efficiency in project formulation, design and execution. The voice of the critics of food aid had been too loud and strident and the voice of the defenders too muted. The defenders of food aid should listen carefully to the critics and vice versa. There should be a case-by-case analysis, jointly by recipients and donors, which should include the range of factors relevant to the risks and opportunities that food aid afforded.

Future directions

Singer identified certain lines of possible future developments in the field of food aid (Singer *et al.*, 1987, pp. 193–205; Raffer and Singer, 1996, pp. 85–7). One possible, and desirable, development was to use food aid to solve some of the intractable problems of the debt burden and balance of payments difficulties of developing countries. The methods of adjustment and conditionality of IMF and World Bank structural-adjustment lending programmes had been generally criticized as being too harsh and having undesirable social consequences, and even being counterproductive in undermining, rather than promoting, future economic growth, calling for 'adjustment with a human face' (Cornia *et al.*, 1987). It has also been recognized that in return for the painful adjustments expected from developing countries, they should be given a greater *quid pro quo* in terms of additional resources. Food aid in structural adjustment lending had caught the attention of those concerned. It could have the special advantage of representing both additional resources to ease adjustment and also of being capable of providing particular relief for vulnerable groups, such as children, landless rural people, unemployed and other victims of 'tough' adjustments policies.

A second desirable and likely development was the increasing concentration of food aid on sub-Saharan Africa (Singer, 1990a). The net food import needs of the sub-region have rapidly increased and have been projected to increase further. Per capita food production has fallen and its revival will be a long-term business, calling for additional aid, including food aid. At the same time, sub-Saharan Africa has carried the heaviest debt burden and is the most affected by the weaknesses in primary commodity prices.

Thirdly, and related to a concentration on sub-Saharan Africa, there was a developing consensus on a broader definition of emergency to include disaster prevention and preparedness at one end, and reconstruction and rehabilitation after disasters at the other. As emergency aid represents an uncontroversial aspect of food aid, this could provide a basis for substantial additions to food aid flows, which in turn would assist the development process. The insight that famine was often caused by a breakdown of incomes or other 'entitlements' providing access to food (Sen, 1981), should further support such protective and non-controversial extensions of food aid. For example, rural public works schemes supported by food aid, or by the proceeds from food aid sales, could be well-designed to maintain rural incomes. They could also be planned so as to cover specifically the 'hungry months' before the harvest and could be stepped up at times of crop failure.

Another line could be the wider use of the potential of monetization. Food aid commodities could be sold in urban areas and the revenue used for rural investment, strengthening the demand for food. Monetization could also help to finance the non-food costs of food aid supported programmes such as emergency food aid, food-for-work schemes and nutrition improvement programmes for mothers and children. All these projects require financial as well as food resources but some food aid agencies, such as the United Nations World Food Programme, suffer from cash shortages. A related desirable development would be better linkage and combinations of financial and food aid, including better co-operation among the aid agencies concerned.

Greater use should be made of the mechanisms and modalities that resulted in the procurement of food commodities in the developing countries themselves for use as food aid. A number of developing countries had exportable food surpluses. They have been hard hit by the protectionist agricultural policies of the major food exporting developed countries and by the resulting low international food prices. Short of a revision of these protectionist policies, developing country food surpluses should be bought at remunerative prices for use in deficit areas, perhaps in combination with the establishment of regional buffer stocks in which internationally financed regional surpluses could be held under international control. Such an imaginative approach could be supplemented by methods to encourage transfer of surplus food from surplus to deficit regions within developing countries, which would require investment in transport and logistics as well as the encouragement of financing local reserve stocks.

Finally, the governing body of WFP should play a more effective role in co-ordinating the policies and programme and establishing institutional coherence among all those involved in food aid than it has done in the past. By providing a multilateral framework, food aid from all sources could be provided coherently and conflict and duplication could be avoided. Singer concluded that as long as food aid was badly administered by donors and/or recipients, it could have no real benefits. One basic pre-condition was the creation of a framework on the part of donors, ideally including a revision of their protectionist policies, that enabled 'food aid to be given for the right reasons to the right countries in the right way'. Similar improvements were necessary on the recipients' side: food aid should be increasingly devoted to two essential purposes, 'to reduce poverty and to help develop domestic food production'. Such were the challenges – and the opportunities – of food aid.

Notes

1   Colleagues in the 'food aid cluster' and others at IDS and elsewhere who have collaborated with Singer on food aid issues include: Edward Clay, Reginald Green, Paul Isenman, Tony Jennings, Richard Jolly, Richard Long-

hurst, Simon Maxwell, Kunibert Raffer, Sumit Roy, Bernard Schaffer, John Shaw, Chris Stevens and John Wood, who have become authorities on food aid and related subjects in their own right.

2   For an account of the history of IDA and its adoption by the World Bank, see Mason and Asher (1973), pp. 295–334; Kapur *et al.* (1997), pp. 1119–60; and Shaw (1998b).

3   Confirmed in a personal communication from Singer of 26 January 1996.

4   Singer was involved in the creation of multilateral facilities for both food aid (WFP) and pre-investment financing (UN Expanded Program for Technical Assistance and the UN Special Fund). The latter two UN bodies were amalgamated in 1965 to form the United Nations Development Programme (UNDP). See Singer (1964b).

5   The classical case of Singer's 'dissenting view' was the terms of trade controversy and the distribution of gains between investing and borrowing countries(Singer, 1950; 1984a).

6   The members of the expert group were: Dr M. R. Benedict, Professor of Agricultural Economics, University of California at Berkeley, United States; Dr J. Figueres, ex-president of the Republic of Costa Rica; Dr V. K. R. V. Rao, ex-vice-chancellor, University of Delhi, India, Director of the New Delhi Institute of Economic Growth, and a former PhD student with Singer at Cambridge University, England; Dr P. N. Rosenstein-Roden, Professor of Economics, Massachusetts Institute of Technology, United States; and Dr H. W. Singer, who was designated as Principal Officer, Office of the Under-Secretary for Economic and Social Affairs, United Nations, New York.

7   Between 1948 and 1952, $13.5 billion of aid was provided by the United States (3 per cent of its annual GNP for four consecutive years), almost one-third of which consisted of food, feed and fertilizer, to the war-torn countries in Europe after the Second World War in a massive reconstruction effort that involved the largest aid programme in history.

8   Keynes, in his *Proposals for an International Clearing Union* (April 1943), which became a basic document for the establishment of the Bretton Woods system, stated that surpluses should be recycled from strong to weak areas and thus offset the contractionist pressures that might otherwise overwhelm in social disorder the hopes for a better post-war world. Keynes felt that the same miracle that had been performed domestically of using finance as a tool 'for turning stone into bread' should be repeated internationally. Singer suggested that this Keynesian vision also governed the objectives of turning the stone of financial and food surpluses in the industrial world, and of underemployed resources and malnourished children in the Third World, into the bread of human investment in healthier and more productive children (Moggridge, 1992, pp. 721–55; Singer and Longhurst, 1986, p. 33).

9   *The Papers of Adlai E. Stevenson: Vol. VIII. Ambassador to the United Nations 1961–1965* (Boston: Little, Brown & Co., 1979, p. 149).

10 Memorandum to the United States Secretary for Agriculture, Orville Freeman, 21 June 1961 (Secretary's Records Section, Food for Peace Program, File IX, US Department of Agriculture, National Agricultural Library, Beltsville, Maryland, United States).

11 Personal communication 26 January 1996. Scrimshaw reiterated his views in Scrimshaw (1997).

12 Singer suggested that a useful way to visualize the importance of the food constraint to economic development in the developing countries was 'to imagine that the developed-country worker spent two-thirds of his wages on oil products and then to consider what a limit this would put on growth in employment' (Isenman and Singer, 1977, p. 207).

13 Additionality in food aid has been increasingly called into question with the decrease of ODA in real terms and the effect of the GATT Uruguay round and the beginnings of agricultural trade liberalization. However, the uncertain effects of the 1996 'freedom to farm' legislation on United States' agriculture, the postponement of reform of the Common Agricultural Policy and the enlargement of the European Union, and the as yet unfulfilled food aid provisions of the Final Act raise doubts as to whether the rapid fall in statistically recorded food aid in the latter part of the 1990s is a structural or short-run phenomenon.

14 At its height, United States bulk-supply food aid to India under Title I of the PL480 food aid programme between 1964 and 1967 reached over five million tons of cereals a year. At its zenith in 1966, it was over eight million tons, 16 per cent of net Indian food-grain production, 80 per cent of net food imports and 58 per cent of the total public food distribution programme, and more than the total global cereal food aid in 1998 (Isenman and Singer, 1977, p. 231, table A1, Shaw and Clay, 1993, p. 59).

15 The UN Charter (Chapter I, Article 2.7) states: 'Nothing contained in the present Charter shall authorize the United Nations to intervene in matters which are essentially within the domestic jurisdiction of any state or shall require the Members to submit such matters to settlement under the present Charter; but this principle shall not prejudice the application of enforcement measures under Chapter VII of the Charter' [entitled 'Action with Respect to Threats to the Peace, Breaches of the Peace and Acts of Aggression'].

16 In 1993, the value of United States agricultural commodities under credit, guarantee and export enhancement programmes, at $7.5 billion, was almost three times the value of agricultural exports designated as 'food aid' and accounted for 18 per cent of the total value of US agricultural exports (USDA, 1995).

17 The IMF's Compensatory Financing Facility (CCF), established in 1963, was widened to include coverage for balance of payments difficulties caused by excesses in cereal import costs. In 1988, the IMF's Compensatory and Contingency Financing Facility (CCFF) was established to provide timely financial assistance to member countries, particularly primary

commodity exporting countries, that experienced balance of payments difficulties resulting from shortfalls in export earnings or sharp increases in cereal import costs.

References

Arestis, P. and M. Sewyer (eds) (1992) *A Bibliographical Dictionary of Dissenting Economists* (Cheltenham: Edward Elgar).

Cassen, R. H. and Associates (1986) *Does Aid Work?* (Oxford: Oxford University Press).

Clay, E. and H. W. Singer (1982) *Food Aid and Development: The Impact and Effectiveness of Bilateral PL480 Title I-Type Assistance.* AID Program Evaluation Discussion Paper no. 15 (Washington, DC: US Agency for International Development).

—— and D. J. Shaw (eds) (1987) *Poverty, Development and Food. Essays in Honour of H. W. Singer on his 75th Birthday* (Basingstoke and London: Macmillan – now Palgrave).

—— and H. W. Singer (eds) (1983) 'Food As Aid: Food For Thought', *IDS Bulletin*, vol. 14, no. 2, April.

—— and H. W. Singer (1985) *Food Aid and Development: Issues and Evidence. A Survey of the Literature since 1977 on the Role and Impact of Food Aid in Developing Countries.* WFP Occasional Paper no. 3 (Rome: World Food Programme).

Cornia, G. A., R. Jolly and F. Stewart (eds) (!987) *Adjustment With A Human Face. Protecting the Vulnerable and Promoting Growth. A Study by UNICEF.* 2 vols (Oxford: Clarendon Press).

FAO (1946) *Proposals for a World Food Board.* Prepared for Submission to the Second Session of the FAO Conference, Copenhagen, Denmark, 2 September 1946 (Washington, DC: Food and Agriculture Organization of the United Nations).

—— (1954) *Disposal of Agricultural Surpluses. Principles Recommended by the FAO* (Rome: Food and Agriculture Organization of the United Nations). Subsequently revised and expanded in five versions as FAO (1992) *Principles of Surplus Disposal and Consultative Obligations of Member Nations* (Rome: Food and Agriculture Organization of the United Nations).

—— (1955) 'Uses of Agricultural Surpluses to Finance Economic Development in Underdeveloped Countries: A Pilot Study in India', *Commodity Policy Studies no. 6* (Rome: Food and Agriculture Organization of the United Nations).

—— (1961) 'Report on an Expanded Program of Surplus Food Utilization' in FAO, *Development through Food. A Strategy for Surplus Utilization*, FFHC Basic Study no. 2 (Rome: Food and Agriculture Organization of the United Nations, pp. 69–117). Republished in FAO (1985), pp. 223–343.

—— (1985) *Food for Development.* Economic and Social Development Paper no. 34 (Rome: Food and Agriculture Organization of the United Nations).

Hopkins, R. F. (1992) 'Reform in the International Food Aid Regime: The Role of Consensual Knowledge', *International Organization*, vol. 46, no. 1, Winter, pp. 225–64.

Isenman, P. J. and H. W. Singer (1977) 'Food Aid: Disincentive Effects and Their Policy Implications', *Economic Development and Cultural Change*, vol. 25, no. 2, January, pp. 205–37. First published as *IDS Communications no. 116* (Brighton: The Institute for Development Studies, University of Sussex, 1975) and *A. I. D. Discussion Paper no. 31* (Washington, DC: Bureau for Program and Policy Coordination, Agency for International Development, 1975).

Kapur, D., J. P. Lewis and R. Webb (1997) *The World Bank. Its First Half Century.* Vol. 1: History (Washington, DC: The Brookings Institution).

Mason, E. S. and R. E. Asher (1973) *The World Bank Since Bretton Woods* (Washington, DC: The Brookings Institution).

Maxwell, S. J. and H. W. Singer (1979) 'Food Aid to Developing Countries: A Survey', *World Development*, vol. 7, no. 3, pp. 225–47.

Moggridge, D. E. (1992) *Maynard Keynes. An Economist's Biography* (London: Routledge).

Oakeshott, W. F., A. D. K. Owen and H. W. Singer (1937) *Men Without Work. Report to the Pilgrim Trust* (Cambridge: Cambridge University Press).

Raffer, K. and H. W. Singer (1996) *The Foreign Aid Business. Economic Assistance and Development Co-operation* (Cheltenham: Edward Elgar).

Ruttan, V. W. (1996) *United States Development Assistance Policy. The Domestic Politics of Foreign Economic Aid* (Baltimore: The Johns Hopkins University Press).

Sapsford, D. and J. Chen (eds) (1998) *Development Economics and Policy. The Conference Volume to Celebrate the 85th Birthday of Professor Sir Hans Singer* (Basingstoke and London: Macmillan – now Palgrave).

Schultz, T. W. (1960) 'Value of U.S. Farm Surpluses to Underdeveloped Countries', *Journal of Farm Economics*, vol. 42, no. 5, December, pp. 1019–30.

Scrimshaw, N. S. (1997) 'The Lasting Damage of Early Malnutrition', in WFP/UNU, *Ending the Inheritance of Hunger* (Rome: World Food Programme and United Nations University, pp. 3–14).

Sen, A. (1981) *Poverty and Famines. An Essay on Entitlement and Deprivation* (Oxford: Clarendon Press).

Shaw, D. J. (1998a) 'The World Food Programme: Linking Relief and Development', in D. Sapsford and J. Chen (eds) (1998), pp. 437–84).

——(1998b) 'The World Bank's Hidden History. A Review Article', *Canadian Journal of Development Studies*, vol. xix, no. 1, pp. 175–86.

——(2001) *The UN World Food Programme and the Development of Food Aid* (Basingstoke and London: Macmillan – now Palgrave).

——and E. Clay (eds) (1993) *World Food Aid: Experiences of Recipients and Donors* (Rome, London and Portsmouth, NH: The World Food Programme in association with James Curvey and Heinemann).

——and H. W. Singer (eds) (1988) 'Food Policy, Food Aid and Economic Adjustment', *Food Policy*, vol. 13, no. 1, February (see 'Introduction', pp. 2–9).

——and H. W. Singer (1995) 'A Future Food Aid Regime: Implications of the Final Act of the GATT Uruguay Round'. *IDS Discussion Paper no. 352*

(Brighton: The Institute of Development Studies, University of Sussex). Different versions of this paper have been published in *Food Policy*, vol. 21, no. 4, pp. 447–60, and in H. O'Neal and J. Toye (eds) (1998) *A World Without Hunger?* (Basingstoke and London: Macmillan (now Palgrave) for the UK Development Studies Association, pp. 305–34).

——and H. W. Singer (1998) 'A Note on Some UN Achievements with Special Reference to the World Food Programme', in M. I. Glassner (ed.), *The United Nations At Work* (Westport, Connecticut and London: Praeger, pp. 186–212).

Singer, H. W. (1940) *Unemployment and the Unemployed* (London: King & Son).

——(1943) *Can We Afford Beveridge?* (London: Victor Gollancz and Fabian Publications).

——(1950) 'Distribution of Gains Between Investing and Borrowing Countries', *American Economic Review*, vol. 40, May, pp. 473–85.

——(1961) 'Use and Abuse of Local Counterpart Funds', *International Development Review*, vol. 3, no. 3, October, pp. 14–16. Also published in H. W. Singer (1964a), pp. 183–8.

——(1964a) *International Development: Growth and Change* (New York: McGraw-Hill Book Co.).

——(1964b) 'An Example of the New Pragmatism: Toward a Theory of Pre-investment', in H. W. Singer (1964a), pp. 18–25).

——(1965) 'External Aid: For Plans or Projects', *The Economic Journal*, vol. LXXV, September, pp. 539–45.

——(1970) 'Some Problems of International Aid', *Journal of World Trade Law*, vol. 4, no. 2, March/April, pp. 347–61.

——(1972) *Children in the Strategy of Development* (New York: United Nations).

——(1976) 'Income Distribution and Population Growth', in H. Richards (ed.), *Population, Factor Movements and Economic Development. Studies Presented to Brindley Thomas* (Cardiff: University of Wales Press).

——(1983) (with the collaboration of S. J. Maxwell) 'Development through Food: Twenty Years' Experience', in WFP/Government of the Netherlands *Report of Food Aid Seminar. The Hague, 3–5 October 1983* (Rome: World Food Programme and Government of the Netherlands, pp. 31–46).

——(1984a) 'The Terms of Trade Controversy and the Evolution of Soft Financing: Early Years in the UN', in G. M. Meier and D. Seers (eds), *Pioneers in Development* (New York: Published for the World Bank by Oxford University Press, pp. 275–303).

——(1984b) 'The Ethics of Aid', *IDS Discussion Paper no. 195* (Brighton: The Institute for Development Studies, University of Sussex).

——(1986) 'Some Reflections on Past Interests and Activities', *IDS Discussion Paper no. 217* (Brighton: Institute of Development Studies, University of Sussex).

——(1987) 'Food Aid: Development Tool or Obstacle to Development', *Development Policy Review*, vol. 5, pp. 323–39. Also published in *Irish Studies in International Affairs*, vol. 2, no. 3, 1987, pp. 51–60.

——(1988) 'A Pioneer's Response to Food Aid Critics', *Ceres*, vol. 123, pp. 44–7.

——(1990a) 'The Role of Food Aid', in J. Pickett and H. W. Singer (eds), *Towards Economic Recovery in Sub-Saharan Africa. Essays in Honour of Robert Gardiner* (London: Routledge, pp. 178–93).

——(1990b) 'Food Aid', in C. K. Eicher and J. M. Staaz (eds), *Agricultural Development in the Third World* (Baltimore: The Johns Hopkins University Press, pp. 242–8).

——(1991a) 'Multilateral Food Aid in Context. A Personal Note' (Brighton: The Institute of development Studies, University of Sussex, 30 August, type-script).

——(1991b) 'Food Aid and Structural Adjustment in Sub-Saharan Africa', in E. Clay and O. Stokke (eds), *Food Aid Reconsidered. Assessing the Impact on Third World Countries* (London: Frank Cass, pp. 180–90).

——(1992) 'The Influence of Schumpeter and Keynes: On the Development of a Development Economist', *Discussion Paper no. 68* (Institut für Volks-wirtschaftslehre, Universitat Hohenheim).

——(1993) 'New Orientations in Food Aid', *World Food Programme Journal*, no. 25, July–September, pp. 3–7. Reprinted in UNESCO (1993) *Culture and Agri-culture* (Paris: United Nations Educational, Scientific and Cultural Organiza-tion, pp. 55–7).

——(1994a) 'Two Visions of Food Aid', in R. Prendergart and F. Stewart (eds), *Market Forces and World Development* (Basingsoke and London: Macmillan – now Palgrave, pp. 207–11).

——(1994b) *Aid Conditionality*. IDS Discussion Paper no. 346 (Brighton: The Institute for Development Studies, University of Sussex).

——(1995) *Aid Conditionality*, ADMP Series no. 13. (Tokyo: Advanced Devel-opment Management Program, Sophia University).

——(1996a) *Linking Relief and Development*, ADMP Series no. 19 (Tokyo: Advanced Development Management Program, Sophia University).

——(1996b) 'Aid Conditionality' and 'Political Conditionality – Illustrating Double Standards', in K. Raffer and H. W. Singer (1996), pp. 153–180.

——(1996c) 'The Future of Food Trade and Food Aid in a Liberalizing Global Economy', in E. Messer and P. Uvin (eds), *The Hunger Report 1995* (Provi-dence, Rhode Island: Alan Shawn Feinstein World Hunger Program, Brown University, pp. 199–209).

——(2001) 'Foreword', in D. J. Shaw (2001).

——and E. Clay (1983) 'Pricing Policies for Food Aid', *Commonwealth Consul-tative Meeting on Food Pricing and Marketing Policy* (London: Commonwealth Secretariat in collaboration with Guelph University, Ontario, Canada).

——and R. Longhurst (1986) 'The Role of Food Aid in Promoting the Welfare of Children in Developing Countries', in J. P. Greaves and D. J. Shaw (eds), *Food Aid and the Well-Being of Children in the Developing World* (New York: United Nations Children's Fund and World Food Programme, pp. 27–66).

——J. Wood and T. Jennings (1987) *Food Aid: The Challenge and the Opportunity* (Oxford: Clarendon Press).

UN (1945) *Charter of the United Nations*. Signed on 26 June 1945 in San Francisco at the conclusion of the UN Conference on International Organizations and came into force on 24 October 1945 (New York: United Nations).

—— (1960a) *868th Plenary Meeting. UN General Assembly, Fifteeth Session.* Official Records Part I. Plenary Meetings Vol. I. Verbatim Records of Meetings of 20 September–17 October 1960 (New York: United Nations).

—— (1960b) 'Provision of Food Surpluses to Food-Deficit People through the United Nations System'. UN General Assembly resolution 1496 (XV) adopted at the 908th Plenary Meeting, 27 October 1960 (New York: United Nations).

—— (1962) *The United Nations Development Decade: Proposals for Action* (New York: United Nations).

UNDP (1994) *Human Development Report 1994* (New York: Oxford University Press for the United Nations Development Programme).

UNICEF (1984) *The State of the World's Children 1984* (New York: Published by Oxford University Press for the United Nations Children's Fund).

US (1962) *Public Papers of the President of the United States. John F. Kennedy, 20 January to 31 December 1961* (Washington, DC: U.S. Government Printing Office).

USDA (1995) 'Agricultural Export Programs: Background for 1995 Farm Legislation', *Agricultural Economic Report no. 716* (Washington, DC: United States Department of Agriculture).

Wallerstein, M. B. (1980) *Food for War – Food for Peace. United States Food Aid in the Global Context* (Cambridge, Mass.: The MIT Press).

WFP (1978a) *A Survey of Studies of Food Aid.* By Professor Hans Singer. Document WFP/CFA: 5/5 – C (Rome: World Food Programme).

—— (1978b) 'Modalities of Operation of the International Emergency Food Reserve', *Report of the Sixth Session of the Committee on Food Aid Policies and Programmes* (Rome: World Food Programme, Annex IV).

—— (1979) 'Guidelines and Criteria for Food Aid', *Report of the Seventh Session of the Committee on Food Aid Policies and Programmes* (Rome: World Food Programme, Annex IV).

Index